CW01496498

Letters from Bishopsbourne

To Rachel

with grateful thanks

Chris Sisson

16 Nov. 2010

LETTERS
FROM
BISHOPSBOURNE

*Three writers
in an English
village*

Christopher Scoble

Published in Great Britain by
BMM
PO Box 422
Cheltenham
GL50 2YN
Tel: 01242 256755
email: info@sportsbooks.ltd.uk
www.sportsbooks.ltd.uk

© Christopher Scoble
First Published November 2010

Book design by Alan Hunns

A catalogue record for this book is available from the British Library.

ISBN 978-0-9541544-1-7

Printed and bound in England
Manufacturing managed by Jellyfish Print Solutions Ltd

For Sheelagh

CONTENTS

Illustrations

Acknowledgements

My first debt of gratitude is to Jonathan Hunt, the leading authority on Jocelyn Brooke, who has been most generous in sharing with me some of the hard won biographical detail of his research and in reading over my text – the errors, of course, remain all mine. We all look forward with impatience to his forthcoming definitive work on Brooke. I am grateful too for the friendly help I have received from John Urmston, the nephew of Jocelyn Brooke, in particular for granting permission to quote extensively from Brooke's works and correspondence and for the touching photograph of Brooke's mother and nurse at the gate of Ivy Cottage, which he took as a young man almost sixty years ago. Likewise I am grateful to Peter Waugh, the son of Alec Waugh, for permission to quote from his father's work and the provision of amusing snippets of information.

I have been generously served too by the biographers of the minor subjects of this book – Bob Gilbert who provided me with extracts from the diaries of A.E.Waite and helped me to locate The White Cottage; and Derek Wood who pointed me to the last letters of J.B.Reade and kindly supplied photographs. Without their work, both Waite and Reade would still be largely unknown. It was a delight to talk to the late James Troughton, the son of Lionel, the Kent cricket captain, who regaled me with stories of life in Bishopsbourne in the 1930s; and I am grateful too to Paul Tritton, the local journalist turned historian, whose book on *A Canterbury Tale* has proved a fascinating mine of information on the making of the film.

For permission to quote from copyright material and reproduce copyright images, I am greatly indebted to Dr Quentin Bone, Deborah Curle, Rachel Galloway, Jonathan Gathorne-Hardy, and Desmond MacCarthy; also to Curtis Brown on behalf of Gillian Tindall, and the estate of Pamela Hansford Johnson; to David Higham Associates on behalf of the estates of Geoffrey Grigson, John Lehmann, Olivia Manning and Anthony Powell; and to Rogers, Coleridge and White on behalf of the estate of Cyril Connolly. I am also grateful to Harvard University Press for permission to quote extensively from the Folger Library Edition of the works of Richard Hooker (volumes I, II and V) and to the Trustees of the Joseph Conrad Estate for their general support. For access to papers and permission to quote from them, I have to thank the Humanities Research Center at the University of Texas and Washington University Library. Any copyright holders who have by chance been missed will, I hope, come forward in due time.

I am indebted to a number of archives and libraries for their usual efficient help, most particularly the Centre for Kentish Studies at Maidstone, Canterbury Cathedral Archives, Canterbury Local Studies Library and the London Library. I am similarly grateful to the Bodleian Library, Bridgeman Art Library, British Library, Canterbury City Council Museums, Corpus Christi College Library, Dorchester Reference Library, Marylebone Cricket Club Library, National Monuments Record, and Sturminster Newton Library.

For their individual help on specific aspects of the book I would like to thank Beryl Graham, Stephen Hardy, Howard Milton, Jane Reynolds, David Robertson, Georgina Troughton; and John Gilkes for yet another of his incomparable maps.

CLS
22 December 2009

It is an article of faith with me that a place consists of everything that has happened there; it is a reservoir of memories; and understanding those memories is not a trap but a liberation.

—Adam Nicolson, *Sissinghurst*

In a book which tried to tell the story of a life it would be necessary to use not the two-dimensional psychology which we normally use but a quite different sort of three-dimensional psychology... since memory by itself, when it introduces the past, unmodified, into the present – the past just as it was at the moment when it was itself the present – suppresses the mighty dimension of Time which is the dimension in which life is lived.

—Marcel Proust, *In Search of Lost Time*

Memory: the past rewritten in the direction of feeling.

—David Shields, *Reality Hunger*

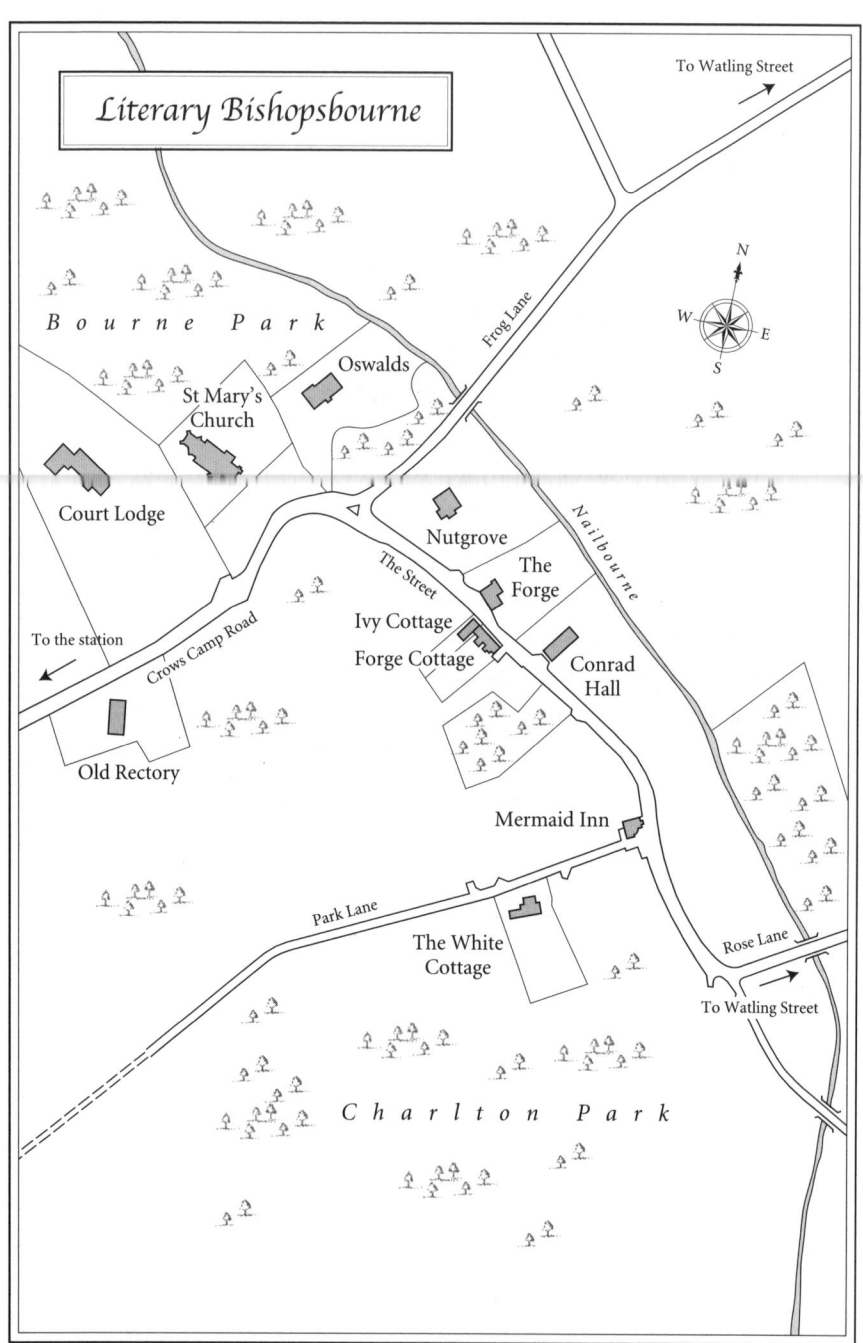

Literary Bishopsbourne

To Watling Street

Bourne Park

Frog Lane

Oswalds

St Mary's Church

Court Lodge

Nutgrove

The Street

The Forge

Nailbourne

To the station

Crows Camp Road

Ivy Cottage

Forge Cottage

Conrad Hall

Old Rectory

Mermaid Inn

Park Lane

The White Cottage

Rose Lane

To Watling Street

Charlton Park

CHAPTER 1

The Village and the Historian

I am inspired by loyalty to place; loyalty to the narrow
streets of Canterbury, the Christ Church Gate and the
great Cathedral itself, standing in the green lawns of the
Precincts. Above all I'm inspired by gratitude and love
for having been born a Man of Kent.

Michael Powell [1]

The late summer of 1943 and a film camera is trundling along The
Parade tracking a young actress through the bomb racked quarter of
the city. The September sun climbs through the morning haze, setting
fire to the tiny globules of dew hanging delicately from the purple
spikes of rosebay willow–herb, that flower of mystery scarce known
in southern England for three hundred years but now brought back
from the ashes courtesy of Adolf Hitler. [2] She is walking purposefully
in jodhpurs and jumper through a film set that could not be perfected
even at Denham – a twilight territory twixt town and country, where
shoes strike pavements of urban urbanity while through the picket
fence alongside stretch sunlit fields of fading summer flowers broken
only by the archaeology of wartime destruction, the painful exposure
of ancient cellars and what was once domestic privacy to the prurient
public gaze.

On a corner she finds her bearings in the wasteland that was once Rose Lane, that haven of the medieval pilgrim where feet could be soaked and rested before crossing the final road to their destination at St Thomas' shrine. The camera turns and pans the opposite side of St George's Street to take in the southern aspect of the cathedral itself, another sight unseen by human eye for perhaps eight centuries, now that the ancient Longmarket and all the little crooked houses that once surrounded it lie wasted too in this sad field of general dereliction. The phalanx of mighty buttresses that bolster the south wall crouch alert on one knee in the morning sun, like a row of archers drawn up in readiness to launch destruction on the next wave of enemy to appear unheralded out of the clear, still, barrage—ballooned sky. The film company, now quietly revolutionising the English cinema, has its toxophilite associations too – they have called themselves The Archers. The camera zooms in on the tower of Bell Harry standing in protective watch over this shattered remnant of the city, a symbol, like St Paul's, of the unshakeable power of collective faith that, unlike mere bricks and mortar, cannot be torn that easily to the ground. The cathedral now on camera waits to dispense its blessings upon a new set of modern–day celluloid pilgrims – the American soldier seeking news of his lost fiancée, the young materialist who longs to play a cathedral organ, and the hapless land–girl (the figure now walking the bombsites) mourning her lover posted missing.

Michael Powell, chauffeured in that morning from his nightly retreat in the George and Dragon at Fordwich where from his hermit cell above the bar he plans the next day's labour, is putting the final miraculous touches to his strange masterpiece, the *Canterbury Tale* to end all Canterbury tales. It has been an awkward film to direct, interleaving mystical themes expressed in atmospheric pictures – the eternal spiritual values of the nation evoked through the subtle glories of the Kent countryside; the nostalgic and civilising power of the past – with a trivial, near ludicrous, detective plot that Emeric has generously served up on him. Mercifully that contorted plot with its "Glueman" has finally spent itself, thus opening the last three reels to a purity of picture and message unparalleled in English cinema. Who better than the surrealist Powell to make a film that mixes real Chaucerian pilgrims with their modern–day counterparts, a medieval working falcon swooping the sky with a spitfire looping the loop, the Pilgrim's Way with the Canterbury–Ashford railway line, the auncient and fabricated village of Chillingbourne with the only too real Wingham and Fordwich, Chilham and Wickhambreaux?

Who better to straddle this chasm between pastoral past and pastoral present than a man born in Bekesbourne parish one hundred years ago, in a farmhouse just a quiet apple orchard walk down to the Nailbourne, that mysterious stream that runs when it chooses through the village and valley that will lie at the heart of this book? Who better to explain to us in pictures steeped in mystical inference the enchantment of these gentle hills and narrow streams, the dancing fields of yellow corn, counterpoint to the sallow darkness of ancient woodlands where neither plough nor sheep has dared to penetrate? For the beauty of the pastures and the fear in the woods have resided here through two thousand years and more of settled habitation, their mystery unbroken by the ceaseless advance of technology, yet kept alive by a handful of writers (whether on paper or celluloid) who have brought to this first corner of England two priceless gifts – their knowledge and their love.

For Powell this project is something of an indulgence, a sentimental return to the haunts of his Edwardian childhood, selecting all the villages and hamlets that share their natural beauty with family associations. "I was creating a story in the county I was born in, the 'garden of England', a chalky country of bare downs and shallow valleys, of chestnut woods and little chuckling streams, of slowly turning water- and windmills, and white capped oast houses with the bittersweet smell of hops drying in the kiln." [3] There has been some indulgence too in the time already expended. The crew has just spent the greater part of July filming the Chaucerian pilgrims up on St Martha's Hill on the Surrey downs (the relic of a Powellite bicycle ride in 1918), an ambitious scene that has now been cut to little over a minute.[4]

Michael Powell was in Canterbury on 16 August to grace the local premiere of *Colonel Blimp* at The Friars, and has been touring the countryside ever since selecting with scrupulous care the numerous villages that will give a share of themselves to "Chillingbourne". He has been scrupulous, and daring too, in his casting, once Roger Livesey and Deborah Kerr, the veterans of *Blimp*, had refused their offered parts, the one wary of the Glueman plot, the other tied by a contractual obligation that even a proposal of marriage from Powell himself could not expunge.[5] Eric Portman has taken Livesey's role, and the rest are new to film – a young Dennis Price invalided out of the army, Sheila Sim, an ex-land girl (appropriately enough) recently discovered on the London stage, and Sergeant John Sweet of the American army, who isn't really an actor at all. Powell himself has spent many hours in the last few weeks pleading with Dean and Chapter to allow filming in the cathedral, but has been bluntly told there is no place for secular activities, albeit aesthetic, within the confines of a consecrated building.[6] It is an opportunity lost to the cathedral authorities given the future celebrity of this iconic film; the scene-builders at Denham are now busy putting them to shame.

Filming in a wartime Canterbury beset by D–Day preparations is no picnic: from time to time the air–raid warning sounds and cast and crew run for cover. Pace is retarded too by the perfectionism of the director of photography, Erwin Hillier, who will wait hours for just the right light or cloud formation.[7] But it is worth it. Today he has been experimenting with a night filter to shoot the bomb sites, producing a strangely dramatic effect around these poignant images of a young girl returning to old haunts only to find them all destroyed.

A few more minutes safely in the can, the director calls a halt to filming for the day, and crew and actors stand down. Or rather sit, the younger ones, on the edge of the broken houses and gardens for swig of beer and bite of sandwich. Then wearily, but cheerily, make their way back to lodgings in the town or outlying villages.

The stars head for the special comfort of the County Hotel; the rest make do with the lesser splendour of the Fleur–de–Lis, next door in White Horse Lane. Had the English soldier of the film, Sergeant Peter Gibbs, been a real soldier out of Jocelyn Brooke, he might well have retraced his steps up the narrow bustling high street to the old West Station to take a train, not west to Chillingbourne, but south east in the direction of the director's birthplace, looping out of the town, through the South Station and past the empty cricket ground, puffing through the deep cuttings that traverse the peaceful orchards and on into the elegant environs of Bourne Park which served in wartime as a military camp. Here, to protect the sensibilities (and the views) of those in the Big House, the train makes a mole-like dive underground through the shortest of tunnels, eventually emerging to brake in the open air and crawl slowly in to the station. The soldier has arrived at the village.[8]

It was not a village really, but more of a hamlet stretching between two landed estates – Bourne Park to the north and Charlton Park the south. They compressed it from either side, thus mercifully forestalling the modern expansion which otherwise would have bound to come.[9] Just a handful of houses, then – 15 in Hasted's day – which gave it at that time the diminished title of Bourne–street. It lay at the heart of the rolling wooded Barham Downs, mid way between the old Dover road (Watling Street in its formal title) and the Elham Valley railway, once the most beautiful small line in the country. Even Hasted, never one inclined to the ecstatic, was moved to remark that the church and village "with the high hills behind them, topped with woods, form a most pleasing and luxuriant prospect indeed".[10]

When the railway arrived in the late 1880s, the old Nailbourne Valley, called after the little stream, the so–called "woe–waters", which rose irregularly every few years and whose rising was supposed to herald disaster, became overnight the Elham Valley, after the pretty downland village further south towards Folkestone, a name that has stuck ever since.[11] Thus the old peasant nomenclature, superstitiously clung to though foreboding evil, was forced by the invasion of the new transport technology to take on a lighter, prettier connotation more in keeping with the demands of tourism and modernity. But in 1939 the Elham Valley railway had been handed over to the military, so it is only in imagination that our soldier from Canterbury in 1943 can alight at the little sunken station (where Churchill had visited two years before to inspect the massive rail–mounted howitzer secreted in Bourne tunnel to give the Germans a fright),[12] climb the path to the road, and then descend the long winding hill to pass on his right the ancient rectory where nearly four hundred years earlier a judiciously literary clergyman had sat at his open study window, gazing out over his newly planted yew hedge, as he fought for the precise mellifluous word to add to the latest chapter of his great work aimed at sweetening with honeyed allurements the recalcitrant drones who opposed the new Anglican dispensation.

As he passes the church over the road from the rectory, he can just make out through the trees on the same side the neatly symmetrical Georgian house called "Oswalds", once the dower house to the Bourne estate, where twenty years before another writer, in exile from his Polish homeland and from literary London, held court to friends and admirers as he tussled with the last frugal offerings to his ever widening band of readers. Then at the fork in the lane, where the signpost stands on its small grass island, he swings round to his right into the main village street – a dozen small cottages down the right hand side of the lane from which they look out over mostly open fields on the other side, where few buildings stand save the forge and the small village hall, with the deep parched course of the ill–fated Nailbourne running along behind them. A moment later he passes the gently sloping dormered end of Ivy Cottage whose occupant, loving this valley even more than the film director, will soon return from the Italian wars to exchange a life of action for a life of writing. From here it is no more than a further fifty thirsty yards to the Mermaid Inn and its encircling houses that mark the village end.[13]

And the history of this place? That has been written by countless generations of anonymous men of Kent, the little people who have tilled the land, felled the trees, trodden the pastures, built the landscape but left no other personal mark to posterity. In fact, like many villages in England, this is largely forgotten ground. Except when a national event has thrust it fleetingly onto the historical record: as on 17 November 1415 when Henry V on his triumphant return from Agincourt received representatives of the Cinque Ports on Barham Down to present him with a golden nef; or when on 25 May 1660 Charles II, on the day of his return to England as lawful King, reviewed troops of horse of the gentry and nobility, together with the Kentish levies on foot, again all drawn up on the Down.[14] Citizens of our village were proudly present there, at the centre of the world for a fleeting second, but then all goes quiet again. George IV used to stay here at Charlton Park when visiting his last mistress Lady Conyngham whose family home was at nearby Bifrons, but that was much lower profile.[15]

Going back further, there seem always to have been people wandering this beautiful valley, as the numerous grave finds have shown. When Caesar made his second invasion in July of 54 B.C., he spent the first night marching from his bridgehead at Deal to a river crossing which some have taken to be the Nailbourne in the area of Charlton Park. There the British were routed and fled into the woods where they fought a fierce rearguard action from a heavily fortified encampment, but ultimately succumbed to the weight of numbers and superior tactics of the Roman army. The only supposed relic of that distant episode is the dip of ground in Bourne Park beside the Dover Road, known as "Old England's Hole", where local legend has it that the Britons dug in to make this last ditch stand.[16] When the final invasion came a hundred years later and the Romans established themselves in the country, Canterbury grew into a thriving market town, key to the south east's defences, and significant signs emerge of Roman settlement here.[17]

At this time, however, the history of the little valley is still shrouded in uncertainty. We know more of how it fitted in to the patterns of settlement as the Dark Ages turned towards the light thanks to the work of a singular historian who, like Michael Powell, knew and loved the Kent countryside and pursued its past with an unfailing zeal. Kenneth Witney was someone university lecturers might be tempted to call an *amateur* historian, for his working career lay elsewhere and he lacked, as a result, the traditional support system enjoyed by the professional academic, rubbing shoulders day by day with other scholars and using them as helpful sounding boards for new ideas. Instead, his intimate knowledge of the Kent countryside, the course of its rivers and trackways, its geology and vegetation, its changing agrarian economy, its ancient administrative boundaries, yielded remarkable insights that more than compensated for this apparent disadvantage. It gave him his reputation as one of the twentieth century's most distinguished historians of medieval Kent. Writers in recent years, whether professional historian or popular author, have found him indispensable to any discussion of the county at this period.[18]

Witney was born in south India in 1916 to missionary parents – his father a Congregationalist minister, his mother a medical doctor.[19] Sent back to England at the age of eight to board at Eltham College, he took every opportunity in the school holidays to explore the Kent countryside, and from here his interest was first fired in the county's complex past. In the mid 1930s he went up to Oxford to read history and there encountered Jolliffe who had just produced his seminal work on the Jutish settlement of Kent.[20] On graduating he joined the Home Office where for almost forty years he was to bring his sharp mind, acerbic wit and gentle bearing to the domestic political issues of the day.

Life was hard for a young Principal in the 1950s bringing up two children on a subsistence wage with very slow prospects of promotion. But he had another string to his bow. On his marriage in 1948 he moved to Tonbridge, a strategic centre for the exploration of the county. About three years later, he started on the research for his major work, *The Jutish Forest*, which was 25 years in the making, and finally published on his retirement from the Department in 1976. Though in scope a history of the Weald from the fifth to the fourteenth centuries, its heart lies in the Kingdom of Kent and its Jutish infrastructure, putting flesh on the distinguished bones that Jolliffe, who died in 1964, had left behind him.[21]

When the Jutish warrior Hengest arrived in Kent around 455, it was as an auxiliary and mercenary of the British king, Vortigern. By the time he was succeeded by his son Aesc, the British had been routed and the Jutish Kingdom of Kent founded on a solid base under the dynasty of the Eskings; it was to survive as an independent nation for almost four hundred years.[22] The small kingdom was divided into provinces – lathes as they were called – which provided the administrative, judicial and agrarian infrastructure of the new state. Each lathe had a royal vill at which the king stopped on his perambulation to dispense justice, receive services from his tenants, sort out administrative problems. In each lathe was a tripartite division of the land – first the royal demesne worked by paid servants or slaves, then the inland owned by the king but let to tenants, and finally the *outland*, land parcelled out to the first warrior followers of the king in recognition of their services. This latter created a distinctive, and almost revolutionary, feature of the Kentish scene – the free holding and disposal of land, giving to the country a core population of free men with a tradition of social and political independence.

The other feature which distinguished the Jutish kingdom from its Anglo–Saxon neighbours was adherence to *gavelkind* – the laws of partible inheritance by which an estate was bequeathed on death equally among the siblings of a family. In the face of such inheritance laws, which would otherwise lead to the splintering of estates, families had to stick together in systems of joint cultivation if they were to maintain viable holdings of land. Out of these essentially family settlements there thus grew up the tiny hamlets – the standard unit of economic life – that are a marked feature of the Kent countryside, contrasting strongly with the large nucleated villages of Anglo–Saxon England.

Each lathe was self–sufficient in agriculture, but this was ultimately achieved only by ingenious contrivance. Though all had a sufficiency of arable, the lands first settled by the invaders, in north and east Kent, were generally ill-provided with pasture-land for sheep and with forests for feeding the large herds of swine with acorns and beechmast during the autumn pannage season. For pasture-land, both the king and the free ceorls in the outland had to look mainly to Romney Marsh, and for pannage to the Wealden forest. Thus, under the system of collective cooperation that prevailed, most of the lathes had allotted to them areas of the marsh and of commons (later divided into dens) in the forest to which the flocks and herds would be driven at the appropriate season of the year.

When, following the ninth century union with Wessex and the later Norman invasion of Kent, the manorial system gradually took over the lathes (though retaining nearly all their ancient administrative features), the manors clung on to the dens in the forest that had once belonged to the original lathe. It was Jolliffe who first suggested that by study of an accumulation of manorial surveys and pre-Conquest charters, it would be possible to reconstitute the whole system under which the forests were parcelled out among the lathes, and by implication develop also a more accurate understanding of the original structure of the lathes themselves.[23]

It was this formidable task that Witney shouldered in the early 1950s. By careful examination of the mass of medieval charters, which start early in Kent, and by judicious use of the complex discipline of place-name studies, he was able to verify or correct Jolliffe's preliminary conclusions on the structure of the lathes and the Wealden dens that belonged to each of them. But it was not just a matter of the study of dusty manuscripts in cathedral archives, museums and record offices. For the seven weeks of the autumn pannage season, great herds of pigs would be driven up to thirty miles over the drove roads and tracks that linked a particular lathe to its own part of the Wealden forest. Thus weekends and holidays would find Kenneth Witney, map and notebook in hand, striding through sunken pathways unused for centuries, attempting to retrace the ancient drove roads that would confirm on the ground the link between lathe and den that had already been posited on paper.

> May the bounds I tread, by minnis, strand and stone
> Restore that realm, articulate and one [24]

It is this intimate knowledge of the terrain, built up over so many years, which gives to Witney's work its incomparable strength.

The eleven lathes described by Jolliffe in his work were expanded by Witney's meticulous study into twelve, many with revised boundaries. Our village of Bishopsbourne in the Nailbourne valley falls within one of Witney's "new" lathes, and it is through Witney that we can locate it accurately within the socio-political framework of the Jutish Kingdom of Kent. By the eighth century, the area was clearly integrated in Borowart lathe (the lathe of the Canterbury men) but there are strong indications that Kingston, which means "the king's farm", now a small village between Bishopsbourne and Barham, was at an earlier date a royal vill, the capital of a small, compact "Kingston" lathe.[25] It is not just the name that suggests it, but also the presence on nearby Kingston Down of a number of pagan burial sites, rich in jewellery, which are to be found at other royal vills. Most celebrated of the jewellery finds is the Kingston brooch, dug up by a local curate in 1771 and one of the finest examples of the sophisticated Jutish style of the reign of Aethelberht when Jutish Kent reached its pinnacle of power, holding sway over most of Anglo–Saxon England.[26] So although a Kingston lathe is still historical conjecture, it fits neatly into the lathe structure of north east Kent, and it somehow feels right. The area of the Nailbourne, sometimes called the Little Stour, is topographically distinct and it does not take much to imagine it a little kingdom of its own, visited for a few days a year by King Aesc or King Aethelberht, sitting in his primitive hall to receive services from, and dispense justice among, the freemen of Bishopsbourne just a mile up the track.

The place is also distinct in standing apart from the system of Wealden dens and drove roads that Witney so painstakingly pieced together. For it is an area of Kent whose later manors mostly had no rights in the Weald, in part because of its distance from the great forest, but mainly because close at hand lay a forest of its own – the forest of Haradun, which bordered on Barham and has left its name today to the villages of Lower and Upper Hardres.[27] It was to this forest then that the men of Bishopsbourne would herd their pigs through the October mists to feed them up for the traditional slaughter at Martinmas, and it is this forest that has left us more than just a corrupted name. On either side of the river valley, the hills are scattered with woods both large and small, the tangled remnants of the mantle that was once this ancient forest – woods for a holy man to wander in at the close of the Elizabethan age, for an old novelist to look up to from his secluded garden, for a small boy to lose himself in at the beginning of the twentieth century. For in the gnarled writhings of the trees and the twisting paths to unknown fears, the forest still lives on.

By Domesday this country had little changed, but its political structure had. With the coming of St Augustine and the christianisation of Kent, under the developing manorial system the King, for the good of his soul, gave away some of his manors to the Church. The manor of Bishopsbourne, however, evaded this process until very late in the day. In the early 11th century, though farmed by Archbishop Stigand, it remained in the ownership of Edward the Confessor; and only with the Conquest was it finally awarded to the archbishop as part of his extensive holdings in Kent.[28]

In the Domesday survey of 1086, the Archbishop is now firmly in charge of the manor of "Burnes" and it is his ownership which later brings to the village its grander title of Bishopsbourne. Here as elsewhere the survey gives us a detailed breakdown of the population of the village (some 117 souls) and its productive resources, including two watermills driven by the Nailbourne.

> Bishopsbourne is held by the Archbishop in lordship. It answers for 6 sulungs (1200 acres). Land for 50 ploughs. In lordship 5 ploughs. 64 villagers (villani) with 53 smallholders (bordarii – lesser landowners) have 30$^{1}/_2$ ploughs. A church; 2 mills at 8s 6d; meadow, 20 acres; woodland, 15 pigs; from grazing, 27d. Total value before 1066 and after £20; now £30.[29]

Kenneth Witney wrote in the 1980s an account of Domesday Kent which still awaits its editor and publisher. In 1989 he started work on a translation from the Latin of the 13th century survey of Archbishop Pecham's Kentish manors, using a 15th century copy in Canterbury Cathedral library which he had studied for his earlier books and articles. When this laborious work was almost complete, misfortune struck. In 1994 he was caught up in a tragic road accident which killed his wife and left him disabled. For the next five years and with some difficulty, he corrected the text and completed the introduction and editorial notes. He died aged 83 in 1999 and the work was published posthumously the following year.

It is a fitting tribute to his tenacity and skill as an historian and will serve well future generations of his Kentish peers. The eighty page introduction is a *tour de force*, a minutely detailed summary of social structure and agrarian practice in medieval Kent in a mature hand, clear and compelling, confidently building on fifty years of writing and study.[30] The survey gives us too a succinct picture of the social structure of the small manor in the Nailbourne valley, where the archbishop held over 500 acres in demesne, the gavelmen (descendants of the free ceorls) 1300 acres and the cottars (poor tenants) just over 50.[31] The archbishop now had two dens in the Weald and his two watermills from Domesday had been translated into one windmill, an indication of the unreliable nature of the spasmodic flow of the Nailbourne. Most of the traditional services of the gavelmen had been commuted into money payments, but together they still had to plough, sow and reap 20 acres of the demesne. This, however, was a mild imposition compared with the 50 acres the small number of cottars had to reap, under detailed regulation as befitted their lowly status.

> Each cotland must reap and bind 4 acres of the lord's corn without receiving food; and keep watch over the bound corn at night, guarding it from evening until the rising of the sun, receiving one meal for this service. They must also lift the corn onto carts and stack it, receiving food three times a day.[32]

In addition were numerous tasks of fetching and carrying, driving the lord's animals between manors, building cattle stalls, clearing out barns, making malt, all for the lord's benefit. But proportionally these serf–like conditions applied to a small number of villagers only.

This lively picture from the mid 1280s is our last glimpse of the village in its tightly controlled medieval structure. The text was preserved by a clerk in the cathedral around the 1490s when his medieval world was vanishing fast. A hundred years later, when the Church had radically changed but the fields and woods remained much the same, a new rector was appointed to the village who was to change its anonymous existence for good.

CHAPTER 2

An Orchidaceous Pyrotechnician

I know from my own experience that a man's work is nothing but a long journey to find again, by all the detours of art, the two or three powerful images on which his whole being opened for the first time.

Albert Camus [1]

With a creaking of brakes like some arthritic aunt, the number five bus in its scarlet and cream livery drew to a halt beside All Saints church and opposite the Monument pub – the last full pick-up before our arrival in town. This combination of church and pub in close proximity gave notice that here was an ancient settlement – the village of Northwood (the northernmost edge of the Jutish forest of Blean) – which formed a substantial manor of the Archbishop of Canterbury at the time of Domesday but then, quite unaccountably, disappeared completely off the radar. This was the church town, the original Whitstable, until superseded by the straggling thread of habitations that ran along the seashore at the foot of the hill. That was known quite fittingly as Whitstable-street until it grew to become a town in its own right. [2] In time the new town lost its attribution of "street" which passed to the older settlement, relegated now simply to Church Street. Thus do the mighty fall, unheard, unsung, without even a mark on the history books.

Oblivious to this historical demotion, with a groan and a chuckle the last few old ladies hauled their shopping trolleys aboard, and we were off, round the corner and down the hill to the old railway bridge which straddled the road at such an acute angle that nothing could be seen of the approach from the other side. The architects clearly had taken no note of the line of the road beneath but since this was the first railway bridge in the world, built in 1830, they could perhaps be forgiven this error in prototype. In those days the early railways took precedence over everything; now the roads take the same precedence, even over people, and the bridge despite its provenance has been quietly dismantled. I would wait with breathless anticipation for the driver to sound his compulsory horn to give him right of way, an echoing blast trumpeting through the great arch which seemed to me the rightful paean to this historic structure. Then on past the railway station and the gasworks, turning finally under the modern railway bridge into Oxford Street where the town proper began, and we alighted. Our ritual progress down the main shopping street took normally two or more hours, calling at fixed points in regulation order along the way, to perform at each the appropriate ceremonial function, the first of which began here at the library across the road from the bus stop.

The library to me was an awesome building, as much from its general demeanour as the intimidating army of books that it housed. Built in 1797 as a private dwelling, Oxford House had in the twentieth century become the main offices for the local district council. In 1935 the administrators moved out to more expansive rooms in the Castle, bequeathing the old house to the library service. By 1950 this interesting change of use – private house to public library – was well established. The building itself was tall in rather forbidding gloomy brick, the façade filled by three large windows and a round-arched doorway with a flight of stone steps leading up to it. The roof was slightly pyramidal in shape with a large dormer window jutting out from the attic front.[3]

Inside was the aura of a house empty for many years but just been put on the market. No carpets or furniture – just bare floors and walls, cracking paint, and a pervading smell of dust and library cards. Entering down a long corridor, past the stairs on the right, we would turn into a miraculous brightly lit room stretching the length of the building and filled with bookstands on every wall and in rows across its breadth. Down one side ran a wooden counter, about as tall as myself, where members made their borrowings and returns. Moving up and down behind it were three or four young women (these were the days when public services were staffed) in square-shouldered blouses or bursting sweaters, burrowing like squirrels on a winter picnic among the trays of cards and pockets, with their russet hair rolled back from the forehead and tailing off in another roll at the nape of the neck. Reaching up on tiptoe to watch, I was fascinated by the complex technology as they riffled at great speed through several rows until they finally matched member's card with borrowed book, chattering lightly as they went – pretty creatures with an authority that made their seeming middle-aged beauty even more entrancing.

At last our books passed through the formal return procedure and, armed with my tickets, I was released to seek out the children's library while my mother browsed among the shelves downstairs. For the children's library was located in what must once have been the front bedroom, looking out over the busy street, another room of bare floorboards, with no furniture other than the makeshift bookshelves that covered every wall. Through clouds of dust I would mount the stairs, my head almost touching the step above, always in a fervour of expectation – would I have the room to myself, would there be a new discovery, would the book I saw last week still be there? I would always make for the corner by the front window where stood the fiction – the old faithfuls like Sam Pig, Just William, Dr Dolittle, or the more exotic Moomintroll books I had only just discovered.

This day there was no competition, I had the room to myself. No obvious choices stood out from the little dark corner by the window; what remained of the old faithfuls there I had already read, so I had to browse diligently like the adults downstairs. At last I alighted on a new book with a romantic title, *The Wonderful Summer*, and intriguing, amusing pictures which invited a further look. The adventure seemed to feature the search for a rare flower, a plot quite out of the ordinary and perhaps therefore a promising choice. Just then my mother appeared at the top of the stairs and came in to see if I had chosen yet; for once she had beaten me to it. When I was undecided, her knowledge of current books was often the catalyst. She took up the book in instant recognition: "Oh! Jocelyn Brooke. He's the man who's mad about orchids and fireworks. I never knew he wrote children's books, but if it's him it's bound to be good".

That the author had written for grown-ups and my mother had read him and liked him, this proved the decisive factor. There was always an exasperating gulf between what she read and what I read, which made the world of children's books seem not real reading somehow. In this case that gulf had been bridged, and I returned home on the bus proudly clutching, if not my first adult book, at least the next best thing – a children's book written by an adult author.

The writing of a children's book was as much a surprise, perhaps, to Brooke as it was to my mother. He was then in the middle of his post-war productive phase, a veritable frenzy of writing in which he published fifteen works in the space of eight years. This one he wrote during his second stint in the army, in charge of the "theatre" at the Royal Herbert Hospital in Woolwich, where he groaned internally as he pounded out each chapter. If it were a difficult book to write, I found it equally difficult to read. It took me a couple of weeks, mainly because of the long words and more complex sentences than I had previously encountered. The line in children's books between extending the reader's vocabulary and leaving him completely behind is a very fine one, and Brooke may have been struggling to find it.

The story is simple enough. An eleven year old boy and his younger sister, awaiting their family removal to Edinburgh, are sent to stay for the summer term and holidays with their bachelor uncle. They are joined by their cousin Vincent, a rather wicked self-portrait of Brooke himself as a child – clever, studious, precocious, arrogant, articulate – execrated by the others alternatively as "a beastly little swot" or that "frightful twerp".[4] They share the predictable children's adventures, falling in the Thames, dressing up as ghosts, looping the loop in an aeroplane, catching chicken-pox and burglars. But like much of Brooke's writing, there is a great deal here that is autobiographical. Uncle Ted is a covert replica of the jolly, balding, middle-aged men that appear in many of the books; and he is looked after by the family's childhood nanny, like Brooke himself. The children are taken to an Italian restaurant and introduced to Brooke's favourite food; they take tea with a young Oxford don and are shown the swans on the lake at Worcester, Brooke's old college.

But most significant of all, and most intriguing for his childhood audience, he introduces his two major life obsessions. When Uncle Ted, who "wasn't really like a grown-up person at all",[5] last visited the children he had bought chemicals from the local chemist and built some magnificent fireworks, the principal interest of his life. He puts on another fine display this time. And when cousin Vincent makes his first entrance, he proudly announces his discovery of *ophrys aranifera*, the rare spider orchid, a specimen of which he then proceeds to display on every conceivable occasion. The other children, put off as much by his Latin as his pretentious boasting, ridicule this miserable "weed" that he has found, but they are soon won over by the search for the even rarer Epipogon, which proves to be the unifying adventure of the book. As with *The Military Orchid*, it is eventually found, but not found – the plant discovered turns out to be a common foreign impostor.

So great is the Brooke enthusiasm for the dual themes of orchids and fireworks that he rather lets them run away with him, abandoning the strict disciplines of the children's author. Instead of a gentle exit as the wonderful summer draws to its close, he devotes two tightly argued pages to an adult explanation of where the deceiving Colonel obtained the questionable foreign plant and how he disguised it as a native, a discussion that might thrill your expert botanist, but not too many children. And he devotes the whole of an earlier chapter to detailed instructions on how to make a range of complicated fireworks, complete with pictures and lists of ingredients – over the head of most children and a major source of anxiety for all parents. But these, of course, were the more expansive days of chemistry sets on the open market, when children, and even parents, were allowed a measure of political incorrectness in flouting what few health and safety rules then lay on the statute book.

The book was intriguing because of these themes, but not otherwise a notable read. The most interesting aspect of any book to me was the issue of place: where it was set or where it was written. Somehow that grounded the creative inspiration in a material context which, far from making it mundane, opened out all sorts of mysterious possibilities, the excitement of names and locations on maps that had yet to be traversed. But the locations of this book were at best neutral. The children's original home was Blackheath, where Brooke's own parents lived and where he was temporarily living when the book was written. And Uncle Ted had a house by the river at Goring-on-Thames, an unknown location to me but one which permitted the author a nostalgic return to his abbreviated student days in Oxford. Whatever hints had been dropped in Brooke's recently published "orchid" trilogy, hints that my mother seemingly had not spotted, there was nothing in this child's book to indicate, what would indeed have brought it to technicolor life for me, that its author was now living and writing only ten miles away from where I was reading it, in a little village just the other side of Canterbury.

As befitting a writer with a highly developed Proustian sense of place and time, Jocelyn Brooke spent most of his life in the village, though in the early years time there was fragmented. This was because Forge Cottage in the main street was a holiday home, and as a child he would arrive there at Easter in time for the spring flowers and stay, at least in the years before school, until the end of the summer. Little wonder then that his recollections of the village in childhood, so potent a part of his writing, were idyllic. Until an adult, he never ever stayed there in winter.

Home of the settled variety was in a house perched on the undercliff at Sandgate, the polite suburb of Folkestone where H G Wells spent his early married life. It was there on 30 November 1908 that Bernard Jocelyn Brooke was born, a delicate, sensitive child who from an early age looked out on the world with a penetrating writer's eye. His father, Henry Brooke, had qualified as a solicitor but quickly abandoned the law to run the well-established family wine business in Folkestone, whose bank-like headquarters (all polished wood and cathedral silence) was known to the family as The Office, and to Brooke himself as "the gin palace".[6] With such a background, wine slipped easily into his portfolio of other passions – music, flowers and fireworks. With his sister Evelyn and brother Cecil both much older than himself, he occupied the role of baby of the family and much enjoyed living up to it. He was brought up in Folkestone mainly by his nanny, a strict Baptist, who by some childish metathesis was always known as "Ninnie". Emily Fagg (her true name), the daughter of a local baker in Dover and aged 27 when Brooke was born, was to turn out the perfect surrogate mother whom he loved passionately and was always terrified of crossing. She continued in that role for the whole of her life, unchanged by her marriage, a constant correspondent when he was away from home, and his faithful housekeeper in later life at Ivy Cottage, the little house perched on the end of Forge Cottage.

Like many writers he spent much of his childhood alone, creating intimately personal worlds out of a vibrant imagination, worlds which in Brooke's case were linked specifically to place, to his beloved wild flowers, and to a sense of nostalgia that could be summoned up out of even the most recent past. Walking through the network of little paths and tamarisk trees that made up the undercliff at Sandgate, he created a make-believe wood peopled with "wild soldiers" and strange animals to impart solid substance to his routine night fears.[7] Though he grew up balanced on a cliff just a stone's drop from the beach, the sea never pursued him as a writer, perhaps because, unlike writers such as Joseph Conrad, he was never at home on the sea. His home was the country. As a nominal town child, the undercliff, this semi-wild, semi-domesticated tract of land, intersected by gravel walks, where he could freely botanise among a strictly limited flora, was his substitute for the country. The real country lay elsewhere, up beyond Caesar's Camp on the downs above the town, reachable by a twenty minute walk.

The barrows and earthworks on the top of Caesar's Camp formed a kind of promised land for the child who, looking up to the hills, longed for the day he could go out and explore them. But even more enticing was the territory that lay beyond.

> The hills behind the town, romantic enough in themselves, engaged my imagination for another reason: for their steep, chalky flanks formed an effectual – and, so it used to seem, an almost impassable – barrier between the familiar, semi-urban world which I inhabited and the vast unknown region which my family were accustomed to refer to, with a comprehensive vagueness, as 'The Country'. Unknown, that is to say, but for the small and strictly delimited area which surrounded the cottage, at the further end of the Elham Valley, where we spent the summer holidays, and which, though indubitably in the country, formed a kind of civilized outpost amid the unexplored and probably dangerous territories of the hinterland.[8]

Right from his earliest years, then, Brooke conceived a picture of the village in which he was to live and write as a familiar oasis of beauty and calm in the midst of a "wild, mysterious kingdom"[9] little different from the deserts and jungles of the adventure stories he read at home, and virtually as unattainable. The image projects right through his most familiar autobiographical writings, and with even more penetrating effect through his less well known Kafka-esque novels where the village itself in one case, as well as the surrounding country, turns into a nightmare of threatening violence. For those steeped in the books, the peace of the village even today seems fragile in face of the silent menace that lurks in the woods all around.

It was in the roaring hot summer of 1911, that harbinger of the great myth of the perfect Edwardian summer, that the Brooke family first rented the cottage that was to become their regular holiday haunt and Jocelyn's spiritual, and indeed material, home. In the following years, the family would make their accustomed trek to the village, at Easter or in July, driving by car from Folkestone. The routine was for Brooke and Ninnie to go on ahead with the bulk of the summer's luggage, taking the train from Shorncliffe station up the Elham Valley line. Outside the carriage, the journey was never so exciting as he expected it to be, his creative eye transfixed by the minutiae of the internal furniture of the train: the pendulous chain of the communication chord with the rubber bulb at the end which reminded him of having his photograph taken; and the cryptic injunction to French tourists on the little enamel plate beneath the window "Ne pas se pencher au dehors", which he conceived as a spell to make the train go.[10]

At long last, the engine would pass under the road bridge and pull up at the village station where Brooke plus nanny would alight, amidst the familiar and ear-splitting sound of belching steam, to be greeted by the local stationmaster as if they were royalty. No matter how familiar the arrival, here was once again an altogether fresh world with its ever-potent sights and sounds.

> We had arrived; and when the train, after a good deal of belching and spitting, had at last puffed away down the chalky cutting towards Canterbury, we would be enfolded in the sudden country silence: that silence which, it seemed to me, differed profoundly not only in degree but qualitatively, in its very essence, from the

silence, say, of the undercliff (haunted always, on the stillest day, by the murmur of the sea), or, even, from the brooding quietude of the Folkestone hills. If it were April, the sudden stillness would be emphasized, rather than broken, by the calling of a cuckoo somewhere among the trees of Bourne Park; and I would sniff, with an acute, never-failing delight, the unique and delicious country smell – composed (if this were a spring visit) of the scent of violets and the fainter, slightly vinous aroma of primroses, combined with the pervasive exhalations of wet earth and wood-smoke and the lingering, steamy, slightly sulphurous odour of the train itself.

By the age of eight, Brooke had started school and the best-remembered annual arrival was now the beginning of the summer holidays when the singular atmosphere of sounds and smells was somehow deeper and richer.

Later in the year – in June or July – we would be greeted by a richer, more complex texture of sensory impressions: the silence now would seem, if not less profound, in a curious way more positive – a dense, palpable element, viscous and fragrant as a honeycomb, composed of the low, perpetual bourdon of innumerable insects, and of the hypnotic cooing of wood-pigeons. No less manifold and closely compacted were the summer odours which assaulted our nostrils: scents of mignonette and sweet-peas from the station garden; of dust, cow-dung, human sweat and new-mown hay; or, if the season were yet later, the pungent tang of hops from the hop-gardens opposite the station – an odour associated, for me, with yet another seasonal ingredient of that country silence: the distant hum – low, monotonous and, after a time, becoming so much a part of the silence as to be scarcely perceptible – of a threshing machine, far away at Langham Park, or at some farm remoter still, beyond Kingston or the wide park-lands of Bourne.

From the platform a narrow path ascended through trees and bushes past the little station house up to the level of the brick-built road bridge, where it opened out through railway picket fences on to the quiet lane that led down to the village. The walk over the last quarter mile of the journey was a crucial ingredient of the whole enterprise, giving time and space to the two pilgrims to register the fact of their physical arrival.

As we emerged from the station the silence was suddenly intensified, and our sense of having arrived, at last, in the country became more immediate and actual. In June the grassy banks opposite the station entrance would be covered with ox-eye daisies and scarlet poppies; the first wild-flowers to greet us, they possessed for me a specialized and symbolic significance, holding forth, as they did, the promise of innumerable other, more interesting and rarer flowers to be sought for during the long succession of summer days that lay ahead. We would walk down the hill to the village, followed at a discreet interval by the porter, carrying our luggage on a trolley; if it were late summer, the hop-garden bordering the road would be crowded with pickers – an alien, ferocious tribe whom I had learnt to place in the same forbidden social category as soldiers, tramps, miners (from the local collieries) and bank-holiday trippers. Earlier in the year, however, the hop-gardens presented only their long, receding and unpeopled vistas of odorous and embowered green; and earlier still, when we had come to the cottage for the Easter holidays, the gardens would be all but leafless – a prospect of innumerable naked poles, with the young tendrils showing only a foot or two above ground. It is these Easter visits which I remember with a particular vividness, for they marked our return to the village after a winter-long absence and seemed, indeed, an integral part of the seasonal process itself – natural and inevitable as the budding of the hedges or the first emergence of primrose or celandine. Turning the corner at the bottom of the hill, I would spare a glance for the two big chestnut trees by the church, for I was fascinated by those fat, sticky buds which, if Easter did not fall too early, would by now be bursting open to reveal the bright green fingers of the unfolding leaves.[11]

Brooke rarely writes about his father, whose world was quite removed from his own, but he does so movingly in a poem that gives an even more emotional twist to the roadside bank opposite the railway station, nodding with poppies in the June sun and the train moving out.

> My father made ladies
> Of the scarlet poppies
> From the bank by the country-station –
> Tying back the silken flower
> With a grass-blade for girdle,
> And frilling out the petals
> To make a crinoline
> For the dark and Southern lady;
> Sprung from my father's hands:
> An extraordinary birth
> From those stiff and awkward fingers;
> So I watched, astounded,
> The long grey face,
> As the fingers fashioned those dark
> And dangerous ladies:

26

> And the train, pulling out of the station,
> Left the silence suddenly deeper
> And the sunlight burning with
> An intenser heat on the roadside
> Where the ox-eye daisies
> And the scarlet poppies
> Like blood and snow contended
> In the June morning.[12]

From the corner at the bottom of the hill, they would catch their first sight of Forge Cottage, a hybrid house consisting of the small brick and tile cottage with its two low-slung dormer windows (backing on to Ivy Cottage) plus the taller, rectangular addition with its three storeys and tiled mansard roof. This quaint amalgam of buildings was surrounded by a little picket fence giving on to the main street. Here was his spiritual, his *real* home.

> Another hundred yards and we were at the cottage: unchanged after our long absence, and seemingly unchangeable; a 'home' which, by contrast with our house at Sandgate, seemed infinitely more homely, with its smaller, more manageable proportions and its air of being rooted and autochthonous, like the apple-tree in the garden, or the dense canopies of ivy which covered the walls and overhung the windows of the cottage itself. Already a blue pillar of smoke rose from the chimney – for one of the maids had been sent ahead on the previous day to light fires and air the beds; in a moment Edna or Minnie, whichever it happened to be, would open the door to us, and I would sniff, once again, with the excitement of some exile returned home after long banishment, the never-to-be-forgotten cottage smell: a subtle, elusive and wholly characteristic odour compounded of paraffin, drying linen, moth-balls and

freshly-scrubbed floors, mingled inextricably with that musty taint of dampness which, in this low-lying valley, with its pervasive mists and seeping subterranean woe-waters, could never, even in the hottest summer, be entirely dispersed.[13]

The tone is elegiac. This is Brooke writing in the 1950s of this particular lost domain at the time that I was just beginning to discover it for myself – a very present reality. But the truth is that, as the writer himself admitted, the same passages could have been written by the small boy of forty years before who had, even at that time, a highly developed sense of nostalgic loss, aware that present joys were evanescent and that the power of place lay less in them than in the recollection of past action and feeling.

The rapturous release that the village atmosphere conferred on this schoolboy was made doubly joyous by the very absence of school. For schooldays were troublous to a solitary, sensitive boy with a very idiosyncratic imagination, which tended to cut him off from social sympathy and open him up, like the fictional Vincent, to teasing and worse. It was in 1916, at the age of seven, that he first went to school. "It was the beginning of a process which was to last nearly twelve years, during which I certainly suffered more acutely than I ever have since. The best thing one can say, I suppose, for the (bourgeois) English educational system is that it immunizes one to a great extent against subsequent horrors."[14]

He started gently enough with morning sessions at a local kindergarten attached to a flourishing girls school where the worst horror he seems to have faced was the cringing embarrassment of kiss-in-the-ring, with Brooke roundly refusing to be kissed.[15] A proper day school in Folkestone followed – The Grange, Shorncliffe Road – which he wrote up amusingly in *The Goose Cathedral*; in later life he was to share the dreadful memories of regimented life there with a pupil from the previous generation, Harold Nicolson.[16] Then at the age of eleven he was sent away to a preparatory boarding school, St Michael's at Uckfield in Sussex, run by the eccentric Anglican clergyman, Harold Hockey and his Christian Scientist wife. Special provision was made for the children of Christian Scientists like Brooke's parents, and like the mother of Denton Welch who followed Brooke there a few years later.[17] Here the horrors of cricket and scouting seem to have been adequately counterbalanced by his intellectual ability and the proclivities of some of the teaching staff for botany, a subject on which he could teach them a thing or two.[18] His ultimate conclusion was that the school "was never quite so bad as one expected it to be".[19]

Then followed his first foray into the public school system when at age 13 he was packed off to the King's School, Canterbury. Five years earlier, Michael Powell had had a splendid time there, lording it over the dormitory with his brash manner and sophisticated tales; but for Brooke it was quite another story. The traditional bullying handed out to all "new bugs", the ragging in the dorm at nights, was a thousand times worse for this particularly sensitive child. It was the first real test in his carefully protected life, and at the end of the first week he and his close friend from St Michael's decided to run away. They walked out of the gates for the normal half-day holiday and then continued on the four miles to Bishopsbourne. Much to the surprise of their unsuspecting hosts, they parked themselves on family friends in the village – the Huggetts, who in the fiction become "the Iggulsdens"[20] – who lived in Nutgrove, the house on the corner where the main street met the beech lined avenue down from the Dover Road. It was not until after the two boys had devoured a substantial tea that it became clear they were running away from school. The Huggetts made a hurried telephone call to Sandgate, and the boys were put on the next train to Folkestone where an irate father arranged for them both to be sent back to King's that same night.[21]

Standing on Bishopsbourne-Bridge station that grim October evening, waiting for the 7.30 to Folkestone, marked a turning point in Brooke's relation to the village. He had expected to be rescued by his village friends but instead had been dutifully handed over to authority. For the first time, the idyllic spell had been broken; even the familiar objects in which he rejoiced now took on a disconcerting aura.

> Mrs Iggulsden, aware of her responsibilities, accompanied us to the station. In the darkness the place had an unfamiliar and unfriendly air: I had scarcely ever seen it except in the daytime. As we bought our tickets I came nearer to tears than at any time that day: the posters of Ramsgate and Margate ("It's ripping!"), the enormous weighing machine, the text of the Explosives Act, 1875, pasted on the wall, filled me with an intolerable nostalgia, linked as they were, inseparably, with our arrival, for the spring or summer holidays, in this village where the happiest times of my life had been spent. I knew – as we waited beneath the dim oil-lamps on the little platform – that after tonight the station would never seem quite the same again, for the familiar objects had become infected by my misery, and would no longer hold for me, as in the past, the promise of an unalloyed and innocent happiness.[22]

It was the first entry of the threatening "real" world into his secret idyll, the invasion of that evil he was to present so powerfully in the darker of his novels.

He was sent back to school to face the event both he and his friend had been dreading – the New Bugs Concert. Discreetly out of sight of masters and prefects, the new boys were hustled into a large classroom where before a baying mob they were forced to stand on a table and do a turn, sing a song, recite a poem, tell a story, in the middle of which (no matter what its quality) they were drowned out by the mob and pelted with rolled up magazines, the force of which knocked them to the ground. They were then made to run an obstacle race under and over the desks, while the mob rained down further blows upon them.[23] While perhaps not quite so appalling as the prep school trials of Hugh Walpole, an earlier and enthusiastic student of the King's School (he was made to stand naked on a bench while his tormentors prodded the more delicate parts of his anatomy with pins and pen-nibs),[24] it was as much the anticipation of these events as their actuality that formed the mind-breaking torture. Brooke had reached the end of his tether and ran away a second time with his friend.

There was a new inquisition at Sandgate, but this time his father proved more malleable and it was agreed that he should not return to Canterbury. He was free! But it was a freedom paid at a heavy price. His friend was forced by a more uncompromising father to return and this, as with survivors of an accident, filled Brooke with a punishing burden of guilt. The episode had a far-reaching impact on his personality – he had been put to the test and had run away.

At one level it strengthened him, confirming his instinctive view of the world – he was an artist, not a bureaucrat.

> My experiences, I suppose, were quite usual: the ferocious initiation ceremonies, the petty cruelties and indecencies, the perpetual sense of injustice and irrational guilt... my fortnight at a public school, if it immunized me successfully against any possible horrors which the future might hold in store, bred in me also an intolerance of tradition, a hatred of all authority and a deep-seated distrust of all institutions from which I am only now slowly beginning to recover.[25]

The flight from King's marks the first of a series of such flights, from institutions either academic or commercial, until he discovered one highly authoritarian institution, the Army, into which, quite by surprise, he fitted comfortably and which brought him unexpected fulfilment.

But the psychological effect of this failure to face up to the challenges of everyday life went far deeper. Any tiny residue of self-confidence that had been stored up from childhood had now drained almost away.

> I continued, if only half-consciously, to be aware of a sense of loss: it was as though some vital nerve had been torn from my body, or a portion of my brain removed, leaving the range of my faculties incomplete. Certain aspects of life would always remain closed to me, there was a whole wide area of normal human activities of which I knew myself to be incapable... My chronic sense of inferiority was... immeasurably aggravated: already habituated to cutting my losses, too prone to nip any crescent ambition in the bud, I became increasingly unwilling to take part in any activity which was in any way competitive, or in which I could not feel sure of excelling.[26]

It was a handicap that was to form the pattern of his life, and set the scene for the lonely middle-aged writer, barricaded in his country cottage, who had completely lost confidence in the power of his writing, the man who would make new friends over lunch but never follow up the second meeting. As he admitted at the time: "This process was to prolong itself well into adult life; it remains operative, for that matter, in later middle-age. In my work, in my social relations and in my sexual life, my temptation has always been to contract out of the rat-race, like some timid and conceited child who says 'I won't play': thereafter to retire, as it were, to a corner of the nursery, and to the undemanding, uncompetitive world of phantasy".[27]

But for the time being, the two escapes from King's had an immediately benign result. His parents took the message and sent him straightway to a gentler institution in the shape of Bedales, the unorthodox alternative school, nestling in the Hampshire downs in the heart of Edward Thomas country. The humanity and friendliness of the place transformed Brooke in a matter of weeks from a difficult, neurotically-timid child into something approaching a normal schoolboy. He was very surprised to find himself happy there.[28] At that time pupils were allowed to work so many hours a day on subjects of their own choosing, and Brooke was delighted to find a biology master obsessed like himself by botany, which now became a serious science rather than the secret, rather shameful, indulgence of his childhood. As a co-educational school, any close relationships were forestalled by the prevailing ethos that sex was "silly", a stance which in Brooke's view created a sexual vacuum that could have been harmful in later years.[29] It does not seem, however, to have prevented him from coming to more or less satisfactory terms with his own homosexuality.

From Bedales in the autumn of 1927 he went up to Worcester College, Oxford to read law like his father, though with rather more interest in the social life that university might offer than in achieving academic excellence. This was his first practical exercise in concerted opting out. He skipped lectures, drank and dined heavily among an elite set of incorrigible aesthetes. In the day he wrote poetry and lay on his bed pondering the elusive nature of his real psyche. Nostalgia for the childhood past was still inescapable. On days he would wander out to Godstow and Iffley to botanise for a few happy hours; and at times would find himself halted outside shops selling fireworks, transfixed by a display of roman candles, rockets and gerbs.[30] As with so many others before and since, the nostalgia of his first summer term became almost instantaneous. "In the summer, in the rain-wet evenings, the gramophones on the river brayed out the tunes of the moment: *Rain, The Man I Love, A Room with a View*. For me, they had already – after only a few weeks – acquired a quality of intolerable nostalgia. My sense of the past had somehow so telescoped itself, that some episode of a month ago or less could seem as poignantly symbolic of my 'Lost Content' as the scenes of my childhood."[31]

The nostalgia, however, was soon to be frozen for good as this first summer term turned out to be his last. He now gave his first public demonstration of his attitude to academic competition. With no work under his belt, he knew his Law Prelim would be a certain failure, and decided to take the provocative way out. He sat in the dark Examination Schools that summer "writing a series of defiant and exclamatory poems in the style of Guillaume Apollinaire".[32] The examiners were not amused, nor was his college; and he returned from a holiday in Paris to find he had been sent down. Given his general behaviour and failure to do any work, it was a predictable conclusion. Brooke later put it all down to his social misjudgments: "I had wasted too much time (I realized it now) on the wrong sort of people – second-rate charmers by whom, in my naïveté, I had been too easily beglamoured, and for whom, in reality, I had cared nothing".[33]

He was now faced with the cold prospect of working for money, with neither the time nor the nerve to do what he wanted most of all – to become a writer. He had had the writer's eye from an early age and had lived all his life on his imagination. In the last few terms at Bedales he had set about the serious task of turning these assets into novels, about half a dozen of them. Later he recalled those autumn afternoons in the school library, grinding out the words with surprising facility – "the dusty indoor-warmth after football, the autumn dusk falling over the school-buildings, the dripping trees – and the warm, almost sexual feeling of release as my pen raced over the lined paper, turning out page after page of facile, middle-brow prose".[34]

His earliest work, composed at about fifteen, was called *Clouds* and was, inevitably, a vehicle for recording his feelings for the village and the country closest to his heart. He was able to treat it later with his usual self-deprecating humour. "The novel, needless to say, was about the country; 'plot' and character, indeed, were plainly the merest pegs on which to hang my rhapsodical descriptions of Spring in the Kentish woods. A rather dim young man called Ian lived near Canterbury: he was married, but his wife didn't like the country, or perhaps she merely didn't like him. In any case, Ian was very unhappy, and the 'story' consisted almost entirely of descriptions of his long, lonely walks through the countryside, interspersed with reflections upon God and War and the League of Nations..."[35] Despite this facetious self-demolition, his most brilliant novels tended later, one might say, to follow the self-same pattern – vehicles for expression of love for the country of his childhood nostalgia. This was both the strength of his writing and its weakness – an exquisite but narrow seam of material to mine, such that, after several novels, he appeared to some to have run out of steam, thus precipitating the rejections and dissatisfaction of his final years.

His reading as a child had been, appropriately enough, childish – Beatrix Potter and adventure stories. He then graduated to popular novelists like Sheila Kaye-Smith, whose strongly topographical writing touched the borders of Kent, and it was not until Bedales that he found Aldous Huxley who became his passion and model for the next few years. At Oxford he discovered Proust who took the place of Huxley as his principal love, and who became, of course, the inspiration of his whole writing life. It was not just that in Proust he had miraculously found a spirit who shared his own special sense of time – not just the power of the childhood nostalgia – but also that ability to see the successive phases of adult life with the clarity of the child's naïve vision.[36]

At Oxford he mixed with other writers and would-be writers, including the writer and journalist, Jonathan Curling, who lived on his staircase and became his special friend, the gently supportive Eric Anquetil of the books. Brooke himself wrote for *Isis* and had published at his own expense his first small booklet, *Six Poems*. So though his year at Oxford had been an academic disaster, it had crystallised through his writing and friends the long-held desire to become a writer. Ambition and reality, however, as most twenty year olds discover, can be quite separate things. His most pressing need now was to find a job, less for the bread it would provide, more to enable him to hold up his head within the confines of a very middle-class family.

There now followed some twelve years of unregulated life for Brooke, drifting despondently from one dead-end job to another, trying to please his family who had found them for him – a period of inter-war angst which crumbled at the end into neurotic illness from which he only slowly recovered. In part his frustration sprang from lack of writing opportunity, but it may nonetheless have been the period of absolute fallow which he needed to set his pen alight after the war was over.

In 1927, the year Brooke went up to Oxford, his father retired from the family firm and in the late summer moved from Sandgate to a large suburban house in Blackheath.[37] At the same time Henry Brooke sold off Forge Cottage but kept in the family the little house attached at right angles to it called Ivy Cottage. It was there that Ninnie now came to live, some time after her surprise marriage in 1923 to William Ford, a carpenter from the next village of Bridge. It seemed on the surface a somewhat strange liaison, she being 42 and he a widower of 70, but it worked well enough, lasting until William's death in 1933. Thus, through Ninnie, Ivy Cottage was now to become a bolthole for Jocelyn, his refuge from London and illness, and later his creative workshop, the focus of his writing life.

But for the time being he followed his parents and London became Brooke's home too, though he still paid frequent visits to Folkestone where his elder brother was now running the wine merchants: "nostalgia drew me back to this haunted coast, I would walk to the end of the Folkestone Leas and look down at our old house beneath the cliffs, now occupied by strangers".[38] At a loose end after Oxford, in the autumn of 1928 he was found a job by his family with a large firm of wholesale booksellers. The chairman was a cousin of his father, who had thought, rather optimistically, that the work might suit his son's literary tastes. The reality was somewhat different: "in fact my job mainly consisted of lugging enormous piles of books up from the basement to the trade-counter. For these services to literature I was paid an 'honorarium' of a pound a week".[39]

In the spring of the following year he was transferred to a bookshop in Old Broad Street owned by the company, and 1930 found him working in another bookshop in Highgate, like George

Orwell in neighbouring Hampstead just four years later.[40] He stuck this soulless drudgery only because it gave him both time and freedom to work at his writing, currently a novel entitled *Surplus Men* (shades of Anthony Powell's *Afternoon Men*) about the thrills of London life played out in bars and nightclubs, which he too was enjoying in his time off. In this, probably the most social, period of his life, he seems, when away from the workplace, to have lived out his early twenties to the full, mingling with other like-minded intellectuals and artists, friends from school and university, and new acquaintances that might hold out the prospect of a love affair. Though his working life was unfulfilled, his sexual life did not appear to be. For a change from the company of middle-class aesthetes, he would spend weekends with his brother in Folkestone, close to the nefarious delights of young working-class men in the pubs and clubs of Dover. "My taste for 'low-life' drew me more than ever to Dover: I invested it, as usual, with more glamour than it really possessed. I liked the pubs full of soldiers and sailors..." [41]

Having sustained the London book trade for two years, he now ended up with a job in a publisher's office, which he soon quitted. He had begun to feel unwell with a disease that no doctor could isolate or diagnose. "I sat in the garden at Blackheath feeling ill and frightened. The more anxious I became, the worse I felt: it was the usual vicious circle. I tried to write, but for almost the first time in my life I found myself incapable of putting pen to paper." [42] He was suffering some kind of nervous breakdown, the panic depression of a young man whose formal working life had already turned out a disastrous failure, and whose only life-line to self-respect, his writing, now seemed to evade him. He was free to write, but could not do it.

The family now decided on a more sheltered workplace and early in 1933 sent him to join his brother in the firm at Folkestone, where he would at least have familiar surroundings and sea air. Here he began to exercise, took up riding and long walks, and immediately began to feel better.[43] But the job, predictably, was another failure "for I was congenitally hopeless at figures, and loathed working in an office".[44] At first he was given the lowest routine work, appropriate to his station, sorting invoices and entering up ledgers. But then the work expanded ominously to the all-embracing task of "learning the business". "Initiative, ambition, 'common-sense' – these were the qualities which I was expected to display... I failed signally to develop these virtues; instead, when I began to feel better, I took to visiting Dover." [45]

He was cheered once more by the pubs full of soldiers and sailors, and as he sat among them recording every move, he dreamed of the imitation of Proust. "I was sustained by the ambition to write (on some far-distant day) a vast Proustian masterpiece. It was to cover my whole life and the lives of everybody I knew; nothing was to be left out – the most intimate bodily functions would be described, of course, in unprecedented detail... The trouble was, though, that I could never bring myself to begin writing the first chapter." [46]

In Dover he resumed an affair with Albert Heron, a twenty year old private soldier, whom he had met in London towards the end of 1932 and who was now stationed in the seaside town with the 1st Battalion, the Seaforth Highlanders. It is one of the few of Brooke's sexual relationships to be documented: the surviving letters from Heron betray a tenderness and angst on parting which indicate the feelings ran deep. Heron sailed for Palestine in December 1933 and Brooke never saw him again. He died in the war but was partially resurrected as Bert Hunwick in *The Goose Cathedral*.[47]

Brooke began to feel ill again and left the family firm at his own request. In 1935 he escaped to Switzerland, for a time in Geneva and then moving about, staying with friends and in cheap hotels, trying to appease his father by not spending too much and, when he was fit enough, by writing the occasional article for periodicals to justify his existence.[48] On his return, still not completely recovered, he went back to stay in the village in the safe haven that was Ivy Cottage, where Ninnie now lived alone since the death of her husband three years earlier. Then in the summer of 1937, as war clouds began to gather, he spent several weeks in the south of France to improve his health, staying first at Cassis and then at the Welcome Hotel in

Villefranche, an early haunt of Alec Waugh.[49]

By the spring of 1938, feeling somewhat better, he resolved on a major life change. He broke with London for good and went to live, as if it were permanently, with Ninnie in Bishopsbourne. After all the barren, dispiriting years, he had at last come into his birthright – returning to his childhood soil, his lasting inspiration, his country of the mind. He began to write again with consecutive endeavour, mostly poetry, preparing the ground for the wondrous spate of books that were to fall from his pen immediately the war was over.[50]

As with many in the late 1930s, Brooke's personal angst seemed to shadow the gathering political crisis of the post-Munich world. "Events in Europe became oddly intermingled with my own state of health; my personal anxiety echoed the mass-dread which was beginning to afflict the whole country." [51] Even the quiet life of the cottage could not dispel the gloomy news of Munich as it came in over the airwaves.

> The flesh is sad, I have read all the books:
> My friends do not visit me, sitting alone
> In this crowded and watchful cottage room
> With the warm, hopeless September rain
> Drenching the garden and the last tawdry flowers –
> Dahlia, phlox, coreopsis; sitting alone,
> Watching the hands of the clock and the streaming
> windows –
> *Lac des Cygnes* on the gramophone, a sense
> Of the world running down, the watery sunset flaming
> In sudden deceptive brightness over the hushed
> Apprehensive village; and at six o'clock –
> With the tea-things spread, the kettle on the stove –
> The bland and hopeless voice of the announcer
> Reciting his banal, sickroom platitudes
> At the death-bed of a world.[52]

The only way out was action. "I would have welcomed the outbreak of war, as I would have welcomed the onset of some acute, definite malady: I longed – as many people longed at that time – for some violent purgation of the crisis-ridden atmosphere... War was the ultimate horror: but secretly – almost unknown to myself – I waited for it with an excited, half-pleasurable anticipation... I had long decided that when war really came I would join up instantly." [53]

He welcomed the war for another reason: after the years of hopeless drift, it relieved him of the constant worry of how to run his own life. And something else too. Though a timid child, whose life was of the mind rather than the body, he had always envied strong physical men, men of action, and had longed to be part of them. His childhood fantasies had been filled with soldiers; he admired their physiques, their uniforms, their bravado. Listening as a child to the bugle calls over Shorncliffe Barracks above Sandgate, he was stirred by the romance of it all. He was stirred too by the real-life soldiers he met, whether friends of his much older brother or those he watched in the bars of Soho or the public houses of Dover. [54] So when he did indeed join up as soon as war was declared, it was another kind of coming home. Perhaps surprisingly, he took immediately to the simple routines, the close proximity of others, the security of constant companionship. He made good friends in his unit that were to last him well beyond the end of hostilities. The army was a novel adventure that was to change his life, and most particularly his writing life.

For the first few months of war, he worked locally at an ARP post in Folkestone, and then signed up for the Royal Army Medical Corps, in a VD unit (the celebrated pox-wallahs) where he was to stay to the end. He remained in England receiving his medical training at Netley and then Shaftesbury, until in the late summer of 1942 he received his posting abroad – to Palestine. He returned to the cottage, in the wake of the Baedeker raid on Canterbury that June, for his final embarkation leave and, nervously awaiting an unknown future, he smelt the same Munich atmosphere of four years before.

AN ORCHIDACEOUS PYROTECHNICIAN

I sit
In the garden-hut, and watch the flying clouds,
And the warm rain falling
Hopelessly on the crimson phlox, the faded
And sprawling ramblers, and remember
Munich, and days like these, and it seems
That this is a new beginning, a rededication
Of the heart to its naked and strict intention.

The soldiers are camped in the Park, the amorous
bugles
Recite their poetry of annihilation to
The bare-limbed rookies running on Barham Downs;
And I walk in the drenched woods
 Through blowsy acres of willowherb
And golden-rod, seeing through a gap
In the trees the sudden burst of sunlight on
The ruined harvest; or I visit the town
And remark, in the blitzed Cathedral, the wind
Stirring the ancient banners through
The shattered windows. But everything is seen
Unpassionately, flat as a photograph:
 Let me be honest, at least: I cannot evoke
The appropriate and elegiac mood
To suit the occasion; this haunted
And tree-muffled village inhibits
The easy and falsified response...[55]

Always, because of his trade, a step behind the actual fighting, he nevertheless played a part at the heart of combat in the major campaigns in North Africa and Italy. Initially, he suffered a stormy crossing of the Bay of Biscay, followed by a short and pleasant transit stay at Cape Town, but from then on the voyage began to pall.

He wrote to his sister: "got very bored with so much water latterly, also with humanity in the mass. I know nothing like a troopship for making one cynical, individualist, anti-democratic and generally browned off with the human race".[56] He finally arrived at Gaza to beautiful weather and a fascinating biblical terrain. Life in the war zone summoned him to let go the nostalgic past and perform "the hard and muscle-bound intention of the soldier". But it was difficult.

> Let me now forget if I can
> The landscape, the remembered hour,
> The obsessive images – the yew-tree,
> The Orchid in the private wood
> And the ruined tower.[57]

North Africa followed and in late 1942, in the wake of the victory at Alamein, he moved up to Tobruk and then on in the spring of 1943 to Barce, where he enjoyed the exotic delights of the Libyan flora and the feeling at last of winning the war.

> The rain holds off, the afternoons are warm;
> We walk to the town, and sit in the ruined
> Piazza, drinking our coffee in the sun:
> Uneasy and a bit self-conscious in
> Our role of victor, feeling out of place
> In this seedy, half-demolished outpost of
> A tawdry and gimcrack Empire.[58]

After the Sicily landings, he spent six weeks in transit at Tripoli and then followed on to Sicily himself in the middle of September 1943. From Syracuse his unit continued up the Adriatic coast of Italy in the footsteps of the 8th Army – Taranto, Bari, Foggia.

This was the real beginning of Brooke's war – the discovery of Sicily and southern Italy which was to draw him back for his post-war spring holidays and to impact so forcefully on his writing. For in the spring of 1944 he was to find a new country which had all the emotional and nostalgic impact of his childhood village – another country of the mind, a new idyll to match the old, making up through distance in space for the lack of distance in time.

His unit was posted to a defunct agricultural college in the little town of Scerni, in the Vastese region at the southern extremity of the Abruzzi. For most of January, he enjoyed a premature wildflower spring which then turned to snow, a strange alternation of climate which was to embed itself deep in his writing mind. A letter to his sister betrays the first signs of the rapture to come.

> ... this is a nice place – in the *depths*, my dear – but the last fortnight has been terrible – very cold, with snow and slush knee-deep everywhere.The previous three weeks were heaven – like April; probably it will begin to be warm in March. Anyway, I can only be thankful (somewhat ignominiously) that I am in a building, and not a slit-trench (the building, by the way, is an ex-agricultural college – a sort of Eye-Tye Wye). The peasants all round are really charming, and extremely hospitable. The country is oddly English-looking, except for the olive-trees, and the small town perched on its hill, which couldn't be anything but Italian. There is a rather nice wild narcissus which I found before the snow came: the sort I *think* (if your memory is still quiz-conscious enough!) which grew in the *rose-bed* at Radnor Cliffe, amongst the irises and Mrs. Simpkins! This made me rather nostalgic.[59]

Even in the midst of war, flowers and the Folkestone childhood were never very far away. At Scerni against the sound of distant gunfire around Pescara, he watched the streaks of snow across the landscape slowly give way to spring flowers and a new sense of hope.

Ringed by its green, soft-contoured hills, this land
Of oaken copse, hedgerow and terraced field
Is seen as if through a glass, a pictured world
From a Gothic missal, static and self-contained;
Delimited by the formal laws, subdued
To the palette's frugal range; a winter land.

Landscape with figures: the people part of the texture,
The kerchiefed women bent to the hoe, or kneading
The pasta, the menfolk felling the winter timber;
Each task a ritual, assigned to its hour or season;
The chapel packed for the festa, the eating of God
A routine like ploughing, part of the seasonal cycle.

Winter was northern, making this land like home:
The classic olive masked by the tactful snow,
The first spring flowers frozen in field and hedgerow —
Coltsfoot and hellebore, the white narcissus —
Speaking a friendly and half-familiar tongue
To the soldier fresh from the South and the desert fighting.

April came up from the South, with lily and tulip
Springing in the young wheat, and the cyclamens
Darting their tongues of dusky and crimson fire
Suddenly sunward from the Plutonic dark,
Heralding May-time and the precocious summer,
The rose-hung hedges, the harvest over in June.[60]

Good relations were achieved with the scattered local peasant families, to whom the unit gave general (not specialist!) medical treatment. Brooke and his colleagues struck up a special friendship with a family of seven in a distant farmhouse, where they stopped one day to ask for wine. They were taken in almost as part of the family, and he wrote home in delight to Ninnie with all the intimate domestic details of pasta making and pasta eating.[61]

One particular day formed the emotional centrepiece of this idyll. They were invited to lunch on Easter Sunday to celebrate the youngest son's first communion. The endless litres of the best dark wine, the half dozen weighty but delicious courses, the post-prandial tarantella round the kitchen, all combined with the spring sunshine and their imminent departure on to the north to make this one of the unforgettable moments of his life.[62]

> And I am the wanderer from another country...
> At ease in the farmhouse, drinking the rough red wine,
> Munching the goat's-cheese and the white fennel, glad
> Of the sun and the food and the wine and being alive.
>
> The woman spins in the doorway, her kerchiefed head
> Demanding a nimbus... Love in this formal land
> Is sculpture, and Faith is a function of flesh, like
> Birth...[63]

After years growing up in a reserved and formal middle-class English family, he sensed the novelty of warm feeling right from the first visit to the farmhouse: "The family watched us out of sight. Looking back across the fields, we saw them standing in the doorway, waving. The house, with its two dark cypresses, stood out brilliantly against the sun-flooded landscape: it seemed like a symbol of happiness, a vision of the good life".[64] Now, on this final visit, the feeling went deeper still: "I knew that with these people, on this Easter day, I had felt happier, I had felt a more genuine sense of the joy of life, than ever in my life before".[65]

In the early autumn of 1944 his unit was disbanded after two years, and he spent the rest of the war stranded in northern Italy ("rather a dismal hole")[66] waiting for the demobilization which was not to come until a year later. In that long wait to go home, he became increasingly nostalgic for Folkestone and the Kentish village of his childhood holidays, now ruled from Bourne House by Sir John Prestige whose baleful influence was suburbanising it ever more rapidly. He feared the changes.

> *I should* have loved to go to Folkestone with you [*his sister, Evelyn*]. The Lower Road sounds lovely: the war has inadvertently produced some curious and romantic effects – willowherb and ragwort suddenly springing up in Cannon Street, etc. I remember a postcard (from Mr. Barron) showing Bishopsbourne *circa* 1913 or '14 – it looked entirely different, far more countrified, with roses all over the forge, and the "front-gardens" full of bushes. It's almost a pity the war hasn't de-Prestiged (or should it be de-Prestidigitated?) the village, which is getting *much* too Letchworth nowadays...[67]

In the barren months of waiting he was thinking too of those peasant villages he had left behind to the south and which had made so deep an impression. The years in the army had opened him up to a new self-confidence, not least in his attitude to writing, and towards the end of 1945 he returned at last to his Kentish village now with a determined will to communicate that joy of life he had stumbled upon in the cool, whitewashed Italian kitchen, with the bunches of drying tomatoes hanging from the ceiling beams, the fire of olive-wood in the open stone hearth, the floury pile of pasta on the scrubbed wooden table, waiting to be cooked.

CHAPTER 3

Jocelyn Brooke

Today "The Military Orchid" has reached me : I've read 30 pages : and so far I'm satisfied – and you know what a delicious sensation that is to a lover of the art of writing. I'll blow my little Sunday Trumpet over it as Linnaeus use[d] to blow his horn to summon his followers when on botanising expeditions he found an interesting plant.

Desmond MacCarthy to Jocelyn Brooke 10 April 1948[1]

I am sorry you drag in the cliché about your literary career being 'nasty, brutish and short.' It may have been nasty and short, but I don't see that it was brutish at all.

John Lehmann to Jocelyn Brooke 8 August 1956[2]

In the autumn of 1945, that time of optimism and hope intermingled with seeds of anti-climax, Private 7523265 Brooke B.J., R.A.M.C. finally received his demob papers and returned to England after an absence of more than three years. He made straight for the village that was now to become the focus of his writing life. Travelling once more down the beautiful Elham Valley, little had changed. The pace of life, comfortable and comforting, remained much as before.

The bus trundled along the valley, through the familiar villages; it was an afternoon in mid-October, warm and sunlit still, but with an autumnal tang in the air. The light lay softly across the stubble fields, touching the far woods to a subdued brilliance of old gold; in the cottage gardens Michaelmas daisies and the last frost-bitten asters smouldered like damp embers. Between Lyminge and Elham there was a slight delay; a flock of sheep crowded the narrow road, their pullulating, woolly bodies milling helplessly between the hedges. The bus hooted, the boy in charge of the sheep scuttled to and fro, vainly attempting to divert this slow, ponderous flow of animate mutton. But the road was narrow, and the bus filled it, we crawled onward, at the sheep's pace, an ineffectual juggernaut – the driver tooting still, for appearance's sake, on his horn, the sheep baa-ing in melancholy chorus: it was we, not they (one felt), who were being led to the sacrifice. 'Disgraceful,' said a man in the next seat to me. 'They want to get organized, that's what they want.' A slick, bumptious townee, he had no patience with country ways – they needed 'organizing': but the woolly, baa-ing mass refused to be organized, we could only crawl helplessly in its wake. There were still moments (I thought) when Nature could interrupt the March of Progress.[3]

He had in his youth lived the "organized" life in London (he was to test it again in two years' time) but he knew it was wanting. For a writer of his themes and sensibilities, it was definitely wanting.

In this rustic manner, he came home to take up writing again, although to be fair he had never really ceased. Throughout his war service he had been writing poetry and had used Ninnie as his arms-length secretary and Jonathan Curling as unpaid agent, arranging typing for him and sending off manuscripts to, among others, Cyril Connolly at *Horizon* and John Lehmann at *Penguin New Writing*.[4] His poems were never as inspired as his prose writing at its best (Olivia

Manning found them "rather stiff and intellectual")[5] but they formed the solid foundation for the images in much of his later work. Cyril Connolly had some typically astringent views on them which reached the unsuspecting poet while on service in North Africa: "Your poems are too wooden, too reminiscent of Auden and Spender – it is not enough to think and feel clearly, as you do – some magic is necessary as well. These are almost prose".[6] A rather chastened Brooke referred to them henceforth with some pugnacity as "my prosy and unmagical verse".[7]

Despite this unpromising start, some got themselves published in various journals, and by his return to England he had a full book of poems (some previously published) all ready for the Bodley Head to accept in January 1946 and bring out later that year under the title *December Spring*. The forty poems track his life from Munich and the late thirties to his wartime itinerary from Gaza through Libya to Sicily and Italy. The book is, nonetheless, full of the Elham Valley, either recorded on leave or recollected in (relative) barrack-room tranquillity; and all the principal constituents of his early novels and the trilogy are here – the scapegoat, Gorsley Wood, Coldharbour, California, the water-tower – which serves to show how deeply developed were the ideas he brought home with him, ready-made for his rapid spate of post-war prose writing. The first stanza of *Metamorphosis*, for example, reads like a synopsis for the whole of the orchid trilogy.

> Cartographer of myth, I chart
> The course of golden and remembered days:
> The legend of the water-tower, the orchis found
> One spring in the Park, but never found again;
> My mother watering the seaside garden, fringed
> With a rainbow made from the spray and the evening
> Light; Aunt Queta arriving from Buenos Ayres,
> High-heeled, powdered like an auricula;
> The fireworks hoarded from war-time – the Italian

Streamers, Devil-among-the-tailors and
The Mine of Serpents flowering suddenly
In the August night...[8]

Now home in the small cramped cottage, still cosseted by Ninnie in her mid-sixties, he returned once more to the little hut at the bottom of the garden, his improvised study, and went to work with a will.[9] By March 1946 he had completed two novels, *The Scapegoat* (published in 1949)[10] and "The Deserter", which never managed to make it into print. But in 1946, much to Brooke's chagrin, both were swiftly rejected for publication, in the case of *The Scapegoat* because of problems with the ending and possibly its homosexual atmosphere. Although, strictly speaking, they are more in the nature of novellas, the fact they were completed so fast gives the hint that they also were the product of the last years of war and had already been a large part written, either in detailed notes or mainly in the mind.

The Scapegoat is set in that menacing period of 1939 with the Germans in Prague and crisis blowing up over Danzig; its personal geography is the equally threatening country of woods, hills and open fields between Folkestone and Brooke's little haven of Bishopsbourne. Into this dark milieu arrives Duncan, a sensitive schoolboy whose mother has just died, to spend the Christmas holidays with his uncle, Gerald, the prototype of Brooke's family of large, balding, hearty no-nonsense homosexuals. Stripped to the waist (Brooke's childhood definition of disturbing nakedness) the two perform a ritual of physical exercises in the bathroom each morning.

The countryside is chief among the characters, spreading a sense of foreboding as Duncan goes walking alone, or rides through the woods suddenly to emerge upon the shadowlands of open fields on their fringes where, blinded by the dazzling sunshine, he stumbles upon an ancient dolmen or the rotting carcase of a sheep, which all add to the atmosphere of impending doom. And again on the fringes of the woods, military camps spring up suddenly from nowhere, symbols of the growing political crisis which will shortly engulf the world.

There is space to fit in one of the Brooke obsessions – a Christmas bonfire party complete with firework display – before the plot thickens. Duncan is sent down from school for stealing; accordingly suspicion and conflict build up in his relationship with Gerald. He makes friends with one of the soldiers in the camp next the woods and steals from Gerald to provide the soldier with money. Duncan is pursued by Gerald to the dolmen stone where he awaits his sacrificial fate; he bites Gerald's hand, symbolically drawing blood, and in a rage Gerald beats him to death.

> From far away, at the barracks over towards Glamber, came the faint nostalgic note of a bugle, sounding reveillé. Gerald turned away, seeing everything clearly at last: knowing that the long initiation was over; the rites observed, the cycle completed.[11]

As this rather abrupt ending betrays, the mythical, mystical element of the book is pitchforked, not very satisfactorily, on to a plot and characters that cannot readily sustain its weight. Brooke struggled over many versions of the ending (and the problem of synthesizing Druidical religion with Freud) in order to satisfy his publishers, and seems in the end to have just given up.[12] Nor does he here demonstrate the brilliant prose mastery of his later works, most particularly of the trilogy. But where he does indubitably score is in the gradual development of the darkling atmosphere, when the relationship between man and boy begins to fall apart and the sense of threat builds up towards the inevitable, ghastly climax. There is power here, and much of it springs from the power of the country itself which Brooke alone is qualified to feel and describe.

At about the same time that Brooke was struggling with various endings for *The Scapegoat*, he had also started work on *The Image of a Drawn Sword*, the second of his "Kafka-esque" novels which first appeared in draft in 1948 and was published in 1950. If the world of *The Scapegoat* is coloured by the gathering threat of Hitler's Germany in the immediate pre-war years, that of *The Image* is overlaid by the immediate post-war threat from Stalin's Russia. As with the Cold War, in the book's looming civil conflict we are not quite sure who the enemy is. Formally England is at peace, but all around the little village cradled in the folds of the Barham Downs there are strong undercurrents of war, made more disturbing by their fragmentary nature – the far-off bugle call from where no barracks exist, the sudden appearance, and then disappearance, of tented camps in farmers' meadows, the soldier's face suddenly emerging from the farmhouse window.

Even though this is a novel, its foundations are clearly autobiographical – in its physical setting, in its action, above all in its psychological furniture. The book is full of undisguised homosexual longing, of sado-masochist events, of ambivalence towards the mother, of guilt over failure of courage, the latter first fired, as we have seen, by Brooke's failure to stand up to the horrors of the King's School. In fact, all the psychological clutter of the author's life, which in later books is disguised beneath a more sophisticated layer of comedy and irony, is here brought painfully and clinically to the surface.

For this is a book about Brooke's post-war adjustment. Coming back to England after the contrasting dangers and boredom of war, nothing could have seemed sweeter than return to Ninnie and his mother in the cottage of his childhood village with the time and the freedom to do what he wanted most in the world – to write books. But the war had presented him with new gifts which he now began keenly to miss – travel, excitement, anonymity, an ordered existence, the close companionship of like-minded men. The quieter kind of order he now found in this increasingly stifling home atmosphere had none of the spice of army life and soon began to pall.

We find this sense of disillusion right from the first page of the book as the hero, Reynard Langrish, returning from work, leaves the bus on the Dover Road and makes his way on foot down the unmistakeable beech-lined lane that leads to Ivy Cottage.

Across the valley, raised slightly above the level of the other houses, a lighted window shone brightly through the gathering dusk. Reynard observed it with satisfaction, aware that his mother would already be preparing tea and that, in another ten minutes, he himself would enter the sitting room and be once again absorbed into the placid fire-lapped comfort of his home. Yet his satisfaction was mitigated by a half-conscious awareness of its falsity; his anxiety to reach home was largely a matter of habit, surviving from an earlier and happier period. Hurrying homeward now, vague, unwitting reluctance seized upon him and, half-way down the lane, he paused and leaned against a gate leading into the fields. Without wholly admitting it to himself, he had come, lately, to feel an inexplicable dread of his daily homecoming. Before he had been in the house ten minutes, he knew that he would begin to chafe at his mother's presence, at the warm, confined ambience of the living-room, the familiar objects ranged unalterably in their places. Sooner or later, during the course of the evening, he would be compelled to escape from the house, to walk aimlessly along the deserted lanes and cart-tracks, possessed by a restless craving to be above and beyond the sight and hearing of his home.[13]

Some of the detail here, especially the warm feelings for home in the past, may well reflect his evening return from work to the house in Blackheath in the early thirties when, despite the bleak nature of his working life, his mother was younger and still a compensating comfort. But the feelings of restlessness and frustration described here were clearly a part of his own very idiosyncratic post-war blues, experienced at the time of writing, and which seemed to be calling him relentlessly back to his true home in the army.

For the psychological themes of *The Image* concern a man pursued in a Kafka-esque dream by soldiers bent on persuading him to re-enlist, to whom he reacts in ambivalent fashion, half-tempted, half-fearful of the consequences of submitting. All of this reflects, of course, the author's own ambivalence towards the temptation of re-enlistment, the idea of which seems to have come to him quite soon after his return to England and the old routine. Reynard, the hero, finally agrees to undertake preliminary training but misses the enlistment date through illness. A few months later he falls by Alice in Wonderland chance into an army dugout which leads along an underground tunnel to a camp just outside the village, where he is forcibly enlisted under emergency regulations. After initial reluctance, he settles happily back into army life until he learns his mother is seriously ill and escapes (twice) to go and visit her.

As he returns home, the idyllic village of Brooke's childhood turns into a place of hellish nightmare. The meadows behind the cottages are full of military police in their encampments and he brutally kills the one who comes forward to challenge him.

> With a single bound, Reynard threw himself upon the tall figure, and, clutching his revolver by the barrel, struck with the butt-end at the man's face. Taken entirely unawares, the corporal stumbled and fell; with the speed of desperation, Reynard seized his rifle and, planting his foot firmly on the man's face, thrust the bayonet home into the heaving belly. There was a stifled cry, and the big body rolled over sideways; seizing the fallen revolver, Reynard struck again, with all his force, at the side of the head; then, grasping the bayonet with both hands, thrust it again and again into the yielding flesh, till at last the limbs were still, and the man lay silent and without a quiver at his feet.[14]

In searching for his mother's house, at the same time striving to evade the enemy police, he becomes hopelessly lost in a dream-like fog. After a long and frightening detour, he emerges on to a blessedly familiar path, the road the author had himself trodden at the beginning of every childhood holiday: "he at last realized with a thrill of joy, where he was: the road was that which led to his mother's house. He must have made an enormous detour, rounding the churchyard and a considerable area of woodland, for he had struck the road, as he now realized, at the opposite end of the village, in the neighbourhood of the railway station".[15]

On entering, Reynard finds Ivy Cottage utterly broken down – smashed windows, gaping roofs, the whole building invaded by vegetation, vermin and damp. He eventually picks his way to his mother's bedroom where the nightmare crescendo of the book reaches its climactic horror.

> Reynard pushed open the door of his mother's bedroom. A current of chilly, fog-laden air struck his face: the window appeared to have been blown inwards by some explosion, and the fragments of glass lay scattered about the floor, mingled with a thin carpet of leaves from the chestnut-tree which grew against the window. A curious odour pervaded the room: a heavy, sweetish taint, recalling the scent of hawthorn-blossom. Upon the bed, a tumbled pile of blankets adumbrated the contours of a human figure… The covered figure on the bed remained silent, without emotion; Reynard paused, irresolute, unwilling to encounter what he knew, now, to be the worst horror of all… Then, with a quick movement, he pulled aside the coverings, revealing the vestigial form of a human face. Upon the bony framework, the last fragments of putrefying flesh clung precariously, like algae to some tide-washed rock; the eye-sockets were turned upward, meeting his own gaze with a sightless,

obscene stare; the mouth lay open, a grinning void of putrescence...[16]

This is the counterpoint to Brooke's image of the idyllic village of beauty, love and security which invests his major works. The difference is one of time. The idyll comes from the period of youthful innocence before the 1920s and boarding school; now that idyll has been invaded by the modern world, a combination of the Hitlerian horror (the author had seen many such dead bodies in the past few years) and the atomic horror yet to come. But it also reflects, in more personal terms, the deep disappointment of the author's return to the land of his childhood, only to meet there the inevitable frustration of those who purposively seek out nostalgia, which Time will not allow us to recapture in routine everyday life. From now on, the author will recapture the true past by writing about it.

Brooke's feelings of frustration at this time are clearly demonstrated by the bitter power of this nightmare prose. In a final climax, Reynard unintentionally kills the love-hate figure of the captain who has pursued him for re-enlistment, and he decides to give himself up to the military authorities in a similar sacrifice to that which ends *The Scapegoat*. *The Image* is a book of its time, capturing all the anomie of the post-war world, but set within the context of the author's very personal dilemma. It reeks of Kafka, but when challenged with this Brooke famously replied that he had never read Kafka – quite possibly true. It also smacks of *1984* a year before that book was published – behind the terse announcements of the military authorities the thought police seem always to be hovering in attendance.

In real life, Brooke was soon to follow the logic of *The Image*. In the autumn of 1947, at the close of that wonderful summer, he rejoined the RAMC at Shorncliffe Barracks in Folkestone, and in one fell swoop had both resolved the book's dilemma of re-enlistment and cured himself of the debilitating frustration stemming from the return to English village peacetime life. But by then he had written a further two novels which were to carry the indelible Brooke imprint.

As we have seen, both *The Scapegoat* and "The Deserter" had been roundly rejected by the Bodley Head, the publishers of his 1946 poems. There may have been a combination of reasons. In the case of *The Scapegoat* it is clearly the work of an apprentice writer and, in addition to the problems with the ending, displays the odd weakness in its prose. Brooke may have been consciously employing a deliberately lean prose style for this book (and later *The Image*), for certainly the contrast with the powerfully confident and accomplished style of the succeeding trilogy is quite remarkable. But the occasional naïveté in the writing was probably not the only cause. Just as likely, it was the power of the scenes of violence and the all-pervading homosexual feeling (more powerful because implicit rather than explicit) that would at this period have raised some doubts within even the most *avant-garde* of publishing houses.

If Brooke, having made the change to civvy street, were feeling the same depth of frustration as his hero, Reynard, the initial rejection of these two books – the writing that was to have given him new life to compensate for loss of the army – must have brought him close to despair. In retrospect, both *The Scapegoat* and later *The Image*, with their troops of soldiers marshalling in the background and their homosexual yearning for the return of army life, can be seen as the perhaps predictable output of a demobbed veteran washed up on the tide of war with no certain place to go. But then, at this low point in his fortunes, he suddenly turned a corner and found the themes which he had been nurturing from childhood, with which he was most comfortable, and which were set to make his name.

It happened almost by chance. Both before and during the war, Brooke had written articles for botanical journals on his first love botany, and in particular orchids. In the midst of this intense post-war burst of novel writing, he had taken up again a project conceived in the late 1920s – a monograph on *The Wild Orchids of Britain*, finally published in 1950. When following the rejection of the first two novels Brooke seemed stranded with nowhere to go, his literary agent, A. M. Heath, suggested that he might build on this interest and write a popular book about flowers.[17] The writer took up the suggestion with alacrity. He was thinking in terms of a chatty book "with a few personal anecdotes sandwiched between the descriptions of plants". But from his earliest writing days Brooke had always leaned towards the autobiographical, and even more strongly towards, one might say, the autobiogeographical. The two failed novels, after all, were both set in his beloved country south of Canterbury and teemed with his current personal concerns. Little surprise that with this new book, then, "the anecdotes took command, and insisted on stringing themselves into an autobiography".[18]

If we now look at *The Military Orchid*, the first book of the trilogy, with this provenance in mind, we can see how what starts in the first part as a focussed account of the development of the author from childhood as obsessive botanist, with the search for the mysterious rare orchid thrown in to create a narrative line, gradually broadens out to embrace his school career, both junior and senior, and finally extends even further to his war experiences in North Africa and Italy. The flowers still remain firmly planted in all these contexts, but it is other autobiographical themes that take precedence – his development as a writer, for example, or as lover of Italy. In retrospect, indeed, the first part of the book seems rather too self-consciously orientated towards plants and flowers, until the chain breaks and the independent writer is finally let off the leash.

Since first publication, there has been discussion as to whether the books of the trilogy are autobiographies or novels – a rather pointless exercise, save for those who love pigeonholes. Some have called them "managed autobiography",[19] but if we must have a category, it is perhaps the word invented by the Edwardian writer, Stephen Reynolds, – autobiografiction – that best fits. In Reynolds' description this category, of which there have been many examples both before Reynolds and since, comprises essentially a selected episode of autobiography, partially rearranged in time and space, written to communicate a deeply felt spiritual experience.[20] Brooke approaches this in his own distinctive way, generally maintaining the integrity of time and space in the mainly autobiographical passages, but adding in the more novel-based parts (primarily in the last two books) semi-fictional characters which are carefully crafted composites of actual people. The result is an intriguing mix of biography and semi-fiction which gives the books their unique flavour.

The Military Orchid was written, like the first two novels, at breakneck speed through the cold wet summer of 1946, and by August it was finished. It is short in length and in the later publication of the combined trilogy as one book perhaps tends to get lost in the larger work. Indeed, in such a format the individual character of each book becomes submerged and lost in a trilogy devised for publishing convenience rather than by express intention of the author. Read in their first editions, the charm of the original publication returns – the delicately drawn jackets, the historical plates, the line illustrations, the surfeit of obscure but pointed epigraphs, all combining to make a work of art, not merely a work of literature. The charm is reinforced by our historical recollection of the famine conditions of post-war publishing – the tiny formats, the coarse thin paper, the slim volumes. When we riffle through the 135 small pages of *The Military Orchid* in its original version, we can perhaps understand how it managed to get written in just those few summer months; and when we sense from the quality of its paper the shortage of supply, we understand too how a book completed and accepted in the middle of 1946 could not achieve publication until 1948. The three books of the trilogy are products of their age – 1940s in subject and feeling; 1940s as manufactured artefacts.

In *The Military Orchid* we are swiftly introduced to the basic building blocks of the Brooke biography. In prime place is that love of the Kentish village south of Canterbury which leaps upon us from the first page in the mysterious, yet comfortingly rustic, form of Mr Bundock.

> Mr Bundock's function, so far as my family was con-
> cerned, was to empty the earth-closet twice a week at

the cottage where we used to spend the summer. This duty he performed unobtrusively and usually late at night: looming up suddenly in the summer-dusk, earth-smelling and hairy like some menial satyr, a kind of Lob. (Perhaps the maids left a bowl of cream for him on the threshold).[21]

The feelings are already established in this richly Brookean opening. A few pages on, the author takes intellectual stock of them.

I suppose for many people, as for myself, some childhood-scene tends to become archetypal, the hidden source of all one's private imagery, tinging the most banal and quotidian words and objects with its distinct yet often unrecognized flavour. For me the village where we spent my childhood summers, where Mr Bundock lurked like a wood-spirit in the warm, tree-muffled evenings, has this quality of legend. Certain basic, ordinary words such as 'wood', 'stream', 'village', in whatever context I may use them, will always, for me, evoke a particular wood, a particular stream, almost always in the immediate neighbourhood of our summer-cottage... A word which, more than most, evokes for me that Kentish village, is the word 'afternoon'. The cool, green, slumberous syllables refuse to be detached from the cottage-garden, drowsing among its trees, the tea-table laid in the shade, the buzzing of wasps busy among the fallen plums – a subdued, perpetual bourdon orchestrating the shriller melodic line of birdsong and the voices of children. In memory, the village seems held in a perpetual trance of summer afternoons: possibly for no better reason than that we seldom visited it in winter.[22]

And possibly also because this compelling image, these sweetly chiselled words, were formed in that desolate wintry summer of 1946 when the world was in limbo, the weather along with it, and Brooke was sensing that despair of resettlement about which he was to write later so powerfully in *The Image*: "I had embarked upon the gradual and depressing process of settling into the old rut, in an England more drab and unaccommodating than even the worst reports from home had led me to believe. It was an England in which even the climate seemed to have worsened: the dreary, sunless summer of 1946 followed by the worst winter in living memory ...".[23]

Yet, at the same time, Brooke fully recognised that with this homecoming, however superficially constraining, he was being given a freedom, especially a freedom to write, that in the 1930s had been stifled by illness and lack of confidence, and in the 1940s by the exigencies of army life. The nostalgic, yet vibrant, prose that now blossomed forth from the window of the garden-hut at Ivy Cottage depended wholly upon this new-found freedom, and the new confidence that facing up to war work, his first proper job, had given him. In 1939, he had thought of the war with fear in his stomach, the same fear that had marked the return to boarding school after the summer holidays; but war was a school where the holidays might never come again. Now he recognised with relief that the war had not been so bad after all, certainly not as bad as the horrors of an English prep school. He had survived and was grateful: "for me, happening to be lucky, the holidays have come again".[24]

As has been pointed out, the quest for the military orchid which provides the unifying theme of the book is, at its most recondite level, a metaphor for the search for physical love, in Brooke's case, of course, for homosexual love. Many of the themes in the trilogy can be found traced out in the poems he had written in earlier years, which shows how close they were to the surface of his imagination, just waiting to burst forth. This one is a case in point. In a poem written in 1942, which Brooke later referred to as *The Military Orchid*, the flower is seen as an image of a Highland soldier's uniform, the sporran forming the orchid's lip – the Highland soldier in question being Albert Heron, his love of the early 1930s.[25] But in the novel the author does not make heavy weather of this, touching on it only lightly with a glancing reference to Proust's "almost too technical"[26] allusion to the fertilisation of an orchid as an image of the encounter between Charlus and Jupien. A year after the poem was written, Brooke himself denied any conscious sexual imagery: "Lehmann said of 'Military Orchid' 'It's rather a difficult poem to publish, isn't it?' and in fact, on rereading, it seems more obscene than I intended, by reason of an equivocal image which appears physiological, though I intended it to be only botanical... Something about a sporran... Shades of Dover, circa 1933".[27]

It would be wrong, therefore, to look upon *The Military Orchid* as a work smouldering with hidden homosexual references and unfulfilled sexual desire. In the beautifully constructed final part of the book, the metaphor is broad and very clear: the author fails to find the orchid but instead finds even greater objects of love – humanity and nature – in the shape of the Abruzzi countryside and the peasant families that inhabit it. The first family that he and his fellow soldiers encounter in Sicily serves as a prelude to the intimate relationship with the Abruzzi family which later takes them in and effectively adopts them. The first provides a moving scene of almost Biblical feeling in the physical conjunction of father, mother and child.

> We had made friends with a peasant-family, and used to
> spend most of our evenings with them. The house lay
> back from the road, down a dusty lane bordered with
> prickly-pears: the children would see us coming down
> the lane and call *Buona sera*. We sat in the doorway of
> the house, in the dusk, eating almonds and drinking
> an excellent red wine from Floridia. Inside the door,
> the mother sat with her youngest child on her knee:
> the father sat nearby, at the table, on which the wine-
> bottle gleamed darkly in the light from a primitive

lamp, consisting of a wick floating in olive-oil; the other children crouched in the doorway, in the dusk. They were the most beautiful people I had ever seen, and the most civilized.[28]

And the landscape in which these holy families have their incarnation holds an equal beauty for an author reaching out toward a poetic vision of winter turning prematurely into spring.

It had snowed for a week: and suddenly the wind came soft and the brown and green patchwork of fields, the silver-grey olives were revealed again. The sun at midday was warm as an English May, the stream-side was miraculously fringed with white polyanthus narcissi, their heavy scent evoking the atmosphere of English drawing-rooms. In the copse, white crocuses sprang like sudden stars, and among the undergrowth crimson anemones flickered like strontium-flames. Next day the snow returned, powdering with soft precision the fields and woods, formal and pictorial as the snow in a Victorian glass paperweight. The anemones, the narcissi were a freak, a vision of Spring in Winter; fleeting as the sudden never-to-be-repeated lyric thrown off by some dull, time-serving pedant; a promise not to be fulfilled in this winter land, this never-turned page of the missal, lying open on the lectern, showing only Winter: the reader away at the wars, perhaps dead by now.[29]

This is an English author writing romantically from an English village in the midst of a cold and rainy English summer. So the similes for this exotic landscape are inescapably English too: the English May, English drawing-rooms, Victorian paperweights. But what that author misses most in this miraculous land of botanic wonders is the nerve-edge of the countryside he knows and loves best: "These fields and woods declared themselves with too much frankness; they had none of that mysteriousness, that hint of the *au delà*, which lurks always in the English countryside, even in the Home Counties, and especially during the winter and early spring".[30] And lurks most potently of all in that exotic valley of woods and hills just a little south of Canterbury.

This book which ends so romantically in the midst of an Italian spring was swept up by his eager publishers in the autumn of 1946. But the shortage of paper in the post-war climate of austerity ensured that the book would not reach its public until 1948, shortly before *The Scapegoat*, on which he now continued to work, was finally published. Though for some time an occasional contributor to various magazines, he now (with two unpublished books in the pipeline) began to move more freely in the London literary world with which, as an essentially rural recluse, he had an ambivalent on-off relationship.

Italy, which had provided the stimulus for the inspired writing at the close of the *Orchid*, was still very much at the forefront of his mind, and it was through his London contacts that in early 1947 he landed a journalistic assignment to report on the post-war culture and economy of Italy, comparing the apparent social buoyancy of that "defeated" nation with the drab desperation of the "victorious" country in which he now lived. For Brooke this was above all an opportunity, both spiritual and literary, to revisit the Abruzzi in peacetime and finally consolidate that dream-like experience which after three years was gradually slipping away into myth. He had always intended to go back there. In the late summer of 1944, when he had left the Abruzzi for the north, he had told Ninnie: "I *much* regret all our friends at the place we spent the winter and spring. They were some of the nicest people I've ever met, and how we did eat and drink! I should like to do a walking-tour of all that part after the war – it would have to be a walking one, since, so far as I know, there's no other way of getting about, and no roads for cars or buses".[31]

He set off for Italy by boat and train in the early days of that notoriously wonderful summer of 1947, but never got further south than Florence. To all the travel agents he consulted there, the Abruzzi was a wild, uninviting country involving a long, difficult and expensive journey – a holiday venue to be treated with caution.[32] He was tempted to believe them: he was fast running out of money; if he fell ill there, where would he find medical help? In any case, he was enjoying himself with friends in Florence and the power of inertia was winning the day. But all these were mere excuses: the real reason behind the failure of his private mission was the very human fear that the reality might not live up to the vision. And what indeed was reality for a writer whose principal theme was the nostalgic past – the experience of the actuality or the experience of the writing?

> Yet at intervals, hauntingly, the vision would recur, and I would resolve to set off the very next day. I realized that the travel difficulties, the fear of illness, were mere alibis, the habitual evasions of a congenitally lazy and stay-at-home disposition... I would start the next day; but the next day it rained, or I remembered that I had a date... How real, after all, was my vision? Wasn't I remembering the nostalgic poems and stories I had written about it, rather than the place, the moment themselves? Similarly, at school or at Oxford, I had written poems and 'novels' about my childhood, thereby distorting the pristine reality till memory and invention became inextricably merged...
> 'Perhaps it would be wiser' said Imogen [*his friend*], 'to keep your illusions'.[33]

And so he did; though the decision not to go south may in itself have taken him a long way towards destroying them.

With *The Military Orchid* and *The Scapegoat* grinding through the publishers' slow presses, and always with a first book the hope of a warm reception and sales, Brooke had now the possibility of an established literary future, writing from his cottage in the country he so loved. To accentuate the point, a new book, autobiographical successor to the *Orchid*, had been gathering force in his mind ever since coming back from Italy. But just as in 1945, on return from war, he had shied against re-entry to a quiet, predictable routine life in England, so now did he shy away from the prospect of an assured existence in the literary world. He had always wanted to write, but had still so little confidence in his ability that the only future he could foresee for himself was the average career of mediocrity, heading inevitably for the downhill path.

> The prospect of becoming a professional *littérateur* depressed me; I preferred to remain an amateur. I knew the booksy racket too well: a *succès d'estime* with a first novel; reviewing for the *Statesman* or the *Times Litt. Supp.*, a talk or two on the Third Programme. Then another book: not so successful. ('I confess to being disappointed with Mr. X's new novel...); more reviewing, more talks; an essay or two on some obscure minor writer for the *Cornhill*; and then the gradual decline, through anthologies, 'introductions' and light middles, to a weekly *causerie* in *John O'London* or a staff-job in the B.B.C...[34]

He was later to nibble tentatively at one or two rungs of this rather bitter ladder of decline, but the comparative failure of his own literary career after an explosive start was very much that of a man who had consciously rejected the role of hack and was not prepared to abandon his country nest or his personal themes to court the barons of literary London.

For the moment, two years of heavily concerted writing now led him back to the escape route for which he had half been longing ever since the day of demobilisation – return to the army. "As for my own writing, I enjoyed it well enough, but I was unable to take it with a proper seriousness. To spend hours, like Flaubert, polishing a phrase, was for me an impossibility; I would rather polish a pair of boots."[35]

So when that long hot Denis Compton summer finally drifted to its close, the autumn of 1947 found him back again at Shorncliffe Camp, the army barracks overlooking the sea and his childhood home on the Sandgate undercliff. At one level it was not so surprising: his money was running short and the eighteen month publishing cycle meant a long wait for financial return. But at a deeper, psychological level there was a certain inevitability about it all: "Like a tattoo-mark, the print of the Army stained my mind, indelibly. The summer continued triumphantly, week after week of perfect weather. I felt fitter than I had felt for two years: and once again, like an adolescent, I was troubled by the old, perverse itch to abandon myself to something which I believed I hated. This time, however, there was a difference: it wouldn't be my first 'experience'".[36]

In the middle of October he took the scarlet and cream bus of the East Kent Road Car Company through the autumnal stubble fields of the Elham Valley to the Folkestone barracks he knew so well. There his intellectual qualification secured him a clerical post in the stores, where he spent a cushy few weeks with minimal work and frequent weekend passes back to the village just fifteen miles away. Eventually he passed his "trade test" and returned to the venereal disease branch of the RAMC. He managed to obtain a posting to the Woolwich hospital, close enough to his mother's Blackheath home for a (most convenient) sleeping-out pass. His re-enlistment was greeted with incredulity by his new comrades and his old literary friends alike, but straightway on his first evening back at Shorncliffe, lying on his bed leafing through an old copy of *Picture Post*, he knew why he was there: "The wireless droned out a swing-tune; from the open window a cool wind, smelling of the sea, played over my bare arms and chest. I felt relaxed, free of responsibility, happy; I was back in the Army".[37]

He had signed on for the standard three years but in the event lasted scarcely one. Perhaps return to these familiar duties was not supportable in the longer term without the special physical and spiritual momentum of war. His earlier service had taken him through Palestine, North Africa, Sicily and Italy – constantly on the move, never sure how long the current location would last, always the nervous stimulus of an unknown future. A more or less permanent posting to Woolwich in a sclerotic post-war army offered little by comparison. And he had foolishly accepted promotion to corporal, biting off more than he could chew. In addition to his normal day job, he had now to undertake night duties three or more times a fortnight, which reduced him to a frazzle. At the same time, he was striving to keep up with his intellectual work: he gave a Third Programme talk on orchids (much to the surprised amusement of his military colleagues) and was struggling with the book that was to become *The Wonderful Summer*. He wrote to John Lehmann. "writing a couple of new chapters for the children's book nearly killed me!".[38]

When change came, it was ostensibly for economic as much as emotional reasons. *The Military Orchid* was finally published in the spring of the following year to instant acclaim. Reviewers fell over one another in the scramble for superlatives. The foremost critic of the day Desmond MacCarthy led the way with an influential piece in *The Sunday Times* headed simply "Distinction".[39] In a sheaf of reviews, the book was found alternately witty, erudite, sophisticated, sensitive, done with rare charm and perception. Elizabeth Bowen spoke for many readers in describing it as "one of those too rare books whose enjoyability makes it seem too short".[40]

MacCarthy had already come across Brooke through an advance fragment of *The Scapegoat* in John Lehmann's magazine *Orpheus* which had whetted quite a number of literary appetites. MacCarthy went overboard in a letter to the author: "I'm craving to go on with "The Scapegoat": I have lived inside that boy, Duncan; I have been alternately terrified and propitiated by the massively commonplace, yet ominously queer Gerald March; the disquieting crushing ordinariness of that farm and village by the sea has gripped me – I must know what it hides". There was acknowledgement too for the prose style: "And accept the tribute of an old critic who has read at any rate more variously than most of his tribe – you can w r i t e –

you know it, but you are not yet famous enough not to be still pleased when told so".[41]

When *The Scapegoat* finally arrived on MacCarthy's desk he found it disappointingly slight: "The fragment had led me to expect more than a psychological study in sadistic homo-sexuality. I was disappointed.... Beware of the modern mistake of thinking that psychology adds to the mystery of life or its poetry. Its effect is in the opposite direction".[42] But he had by then read *The Military Orchid* and pronounced himself "satisfied", following it up with heavy praise in his column in the *Sunday Times*. Although Brooke knew the review would be good, it nevertheless came to him as a bolt from the blue – the first major review he had ever received.

> One Sunday morning I opened the paper to find that my book had received a long and glowing review from an extremely eminent critic... I read and reread the article throughout the day, still half-inclined to suppose that either myself or the eminent reviewer had suddenly gone mad... My book received other reviews – less exciting than that first, intoxicating paean of praise, but quite flattering enough to nourish my newly-acquired but already insatiable vanity. Resigned for many years to being a perpetual failure, I had now suddenly been injected with the potent, habit-forming toxin of success, and it had flown – as such poisons will when one is unaccustomed to them – straight to my head.[43]

As the first novelty wore off, the acclaim became more of a burden than a blessing for it served only to point up his current predicament. Here he was, trapped in the army by overwork just as the siren of success was beckoning temptingly from outside. He needed to return to the world of culture if he were to have once more the space to write. The favourable reception of the book, however, coincided fortuitously with two other events that were to assist his release: out of the blue, the military authorities reintroduced the pre-war policy of buying out of the army; and about the same time Brooke received a call from his producer at the BBC suggesting he might apply for one of the posts of talks producer then being advertised. His highly praised new book was selling well enough to realise the hundred pounds needed to buy himself out.

So at the beginning of 1949 he joined the BBC as talks producer on the Third Programme, but his progress in this novel species of paid employment followed predictably the pattern of the past. He was quick to recognise that a small self-regarding literary clique stuck in a large bureaucratic organisation was not the life for him; he resigned after only four months. There was another contributory factor. He was beginning to find living in London, at the old family house in Blackheath, too much of a strain and wholly unconducive to writing. He returned to the little cottage in the Kentish village where, cosseted once more by Ninnie and his mother May (known within the family as The Owl because of the thick tortoiseshell frames to her spectacles), he could begin his settled writing career in earnest.

He had by now completed the second book of the autobiographical trilogy, *A Mine of Serpents*, the book he had had in mind ever since his Italian trip two summers before. In the new biography, his passion for fireworks takes the place of his botanical obsessions, and indeed the firework of the title supersedes the orchid of the first book as the object of desire and single-minded pursuit; but less securely so, as the firework theme, more closely associated with childhood, tends naturally to dissipate as the narrator moves on into adult life.[44]

The narrative of the new book is neither so well controlled nor organised as the first. That had followed what seemed a natural progression through childhood and schooldays until, in the final part, it brought the reader up to date with a shock, suddenly thrusting him into the sharply contrasting scenes of army life in wartime. Within its narrow compass, it had a perfect symmetry.

A Mine of Serpents builds once more the story of the narrator's past, but this time within the contemporary setting of the 1947 journey to Italy and its crucial dilemma – to go, or not to go, back to the Abruzzi. Brooke creates more of a novel this time round by introducing two semi-fictional characters symbolising two distinct episodes of his life: Hew Dallas, the aesthete, to represent the Oxford days and Basil Medlicott, the ageing hearty, the London of nightclubs and homosexual haunts in the 1930s. Both characters carry with them an intangible air of mystery as they drift in and out of the narrator's life, each time in new and surprising guises, but neither really develop as human beings out of the symbolic figures we first meet. This narrative can be seen as a set of chinese boxes, moving boldly in and out of different time periods,[45] but in truth these movements seem more haphazard than in the previous book, leaving the reader on occasion stranded and struggling to catch his bearings in time and place. The introduction, quite out of context, of a warmed-up article on the author's great-grandfather, the writer Joseph Hewlett, is perhaps indication of Brooke tending here to fall dangerously close to pot-boiler mode, rather than stay in full aesthetic control of his creation, as we have in the past come to expect.

But Brooke was always one to assert the prerogative of the writer to write about whatever he chose, and these are minor criticisms of a work that has most of the combined strengths of its predecessor: a delicious prose style, an acute perception and sensitivity, a narrative that, opening this time with the start of a physical journey, entices the reader irresistibly on to the end, even though there is perhaps no firm destination ever to be reached. Once again, the narrative is held together by the mythical power of the countryside south of Canterbury, and in particular the new image of the ghostly, yet protective, water-tower that presides like a god over its kingdom – the child's imagined subterranean world stretching beneath the downs all the way to the tunnels in the cliffs at Dover, a world from which the miners of the Kent coalfield emerge from time to time to clamber like monkeys over the iron balustrades of this building of mystery, whose practical purpose in this world is impossible to fathom. On those occasions when the family took the car, rather than train, for their spring or summer holiday, it was the tower that marked their return to the country: "or sometimes, we would go, more excitingly, by car: actually penetrating the mysterious barrier of the hills, driving through Swingfield and Denton and along the high plateau of Barham Downs, until at last we would see, gleaming above the far woodlands, the white, familiar peak of the watertower".[46]

For although the tower appears at times as a symbol of the mysterious, dangerous underground world from which it springs, a phallic symbol like the military orchid, it appears more frequently as this other nostalgic symbol of comfort, of safe return home. When the picnic parties of Brooke's childhood become lost in the woods, the white tower appears miraculously out of the trees on the other horizon to give them back their bearings. At the touching close of the book, beginning to despair of the prospect of a writer's life, the narrator takes a trip to Chatham to put out feelers for a possible return to the army. But he is undecided, nervous of the future. At Canterbury, he continues on the Dover train rather than take the taxi or bus home, and sees the tower for the first time from a completely new angle, both physical and metaphysical, a relic of comfort but also a symbol of challenge.

> Instead of leaving the train at Canterbury, as I usually did, I went on to Bekesbourne. The station was silent and apparently deserted, isolated among high, empty-looking fields. The rain fell gently; I looked across at the line of woods on the horizon, and gave a sudden start of surprised recognition: there, protruding nakedly from the dark mass of trees, gleaming with a tarnished whiteness against the grey sky, was the watertower. I had scarcely ever seen it, before, from this aspect: I was on the 'wrong' side of it, beyond the frontier-line of the woods. Over there, on the other side, was familiar country; mute, non-committal, the tower stood between two worlds, guarding the frontier: its white cap poised,

like a silent, hovering bird, between the future and the
past.[47]

Published in 1949, the book was received with equal delight to its
predecessor. The success of *The Military Orchid* had created firm
expectations in the mind of the reviewers, and they were not
disappointed. But the most distinguished reviewer to give this second
book a push was Anthony Powell in the *Times Literary Supplement*,
who by contrast had not read the *Orchid* and was only vaguely aware
of Brooke's existence, and that as a largely botanophil writer.[48] His
review was full of praise for this uniquely distinctive voice and Powell,
who met and befriended Brooke four years later, was to become a
convinced champion of the new writer and continue to wave the flag
long after Brooke's death.

In a note at the front of this new book, Brooke had linked it with the
Orchid as a complementary work – "two sets of variations on the same
or similar thematic material".[49] He now set out to write a new book
to form "the third volume of what may loosely be called a 'trilogy'",[50]
sensing that, though his autobiographical material was seemingly
inexhaustible, this work would put a definite end to the series. In his
introduction to *The Goose Cathedral*, he openly acknowledges that this
is "autobiografiction", the form to which the writer Stephen Reynolds
had given the name back in 1906. And the reasons for choosing it over
fiction or autobiography were almost identical to those of Reynolds. In
his 1908 preface to *A Poor Man's House*, which Reynolds had originally
planned as a novel, he had written: "Fiction, however, showed itself
an inappropriate medium. I was unwilling to cut about the material,
to modify the characters, in order to meet the exigencies of plot,
form, and so on. I felt that the life and the people were so much better
than anything I could invent".[51] Brooke in 1950 uses much the same
arguments.

The present volume, like its two predecessors, is neither
entirely fictitious nor entirely autobiographical; by way

of apology for this hybrid breed, I can only say that, as a method of composition, I happen to find it useful. To force my material into novel form would involve a Procrustean distortion of the theme which, for me at least, would make the book pointless, and not worth the bother of writing. On the other hand, 'straight' autobiography is ruled out for more obvious reasons – the law of libel being one.[52]

The Goose Cathedral is clearly the most mature book of the three. Brooke has by now slipped into the pattern of this fictional-autobiographical structure and shows himself very much at ease within it, both in prose style and in narrative building. With fewer of the metaphorical fireworks of the other books, it may seem at first read rather quiet and slow, but it has a unity of approach and feeling that the others perhaps lack. It begins and ends with the striking immediacy of army life – starting at the moment of the narrator's re-enlistment in October 1947 and ending in the barracks a few weeks later, settled back into military life and still waiting his formal posting to Woolwich. In between we have three episodes from his early life – childhood botanising on the undercliff at Sandgate, the wider world of Folkestone, the horrors of his first serious school – interspersed with three from his adult life – the early thirties at a loose end in Folkestone working for the family firm, mid-thirties in London and the introduction of two new fictional characters, Pussy Wilkinson and Bert Hunwick, in the style of Basil Medlicott, and finally the gloomy hopelessness of the immediate pre-war period.

This is the Folkestone book (there is little of the village near Canterbury) and it is the unity of place that more than anything else provides the unity of feel. Like the previous book, but even more effectively, the narrative is bound together by the presence of a symbolic building, the Goose Cathedral,[53] the ornate neo-Gothic boathouse on the foreshore whose continuing changes of use – from lifeboat station to private dwelling to seaside café – mirror the cycles of the author's own life, which finally collapse around him as the despised technocrats of the modern world take over. "It was as though, in the shadowy, haunted spaces of the Goose Cathedral, the whole of my past, the whole, carefully built-up structure of my life and personality, had collapsed like a card-house. My innumerable *personae*, my *bovarysmes*, lay scattered like shot birds about the spiky, turreted pile of the boathouse..." [54]

There were more plaudits from the reviewers as the book came out in the autumn of 1950, but now Brooke was no longer a new voice and the praise was inevitably a little more restrained, if still just as positive. Robert Kee in the *New Statesman* saw this "apparently easily woven symphony of narrative and reflection" as "quite simply the theme of life itself", and the three books together as catching more subtly than other contemporary works "the dying fall of our time". [55] The unified strength of the new book seemed to give a unity to the trilogy as a whole and marked a significant rounding off of the project that had made Brooke's name. What would he do next: branch out into new fields, or find a safe niche on the literary ladder he had earlier so scornfully rejected?

The answer was simple. He would not strive to repeat the formulaic success of the trilogy (at least not for the time being) but would frankly please himself, launching into those things, often on a small uncommercial scale, which interested him most. Thus he produced two botanical works – *The Wild Orchids of Britain* in 1950, on which he had been working for some time, and the more populist *The Flower in Season* in 1952, both of which showed off his botanical expertise to a genuinely scientific audience. In that latter year too he published a new volume of poetry, *The Elements of Death* and, using his well accredited literary critical skills, in 1951 a work on a favoured author who regularly crops up in the pages of the trilogy, *Ronald Firbank*. In the same vein, he used his current influence to resurrect that *wunderkind* of the 1940s, the writer and artist Denton Welch, by editing his diaries, also published in 1952. [56]

Such was Brooke's reputation at this time for these literary sideshows that in 1954 he was commissioned by Heinemann to compile a Festschrift for Somerset Maugham to be presented to the old author on his 80th birthday. It was not so strange a choice. Brooke and Maugham had some local interests in common: both had endured a miserable time at the King's School, yet had retained a deep nostalgic love for the countryside around Canterbury. In his later years Maugham was occasionally to be seen retracing his childhood haunts in Whitstable from Joy Lane to the graveyard at All Saints church where he tended the graves of the uncle and aunt who had brought him up there. But the enterprise was a disaster. Maugham's personal and literary reputation at the time was enough to frighten the horses; most of the distinguished literary figures approached to write the essays on him for the compilation cried off with polite excuses. Anthony Powell and Raymond Mortimer were the only two to offer their services and accordingly the project had to be aborted.[57]

Thus in the early fifties these varied and idiosyncratic works poured forth in a regular stream from the little cottage in the Kentish village, riding on the critical success of the trilogy and the earlier novels. For the children's book *The Wonderful Summer* had been published in 1949, and *The Image of a Drawn Sword* followed the next year. Brooke had very sensibly given himself a break from the most demanding creative work, but it was only a short one. He knew he was not cut out for straight novels, which is why he had taken the autobiographical route; but he also knew he could not fall back on the identical formulae of the trilogy if he were to carry credibility among the salivating critics, now sharpening their knives in readiness for the first failure.

He was now an established writer, acknowledged at least by his colleagues in literary circles as a brilliant *petit-maître*. He had always been sociable, especially in pubs and clubs where drink lifted his spirits and banished his natural shyness, but it was a sociability very much on his own terms. He would appear now and again in the village pub, or take tea at the old rectory, but work kept him more often

holed up in Ivy Cottage or striding alone the woods and footpaths of
his childhood memories.

> From the green and tunnelled lane
> Of May-time beeches
> Fresh from the night's rain,
> I come to the flattened reaches
> Of Barham Downs, where the wind
> Stirs taw-grass and clover...
>
> And crossing the rising land
> By wind-blown hedge
> And hollied copse, I stand
> At last on the naked edge
> Of the known and childhood world,
> Seeing the white-capped tower
> Like sudden flag unfurled
> Above the dark woodland...[58]

He maintained close contact with his old friends of the twenties
and thirties through the occasional visit, but more usually by
correspondence. With his now established reputation new
acquaintances, mostly literary, came thick and fast, but he was slow
to pursue them to friendships, often failing deliberately, as he himself
admitted, to follow up a first meeting. He needed these relationships,
but was happier conducting them from behind his typewriter in the
comparative safety of his own home.

Two writers who first met him during this period of the early
fifties, Anthony Powell and Olivia Manning, have left us with brief
portraits of how he looked and behaved. Powell first met him in 1953
having written to thank him for an article in *Time and Tide* praising
Powell's first novel, *Afternoon Men*.[59] They met occasionally and
corresponded fitfully from then on, but Powell realised early that
Brooke preferred writing letters to meeting face to face.

I was never a close friend of Jocelyn Brooke's, but we corresponded quite often, and he was one of the people to whom one wrote letters with great ease. He speaks more than once of his own liking for that sort of relationship, a kind that did not make him feel hemmed in. There are several incidents in his books when the narrator refuses an invitation from someone with whom he is getting on pretty well so that it was no great surprise when, a few months after Brooke had stayed with us for a weekend, he politely excused himself from another visit on grounds of work. The reason may have been valid enough, writing time always hard to conserve, but one suspected his sense of feeling 'different', unwillingness to cope with face-to-face cordialities of a kind that might at the same time be agreeable in letters.[60]

This lack of natural cordiality, brought on perhaps by shyness, could be overcome by alcohol, on imbibing which he could swiftly become somewhat over-cordial. Powell noted this weakness also: "Brooke liked a fair amount to drink, and, after lunching with one, was inclined to say: 'Shall we be *beasts*, and now go to *my* club, and have another glass of port?'"[61] Olivia Manning, on Brooke's first visit to her house in St John's Wood, also noted the two sides to his sociability. He had been visiting a composer friend whose studio was next door to her, and he followed her quietly enough as she showed him round her garden.

Jocelyn was surprised by the size of our garden and by some of the things a pre-war garden-loving tenant had planted there. The composer, with his guest out of the way, had returned to his twelve-tone composing and, as Jocelyn and I wandered round in the spring sunshine, the air was full of speculative chords that never reached resolution. Jocelyn was sober and subdued. He was lean and lumbering, with a narrow, weathered countryman's face, tight mouth and long, jutting nose. His eyes were strikingly dark and gave him a startled expression. He had little to say until we reached a helleborus that was massed with small green flowers. Perhaps it was a *Helleborous olympicus*. Whatever it was, it caused him to stop and stare, and he said it was an unusual kind. I felt proud of it. Later that evening we met in the Ordnance Arms. Jocelyn was neither sober nor subdued. Soon he began to tweak the hair of the composer's wife and, meeting with disapproval, he went off in search of wilder woods.[62]

Manning, who was distinctly ambivalent towards both the man and his works, is not perhaps the most reliable witness as to character. Anthony Powell, in his more accustomed stance of open generosity, is gentler, even in his physical description of the man.

In appearance Jocelyn Brooke was tall, pale, not bad looking, with an air of melancholy that would suddenly leave him when he laughed. Photographs give him a haggard air, a stare as if mesmerizing or mesmerized (perhaps assumed for fun), that hardly does him justice. He often reminded me of George Orwell, not in feature so much as a kind of hesitancy of manner, thinking for a second or two of what had been said, but he had none of Orwell's wish to set the world right, and his laughter was quite un-Orwellian.[63]

It is noteworthy that Olivia Manning should have seen him as a weathered countryman, for in many respects that was what he now was. Despite his new-found minor celebrity, he could stand the life of London club-land, even among sympathetic writers like Anthony Powell, only for so long. A natural instinct soon drew him back to the cottage and village where he could write in peace and draw sustenance from the natural world that surrounded him there.

The success of the trilogy had set him a new and puzzling problem – how to write more and yet *different*. Though it may be an accepted phenomenon that many authors write the same book over and over again, they have at least to try and make them look distinct, if only on the surface. But leaving behind the botany and the literary biography of the past three years and returning to fiction, he now found himself unable to evade the obsession with his own past that was so central to his writing. Thus in his next quasi-novel, *The Passing of a Hero*, we follow the familiar Brooke narrator through prep school, to Oxford, on to London working in bookshops, and finally to the beginning of the war. The book takes a more overtly novelistic form by setting out to chart the career of a third party, one of Brooke's Oxford aesthetes, Denzil Pryce-Foulger, the hero of the title whose claim to our interest lies in his failure to realise his scholastic potential. Pryce-Foulger publishes a book so out of his style that no-one believes it is his – a theme Brooke is to return to in his last published novel, *Conventional Weapons*. The impact of this new work is slight compared to the trilogy, and the critics were quick to notice. The attempt to disguise it as a novel by running a fictional hero throughout (unlike the episodic heroes of the trilogy) just does not come off. It was now that Brooke became depressed with his writing career ("nasty, brutish and short") and spoke to friends of being "written out".[64]

Worse was to follow the next year (1954) when Brooke published *Private View*, a potboiler of a book, in part based on a magazine article and a radio talk. It contains four portraits, two of which – Alison Vyse and Kurt Schlegel – had appeared as minor characters in the trilogy; and a third, Gerald Brockhurst, marks a return to the Gerald March figure of *The Scapegoat*. Once again, these characters are set against the backdrop of the narrator's own progress through childhood, university, working life and war, but as ever the narrator ends up stealing the show and these four figures become the backdrop to him. There is in places here some very fine, strongly confessional, prose writing, and the book is more open in its homosexual content than previous works, but these strengths are overridden by the rather strange "four portrait" format, which seems to denote a lazy writer too nervous to tackle a proper novel in which all of these characters might perform together their interlocking roles.[65]

These two comparative failures were, however, to reap their ultimate reward. By leading Brooke back into that closed world of the nostalgic past, where his real heart lay, they now paved the way for his eventual masterpiece which was to put even the delights of the trilogy into the shade.

In March 1953 Brooke made a pilgrimage back to Sicily where he had been posted during the war in the aftermath of the allied Italian landings. He always took his continental holidays in the early spring to catch the flora at its most beautiful and abundant. It was a similar expedition to his Italian journey of 1947 that had given rise to *A Mine of Serpents*, but this time he was going by air. Olivia Manning noted the tension: "I saw him just before he set out on this journey by air, and as we were both equally scared of flying, the meeting was overhung with funerary gloom".[66] This new adventure now stimulated ideas for a new book that was to take the trilogy, and indeed all his writing, one step further in maturity.

Like the first two books of the trilogy, *The Dog at Clambercrown* is about a search – in fact, two searches. The literary motive of the return to Sicily is to trace the "fair fields of Enna" and take his earthly bearings on the myth of Persephone, which, with its strong botanical element, had captured him in childhood. The second pursuit is of the equally mythical country of Clambercrown where the Dog public house presides over an image of a lost world, of legendary status for the young Brooke because, though frequently talked of at home, its precise location is seemingly unknown. Both territories, one lying in the midst of the barren rocky mountains of Sicily, the other in the impenetrable wooded hills beyond Bishopsbourne, represent for

Brooke "the forbidden kingdom", the country of the mind in which most writers find their inspiration, and he more than most.

Both searches end in ostensible failure: the supposed magic of Sicily is ruined by the impact of the modern world – disgruntled natives and puerile tourists; the legendary public house, once located at the crossroads just south of Lynsore Court, turns out to have recently closed, leaving just an unprepossessing private house.[67] But each search produces an unexpected discovery and a fresh understanding: in Sicily a renewal of Brooke's earlier encounters with the *real* natives of Italy, as a friendly extended family that runs the wineshop in Pergusa (like the Abruzzi family of ten years before) takes him in for a riotous Easter Sunday festive meal. And back in Kent in 1925, struggling through the August heat on the way to discover *The Dog*, the adolescent Brooke goes through a pleasure/pain climacteric, spreadeagled naked in a woodland clearing, a dramatic break with innocence which seems to give structure and understanding to his uncharted sexual desires. What we seek and what we find, says Brooke once more, are two quite different things.

With *The Dog at Clambercrown* Brooke pulls in all the structural threads he had used to such effect in the trilogy. He begins, as in *A Mine of Serpents*, with a continental journey, the usual telling detail (this time of air flight) heightening the feeling of nervous anticipation. We sense the fear of take-off as he waits at the terminal for the fog to clear, and the great relief as he meets the beauty of the warming sun once above the clouds.

> The aeroplane reared itself dimly in the gloom: we mounted the gangway, took our seats; five minutes later we were roaring down the run-way; another minute and we were, miraculously, above the fog, in the brilliant sunshine of a March morning. As we climbed, the belt of fog fell away: London lay like a plate of brown soup below. Presently the brown thinned out into a patchy whiteness: here and there the Surrey

1. September 1943 – The Archers shoot the cathedral. St Thomas' Catholic Church, site of Conrad's funeral, stands desolate on the right.

2. Director of Photography, Erwin Hiller, spots a cloud advancing.

3. Michael Powell sets up at the Christ Church Gate.

4. Kenneth Witney, historian.

5. St Mary's Church, Bishopsbourne.

6. Whitstable Library in the 1950s.

7. Ninnie (Emily Fagg) and Jocelyn, Sandgate *c* 1909.

8. A youthful Jocelyn.

9. Forge and Ivy Cottages *c* 1920, *left to right* Jocelyn, Ninnie, Alice and The Owl.

10. The cottages today, with the façade of Ivy Cottage on the right.

11. Jocelyn Brooke, author.

12. The Dog at Clambercrown today.

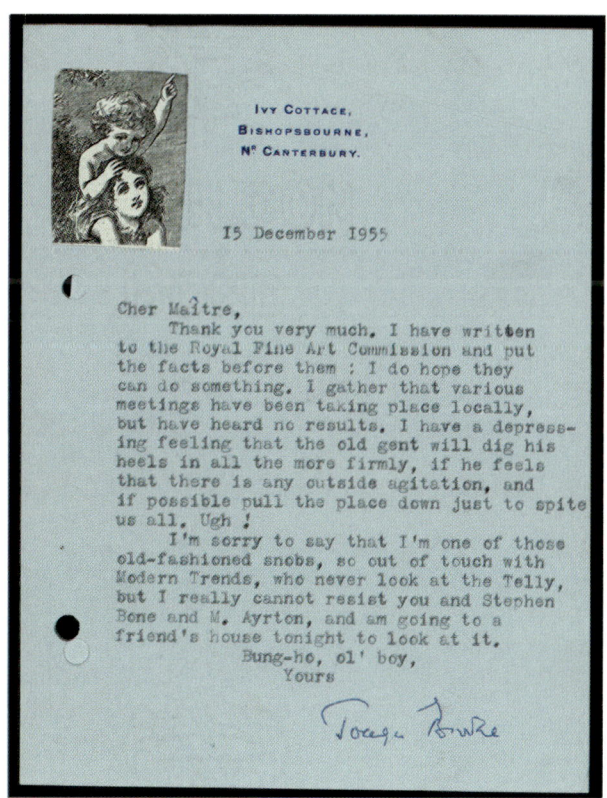

IVY COTTAGE,
BISHOPSBOURNE,
Nᵣ CANTERBURY.

15 December 1955

Cher Maître,
Thank you very much. I have written
to the Royal Fine Art Commission and put
the facts before them : I do hope they
can do something. I gather that various
meetings have been taking place locally,
but have heard no results. I have a depressing feeling that the old gent will dig his
heels in all the more firmly, if he feels
that there is any outside agitation, and
if possible pull the place down just to spite
us all. Ugh !
I'm sorry to say that I'm one of those
old-fashioned snobs, so out of touch with
Modern Trends, who never look at the Telly,
but I really cannot resist you and Stephen
Bone and M. Ayrton, and am going to a
friend's house tonight to look at it.
Bung-ho, ol' boy,
Yours

Jocelyn Brooke

13. Jocelyn Brooke to John Betjeman on the campaign to save Bourne House.

14. Bourne House in the 1950s.

15. Bourne Park today, the old cricket ground to the left.

hills appeared, black crests of pine and beech islanded in a level, waveless sea. Oxted, Limpsfield, East Grinstead – I thought of the stockbrokers' wives and the retired Anglo-Indians drooping in a hundred Tudor snuggeries over their morning coffee... A few minutes later luncheon-trays appeared: soup, roast chicken and salad, a carafe of Swiss red wine. Some thousands of feet below, I thought, in the grey, wind-swept streets, the pubs would be opening: big black pints of mild slopping on the mahogany counters; and beyond the steamy windows the drifting fog and the bleak March wind catching at the throat... My spirits suddenly lifted; the wine tingled on my palate, a sudden foretaste of 'abroad'. Looking down, I saw the vague, irregular outline of the French coast. Through the windows the sun fell hot on my cheek; I finished my quarter-litre of wine and asked for some more.

And then comes the give-away that proves that this is fiction after all. "A physical coward in most other respects, I have, curiously enough, no fear of flying." [68]

He ends the book, as in *The Military Orchid* and *The Goose Cathedral*, with another vignette of army life, this time his experience in the Woolwich hospital during his period of re-enlistment in 1948. With quiet hilarity, he traces his relationship with the larger-than-life Colonel in charge of the hospital whose thesis on the history of the treatment of venereal disease in the army takes precedence over all the daily routines.

The heart of the book is travelogue and autobiography – a uniformly gentle description of his journey through Sicily, from Taormina *via* Syracuse to Enna, mostly in miserable weather which sets the tone for his continuing loss of romantic illusion; and of the familiar pattern of his English life from childhood among the "little paths" on the Sandgate undercliff and in Bishopsbourne summers, through Bedales and adolescence, to war and the army. We have too the equally familiar Brookean dissertations by way of asides to the narrative, this time with highly perceptive critiques of D H Lawrence, Joyce and his schoolboy love, Aldous Huxley. With these threads from the trilogy he combines a significant new element – the mystical atmospherics of his two early novels, *The Scapegoat* and *The Image of a Drawn Sword*, which we encounter in his gradual working up of the dark and threatening aspects of the wooded hills of the Elham Valley and finally, most strongly of all, in the strange climax in the woodland clearing near Clambercrown which mirrors, but with more mature intensity, the sacrificial climax of *The Scapegoat*.[69]

So, one might think, much the same recipe as before, with little development to show for eight or nine years of concerted writing. But as many critics have noted, Brooke was a writer who could produce quite freshly inspired works drawing on the same material and formats. *The Dog* represents the peak of his achievement, the final fashioning of all the elements that had gone before into a concerted whole. This is now a richer mix than the autobiografiction of the trilogy. With the casting of the philosophical-come-mythical net over the territory of Clambercrown and the fields of Enna, we move from Stephen Reynolds and Henry Ryecroft to the darker, more threatening landscapes of a W.G. Sebald or David Seabrook. Whereas the books of the trilogy seem to make self-conscious jumps in time and space to different narrative streams, in the new book the writing flows seamlessly and naturally. It is richer, more powerful, because it is in some ways more restrained, the author sitting back to let the narrative proceed under its own direction. Brooke takes his earlier biographical accounts as read, but builds on them in a way that makes them comprehensible and fresh to both new and old reader alike.

Central to the vision is still the Kent village in which his childhood imagination had first been fired, but he introduces it late in the book and creates the atmosphere of this very special territory less by straight physical description than by more peripheral means – for example, introduction of the strange, off-beat yet beautiful, place-names of East Kent — Stelling Minnis, Bladbean, Old Wives Lees, Wheelbarrow Town — which culminate in the place-name which is not a place-name, Clambercrown itself.[70] This use of names plucked off the map, familiar to all citizens of East Kent, gives a reality to the text which adds spice and conviction to counterbalance the more mystical flights of the author's imagination. It anchors the narrative in old Kentish earth.

Brooke stands back on this occasion not just from the narrative but from himself and his achievement, as if this were a final retrospective, bidding farewell to his writing life. He indulges in a certain self-mockery of his claims as a writer: the big novel he wrote at Bedales about the youth wandering in the Kentish woods had put the Elham Valley into literature, perhaps like Hardy with Dorset.

> ...my novel consisted almost entirely of verbose and juicy descriptions of rural scenery, full of words like 'lush' and 'redolent', and with as many local place-names as I could squeeze in without sounding like a guide-book (a danger which, indeed, I too often failed to avoid). Needless to say, the scene was set, for the most part, in the Elham Valley; and in describing, nostalgically, that long-familiar countryside, it was as though a new dimension had been added to those remembered fields and woodlands, so that when we returned to the cottage, for our summer holidays, it seemed to me that Gorsley and Forty-acres, the water-tower and Mr Adams's farm had acquired a deeper and more poignant reality. Their outward lineaments remained the same; but they had now become, as it were, a part of 'literature', I saw them through the romantic haze of a novelist's imagination. It was rather as though one should visit Dorset after being immersed in the novels of Hardy... The only difference was that, in the case of this particular countryside, I happened to have written the appropriate 'regional'

> novels myself: the Elham valley, in fact, had become for
> me already, as it were, the Brooke country.[71]

This is intended as gentle tongue in cheek; but in fact, as the Brooke legacy has turned out, it could not be much closer to the truth.

With the passage of time, his earlier literary works have themselves become in this new book an integral part of the Brooke biography. He mentions *en passant* *The Military Orchid* and "a novel of mine called *The Scapegoat*".[72] His self-deprecation as author remains consistent: "As a writer, I suffer from the amateur's failing of taking perpetual short-cuts; chronically lazy, I find it nearly impossible to write within a conventional framework, and am apt to employ the loosest form available or the form in which, at the moment, I seem able to work most easily. Yet I have always wanted to be a novelist..."[73]

He describes the beginning of his public literary career, the excitement and disbelief with which he read the Desmond MacCarthy review of the *Orchid* that established his reputation. He soon becomes dismissive of success and "my little book – pathetically 'slim' and printed on dingy 'utility' paper".[74] Here was a case where the corners had been cut: "I was convinced, in my more rational moments, that the eminent critic had, perhaps from sheer kind-heartedness, grossly over-praised my book; I knew, in my heart, that it was a scrappy, slipshod affair, which I could greatly have improved upon if I had taken more trouble".[75]

Whether this is fair self-criticism or false humility, it is certainly true that the three books of the trilogy were written, contemporaneously with other works, far faster than the *Dog*. With the latter book, there is a much longer gestation period and writing time, the visit to Sicily of March 1953 not appearing in print until October 1955, with only bread-and-butter reviewing in competition. There are clear signs that greater pains have been taken by an author who has the freedom and space that only established reputation can afford. The prose is richer, the ideas and descriptions emerge subtly from the text, inferred rather than stated; the scenes slide smoothly from one to the next like the "proper" novel he could not write, the narrative shows signs of careful crafting – witness the way the descriptions of the Proustian childhood walks early in the book come full circle to meet up again at the final discovery of the Clambercrown.

We can see this perfectionist streak in a letter Brooke wrote to John Lehmann soon after publication which finds him still worrying about the structure of the book and in particular the placing of the seminal picture of Aunt Cock which prompts thoughts of the forbidden kingdom beyond the hills.

> ....as so often you put your finger on what I always suspected to be its weakest spot – the link-up between the childhood parts and Sicily. As a matter of fact, in the first draft the book began with Aunt Cock, and then switched very abruptly to the first travel section; a friend who read it in typescript suggested it would be better the other way round, and I think he was right on the whole, but the transition from the journey to Aunt Cock does seem to me rather "contrived".[76]

Thus explodes the self-constructed myth of the careless author tossing his material in at random. The pains taken show only too strongly in every page of this tightly knitted text.

Though he was to write a few more books in his life – two published, most not – this is the last big book and a conscious public farewell, finally, to the autobiographical stream that had begun so promisingly with the *Orchid*. In a lyrical passage – focussed on Bourne Park, the local country seat (akin to Wells' Bladesover) – he seems to sum up the main thrust of his writing life, the continuous journey through the countries of the mind; and now, in middle age, betrays himself almost for the first time into a gentle lament for the passing of the old world.

> In retrospect, then, Bourne seems a summer land, lapped in a cool, tree-muffled silence, stirred only

by the gentle rippling of the Nailbourne and by the cooing of wood-pigeons. Yet the channels of memory which radiate outward from that still centre of our rural province lead me to many and distant countries of the mind: some leafless and ice-bound, frozen in a perpetual winter; others vibrant with the shrill, tender green of early spring, and odorous with the first primroses and violets; others, again, humid and leaf-strewn beneath the fading suns of autumn, and sonorous with the thresher's drone... Today, as ever, the rose-pink mansion, standing foursquare among its enveloping trees, remains a symbol of order and stability; yet the house is now untenanted and threatened by the doom which overhangs all such survivals from a pre-atomic age. Bourne may just outlast my life-time, but the world which it represents – that world which survived into my own childhood, and which, with all its injustices and cruelties, its poverty, disease and hardship, was perhaps happier than ours – that world has gone for good: vanished into a limbo more remote than those romantic, unattainable lands which, in that far-off epoch, I imagined as lying beyond the hills and woodlands of Langham Park and Woodgate. The days and years wheel outward, in an ever-widening circle, from that still centre: days which one remembers with a recrudescent nostalgia – the March sunset stirring the heart with a sudden, romantic wildness and a bitterness as of some old and inescapable remorse; 'days which our Ancestors called their Monthes Mind, whereon their Souls, after their deaths, were had in special remembrance'...[77]

But nostalgia, in its Greek derivation, begins and ends at home. The final pages of the book, presaging the final pages of his life, find

Brooke, the re-enlisted soldier who had bought himself out, departing Woolwich Barracks to return once more to that village in the country whence all his books had sprung.

> I returned, two days later, to the country – to that cottage in the Elham Valley where, since the war, I had lived with Ninnie and my mother. Driving out from Canterbury, it seemed to me that the wheel had come full-circle: my life during the past year had been, as it were, another 'north-west passage', leading me back circuitously – like that half-remembered journey to the Clambercrown a quarter of a century ago – yet with a predestined certainty to the place where, perhaps, my roots went deepest. From the hill above Bridge I looked down across the park to Bourne: the long pink façade, so elegant and so self-assured, was itself unchanged; only the broad avenue of elms behind the house had gone, revealing a prospect of fields sweeping upward, naked and treeless now, towards the fringes of Gorsley and the haunted thickets of California. In the autumn twilight the belt of woodland showed densely black against a clear, greenish sky, in which a single star hung, like a beckoning signal, over the darkling lands beyond. As the taxi turned down the lane to the village, the last fires of the sunset blazed through the bronze canopy of the beeches; in the windless air, the smoke rose vertically, in thin blue columns, from the cottage chimneys. Turning the corner into the village street, I saw the lights of our own cottage shining forth warmly in the thickening twilight; and I knew that the long uneasy quest was once more at an end, and that I had come home again.[78]

And this time it was for good. Only death would remove him now.

CHAPTER 4

INTERLUDE

A Reluctant Occultist and a Looming Youth

> I used to know Bishopsbourne well 30 years ago. My
> brother lived in the house where Conrad died. I hope
> the place is not greatly changed.
>
> *Evelyn Waugh to Jocelyn Brooke 18 February 1961*[1]

The Brooke family was not the only one to turn its back on the
excited summer crowds milling on the Kent coast to head for the
quieter pleasures of a tiny village tucked away in a remote valley – to
exchange, in their case, the serene clamour of the Sandgate beach for
the silent woods and fields of their beloved Bishopsbourne. In 1927,
the year when Jocelyn's father sold off Forge Cottage to retire to
London, another writer bought a cottage in the village determined to
spend his summers working peacefully there and thus escape, in his
case, the even more boisterous environment of his permanent home
on the High Street at Ramsgate.

If Jocelyn's books were strange, his were even stranger – and he
had been writing them then for over fifty years. At times in his writing
life Brooke was to grapple on the fringes of mystical themes – in
The Scapegoat with the assimilation of the Druidic religion and Freud,

and in his last unpublished autobiographical (almost occult) novel, "Furious and Deadly", with another Freudian theme, the relation between sex and the supernatural. This new author, who now joined the village just as Brooke was leaving for London and Oxford, was a professional writer on the supernatural, a world expert on the history of occult groups and rites, who longed for acceptance, not as a writer on occult magic, but as a serious student of mysticism.

He had been born Arthur Waite (A.E.Waite was his writing name) in Brooklyn, New York in October 1857, the son of an American captain in the merchant marine whom his mother, Emma Lovell, had met on return home from a trip to Canada. She accompanied Captain Waite as his common law wife on many an Atlantic crossing, but not the one in September 1858 when he died in mid-ocean, of exposure through sleeping on deck of the waterlogged vessel, and was subsequently buried at sea. Three days later Waite's sister Frederica was born in New York. His mother could not settle happily with her American in-laws and soon returned to England with the two young children, but here she fared little better with her own family, who disapproved of her unmarried condition. In her isolation, she turned to religion and found solace in the authority and ceremonial of the Roman Catholic Church.

Inevitably, the social isolation of the mother was visited on the children. Waite grew up without a father and in the disturbing knowledge of his illegitimacy; he too lost himself in religion. He rapidly became an ardent Catholic, and while serving as an altar boy found a deep love of complex and symbolic ritual which was to sustain him throughout life and mould his writing career. It was a "love of the Altar and of all that belongs to Rites. It gave me the sense of the Sanctuary, of a world and a call therein".[2] And as a child, shuffling in genteel poverty from one North London house to another, what indeed he needed most was sanctuary.

1874 marked a crucial point in his adolescent development. In September his sister died following a bout of scarlet fever, just two weeks before her sixteenth birthday. His mother was inconsolable and continued to mourn for many years, shutting herself off emotionally more than ever from her son. Waite himself was deeply affected and, although he remained in the Catholic Church for some time to come, its doctrine and ritual gradually lost meaning for him.

As an introverted child in an introverted family, he had been an avid reader from an early age, stirred by fantastic tales of Arabia and later romantic and blood-curdling stories of the kind that appeared in the "penny dreadfuls". After his sister's death he turned to writing poetry, published in literary magazines, and sought and received advice on them from Robert Browning. By the age of 20, he was now *writing* the romantic and fantastic tales he had been reading since childhood; and his career as a writer with a prodigious output had just begun.

In the years following Frederica's death, his loss of faith in the Christian doctrine of the after-life turned him towards spiritualism as the natural substitute. As with all his ventures into the occult, he never did anything by halves. Before starting to take part in séances, he studied avidly the spiritualist literature, soon becoming a minor authority, and made acquaintance with most of the leading figures in the movement. In the 1880s he attended many different series of séances, which seemed for a time to give him reassurance, but he eventually grew disenchanted with the naiveté of those who sought out merely physical phenomena, and began to expound the merits of mystical over psychic experiments.

It was in the late 1880s that Waite met Arthur Machen, the writer of the macabre, who like Waite retains his cult following today but in a rather different field. It was the beginning of a close friendship that was to last the whole of Waite's life. At this time both men were immersed in the literature of occultism – Machen was compiling catalogues of occult books for the publisher George Redway, incidentally building the foundations for his early fantastic tales, while Waite was gathering the raw material for the historical and critical studies of the occult that he was planning to write. And what plans they were. In the course of the 1890s, his most prolific decade, he wrote ten books, edited or translated fifteen others and established the first independent journal in the field of occultism, *The Unknown World*. His works ranged from alchemy to hypnotism, from mysticism to black magic.

In 1888 Waite had married Ada Lakeman, the younger sister of his first and only love, Dora who had unfortunately married someone else. It was not, therefore, destined to be a particularly happy marriage, for although Waite was fond of his wife and Sybil, his only child, and cared for them financially through difficult times, he abandoned them emotionally as he lost himself in his esoteric work. His studies involved immense labour and with his brilliant memory he became a leading authority on a wide range of occult disciplines. He would regularly write through the night, four or five in the morning was his usual time for bed.

His writing and journalism allowed him a reasonable standard of living, but it was a hand-to-mouth existence until in 1899 he secured a reliable job as London manager of Horlick's, the American malted milk company, and later private secretary to the English partner James Horlick. Out of this job arose *Horlick's Magazine*, a literary journal intended initially as an advertising vehicle directed at the colonies. For a time it throve, publishing stories by leading popular writers of the day, including Waite's friend Arthur Machen. As editor, Waite loaded the magazine with his own essays on obscure aspects of the occult and with his latest poems; it ran for fifteen issues before the company put it to rest. His work with Horlick's lasted until 1909, and from then on he lived by the pen alone.

Waite's immersion in occult affairs was not just confined to reading and writing. His explorations took a practical, physical form through his membership of occult associations, the most renowned of which was the Hermetic Order of the Golden Dawn which he joined in 1891. It had a chequered history right from its inauguration – later found to be based on forged documents – but was widely welcomed by the occultist establishment of the day as a new vehicle for the pursuit of occult studies. Controversy soon broke out within the association, ostensibly over such matters as the form of ritual, but rapidly developing into an open power struggle for leadership, in which Waite was closely involved. But in any case by the mid-1890s he had become thoroughly disillusioned with occultism, which failed in his view to provide in its systems a path from man to God. In later days he saw his book *The Occult Sciences*, published in 1891, as marking the end of his trust in the occult: "it was the last flicker of a dying belief that there is something which corresponds to factual reality in things called occult. Those who believed therein, or so dreamed, those above all who laid claim on Secret Knowledge, had wearied me of all its ways".[3]

From 1903 Waite played little part in the Order, for he had turned to freemasonry as a new experiment in the way forward. Over a period of years, he joined both at home and abroad every Masonic order that was open to him, collecting the rites as small boys collect postage stamps, in order to disclose more aspects of the Secret Tradition he was determined to track down.

Eventually this too proved a cul-de-sac, and in the period of the First World War he found a degree of fulfilment by turning from magic to mysticism (he wrote his best mystical works, like *The Way of Divine Union*, at this time), and realised his ambition for control by founding his own sect, the Fellowship of the Rosy Cross, in which he was free to design his own rites and retain the spirit of mysticism, all against the background of the Christian belief he was never to shed.

He came to the village by a circuitous path. For some time, the family had used the Isle of Thanet, most particularly Ramsgate, as an escape from London when recuperating from illness or for just a holiday change of air. When war came, he and Ada began actively to seek a house out of London, and alighted on a 300-year-old cottage in Ramsgate High Street which they bought in 1916 as a holiday home. But immediately following the war, money was tight and it became clear that Waite could not live off his writing alone; at the same time, his punishing routine of work was breaking down his constitution, and sea air was recommended. So he sold up his house by Gunnersbury Park, where he had lived for twenty years, and took the family, including his daughter Sybil, now 30, to live permanently in Ramsgate. The money from the house sale was invested on Sybil's behalf to boost the family income.

Life was not easy in Ramsgate. The cottage roof, bomb-damaged in the war, was crumbling and the cellar inherently damp; Waite lost many hundreds of his valuable papers by storing them there. In 1924, Ada died of cancer; although she and Waite had little in common and he had neglected her for his work, they were nevertheless very fond of each other, and her death was a heavy blow. Predictably, he threw himself back on his studying and writing, and the work of the Order he had founded. The emotional life in the Ramsgate house was not easy either. After his wife's death, Mary Schofield, a member of the Order who idolised Waite, took upon herself the duties of his private secretary, much to the annoyance of Sybil who saw herself in that role. The relationship between Waite and his secretary grew closer (they were to marry in 1933) and the tensions with his highly neurotic daughter even stronger. The local doctor prescribed rest and change for both Sybil and Waite.

Thus it came about that in 1927, after her mother's death, Sybil purchased at her father's direction a small house, The White Cottage, in Bishopsbourne, the village where writers both before and after him would find the peace to continue their work. Since living in Ramsgate, they had become used to spending a few weeks each summer in Bridge, the next village, and had had their eyes for some time on the Bishopsbourne cottage, as Waite explains:

> When Lucasta [*Ada*] was still with us, we used to leave Ramsgate occasionally – especially in summer weather – and lodge with the excellent Mrs. Fairbrass at Bridge, by Canterbury, sometimes for weeks together. So we knew all the villages about and among them Bishopsbourne, which has precious memories

of Hooker, if not of his *Ecclesiastical Polity*. It is a single street with a single midwise turning [*by the pub*], giving on a green lane; but down that lane we did not happen to go till the last occasion on which Lucasta was with us. We found a roomy, half-timbered White Cottage, embowered in hedges and bushes, trees and creepers. We fell in love with it there and then, in part for itself and in part for the radiant span of meadows beside and behind it, and a wooded park [*Charlton Park*] beyond. With all her heart and soul would Lucasta have tended it and made it beautiful, within and without. But the place was occupied and Lucasta went away. From time to time, but mostly for shorter periods, Sybil and I stayed subsequently with Mrs. Fairbrass, who had, among other things and many, a heart of gold, very tender also and true in the memory of my wife. We were at Bridge one time in 1928 [*1927 in fact*], when our hostess burst in on a morning at breakfast and told how the White Cottage was empty, for the tenant had died suddenly. This time we saw it not only from without but went over it often and more indeed than often. It was to let and not for sale; but Sybil resolved to buy it for her very own. It has been since our fair weather residence, away from a sea-town's crowd.[4]

They had first seen again the "old White House" in the May of 1927, Sybil bought it that July for £500, and they moved in at the beginning of August.[5] In subsequent years a routine soon developed: they would head for the village in early May and stay for the whole of the summer, returning to Ramsgate (and Broadstairs to where he later removed) in late October or early November when the cold days of autumn arrived. For Sybil it was a worthwhile investment: for half the year she could have her father to herself and escape the ministrations of her much loathed stepmother.

The process of moving back and forth to the village was always chaotic since Waite insisted on taking with him a large part of his very extensive library, without which he could not write. Though his work still took up most of his day and night – he would as a rule start about lunchtime and continue into the early hours of the morning – he was not entirely oblivious to the village life going on all around him, and on at least one recorded occasion during his first full summer there wandered over to Charlton Park to watch the last cricket match of the season.[6] Five years later he may have had the chance to see another much younger writer playing in the village team there. Like Brooke, he loved nature and went for many of the same long walks through the wooded countryside; his diaries of this time make careful note of the flowering of plants and the call of the first cuckoo.

Sybil was a regular churchgoer and Waite, who still retained some vestige of his Roman Catholic upbringing, would occasionally accompany her to services at St Mary's, especially during that first full summer when life in the cottage was new.[7] In those drowsy summer village days, even minor distractions from the routine took on the form of major incidents. In early July of 1932, Waite's unusual nocturnal habits proved successful in foiling a burglary or, even worse, an abduction: "I was in the course at night of dictating to Phyllis *[Phyllis Leuliette, a friend of Sybil's who acted on occasion as his scribe]*... when we heard a noise in the back garden. Sybil had retired, but began to call out. It proved that a man was in the act of placing a ladder against the wall under one of her windows. I roused up the Post Office, telephoned Sergeant Castle, & he came over. Naturally the man made off when we proved to be about".[8] But generally the writing went smoothly on without like interruption.

He had arrived in the village in his seventieth year when age and illness were beginning to take their toll, so although he kept up with his writing he was no longer bursting with the new books and ideas that had filled his mind thirty years before. Rather he used his time now to consolidate his achievement with new and revised editions of his major works. In 1926 when he published *The Secret*

Tradition in Alchemy, he announced in the preface that it "completes my examination of the Secret Tradition transmitted through Christian Times... If I am spared for further efforts in these directions, they will belong to the work of revision..."[9] Thus the revisions were published in sequence — *The Holy Kabbalah* (1929), *The Holy Grail* (1933) and *The Secret Tradition in Freemasonry* (1937) — much of the work being carried out through the long days of those peaceful village summers.

He wrote much of his last book there too — a set of memoirs entitled *Shadows of Life and Thought*, which he began in February 1936. By the start of the following Bishopsbourne summer the work was well advanced, but the process of writing, now in his eightieth year, was proving especially tiring: " I fell asleep over them [*the memoirs*] and who will keep awake? "[10] Perhaps not many today, for they form a strange book with its emphasis on the inner life, and even where outer events are recorded they are couched in such opaque, ambivalent language as almost to become mystical occurrences themselves. He explains the motivation in his preface, written at Bishopsbourne: "Despite our sleep and our forgetting, there come also to a few in the stillness, luminous and beautiful to see, the far reflections from pre-natal modes of being: they are better than all mundane retrospects". Above all he is not going to dish the dirt: "there is much that remains over concerning occult pretenders and exponents of new thought, who had left wives across the ocean ways and found some casual substitutes in England and elsewhere. There are also illustrations of mendacity and imposture among the emissaries of Hidden Masters... but I have held back the chronicles concerning them".[11] The intimate details of the bitter battles for the soul of the Golden Dawn still awaited their historian.

He closes his memoirs, as one would expect, with a summary of his personal spiritual journey, his quest for a state of pure being, and reminds his readers that this can be found most easily in the peace of the country, even if his own village did not in fact come complete with a permanent river of lapping waves.

> It is of this state that I would ask those who read to think
> with me a little, when the summer of the world about us
> is like a summer of the world within; and though some
> may be holding these pages within the city and its walls,
> that which is here set down is being written where the
> lapping waves of stream and river lisp intelligible voices,
> where hours of earth are like unto hours in Faërie...[12]

The opening of the Second World War found Waite, now an old man, worrying about the preservation of his beloved collection of books: "Canterbury and part of the Elham Valley are to be used as safe for the evacuation of Chatham and I must be at Bishopsbourne to prevent if possible the White Cottage and its great uncatalogued library from falling into the hands of Heaven knows whom".[13] But, as with many old men, such domestic worries were overtaken by events. Waite, who for much of his life was a determined hypochondriac, had been convinced for some years that his heart was failing, and in 1940 his own prognosis was proved to be correct. The annual shuttle between houses now had to cease, and Sybil bought for him a new permanent home in Gordon House, Bridge so he could remain in close touch with the village he had come to love. A friend who stayed near him in Bridge during the last illness recalled: "I was with him during the greater part of the last day of his life. His thoughts were with his work almost to the end".[14] He died on 19 May 1942, a fortnight before the bombs fell on Canterbury, and was buried in Bishopsbourne churchyard to the right of the lychgate as you go in.

His name has survived as the first man to attempt a systematic study of the history of western occultism viewed as a spiritual tradition, and to turn "rejected knowledge" into a fit subject of study within the history of ideas. He is remembered most today in "New Age" circles for what he would have regarded his minor works – the translation of the writings of the French occultist Éliphas Lévi, and the brilliantly innovative tarot cards designed under his guidance in

1910. His more serious work on mysticism is largely ignored, a fate bemoaned by his biographer:

> Waite's true legacy is in his philosophy of mysticism, but until such time as it is analysed in something more than a superficial manner, and its originality and genius recognized, he will not be accorded the place in the history of thought that he deserves. Until then his reputation will be shrouded in a manner analogous to that of his grave at Bishopsbourne: a grave that has for many years been covered by a rank and spreading growth of Deadly Nightshade.[15]

But perhaps things are not quite so bad as that. The growth may be that of its gentler sister, the woody nightshade, and not the "furious and deadly" of Jocelyn Brooke.

In the summer of 1928, while Arthur Waite was settling into the village, a rather younger writer came down from London for the weekend to play a game of cricket in Bourne Park.[16] He was invited down by the new owner, the engineer Sir John Prestige, who had recently bought the estate and hoped to revive its cricketing glories of almost two hundred years before. For the young author, Alec Waugh, was crazy about cricket and would play anywhere at anyone's invitation. When four years later he was looking for a house in the country to rent, he remembered that cricket match and, more particularly, the beautiful village in which it was played. He had a cricketing friend in the village, living at Court Lodge by the church – the distinguished retired captain of the Kent county side, Colonel Lionel Troughton. They had met in the war both as prisoners of the Germans, and Troughton no doubt had a share in that first invitation to play at Bourne Park and in finding the house to rent.

Waugh had been born in Hampstead thirty years before in July 1898, the son of the writer and literary critic, Arthur Waugh, who a little later was to become managing director of the publishing house of Chapman and Hall, now fallen on rather harder times than those it had enjoyed in the mid-nineteenth century when Dickens was its foremost client. Alec was the apple of his father's eye, taking precedence over his younger brother Evelyn, whom Arthur never really understood. Arthur Waugh showered his eldest son with attention and instruction, in the arts of writing, acting and literature, not to mention cricket, about which the older man was equally obsessed. Alec was sent to Sherborne School in Dorset (his father was there in the 1880s) where he distinguished himself on the sports field but left under a cloud at the age of seventeen. He joined the army forthwith and a little before Christmas 1915, in any free time he could squeeze from his military training, he began his first novel which, despite its considerable length, he polished off in a matter of six or seven weeks. It was a first-hand account of contemporary life in a boys public school and was soon to clarify what that particular cloud at Sherborne had all been about.

The Loom of Youth is typical of the style of many of the novels Alec Waugh wrote in his life time – a detailed narrative that drives on successfully, interspersed with philosophical asides about life and virtue, in this case generalised and a little trite as one might expect from a teenager of that time. Much of it is taken up with the author's obsession with sport, and individual games of cricket and rugby are relived at length, rather obscuring the fact that this is also an institution of academic learning. But gradually the book develops a pointed critique of the public school ethos as outmoded (partly for its emphasis on sport!) and unfitted to prepare children for the real world, relying as it did on such subjects as Latin and Greek.

The furore the book caused was partly about this, but mainly about the rather frank treatment (for the time) of homosexuality in public schools: it was perhaps an unfortunate coincidence that the first chapter was entitled "Groping". While all the heroics are going on on the rugger field, eighteen year olds are quietly taking their thirteen year old friends out for walks. The hero Gordon Caruthers falls for Morcombe, a boy of his own age who has read *A Shropshire Lad*, and with whom he feels "indescribably happy". Now in the long hours of morning study "more than once there came over him a wish to plunge himself into the feverish waters of pleasure". Our hero, however, resists this temptation and later is revolted by the whole episode, amazed that "he could ever have wished to dabble in ugly things".[17] This is just a fleeting moment in the novel, handled lightly and with great delicacy, so much so that many who bought the book out of prurient interest complained later that they missed it altogether.

It went the round of all the publishers who rapidly dismissed it for these offensive elements. Arthur Waugh, ever keen to promote his first born, claimed later to have contemplated recommending it to his own Board, but secretly he was highly nervous of the likely consequences of publication.[18] The book was put on the shelf as patently unmarketable. At this point in the story in stepped Thomas Seccombe. Seccombe was one of those shadowy figures who then hovered on the margins of the literary world, critic, editor, teacher and occasionally writer, rather like Edward Garnett or Arthur Waugh himself, though less well known. He had made a name in the 1890s as assistant editor of the first *Dictionary of National Biography* for which he had written more than 500 entries. Like Garnett he was an ever-active spotter of youthful talent and inspired his protégés with his love of literature. In 1902, when a temporary English lecturer at Manchester University, he had spotted Stephen Reynolds and set him off on his writing career.[19]

He was Professor of English at Sandhurst when Alec Waugh joined the Royal Military College after his expulsion from Sherborne. In looking after his young students Seccombe provided a welcome relief from all the square-bashing and macho exploits of the main syllabus.

> He kept open house on Sundays. Half a dozen or so of us would go up in the early afternoon. He had a seventeen year old and attractive daughter [*Alec had ever a quick eye for the local talent*]; and a schoolboy son, Lionel, who was

102

in the 'thirties to make a name for himself on the BBC as a reporter on athletics. We would have a solid tea and play nursery games like 'Up Jenkins'. It was a congenial counter-atmosphere to the RMC.[20]

It was on such an afternoon that Alec happened to mention he had written a novel, and Seccombe took it up with enthusiasm. He showed the manuscript to the publisher, Grant Richards, who far from being dismayed by its contents saw controversy and profit written all over it. He got Seccombe to write an enticing preface which, above his signature, was bound to catch the eye of the literary editors. The literary column of the *Nation* was first to fire the interest of readers.

> I have read few books that have interested me more than Mr. Waugh's *Loom of Youth*. It is in one respect an almost miraculous production. Here is a boy of eighteen who diaries his school life, reproduces its talk and atmosphere, and builds up a merciless memorial of its evils and shortcomings... It seems to me that it is a revolutionary work – if only the parents of England will read it, and having read, act on it. If they do the one without the other, it is on their conscience that they risk the ruin of their children's characters and mind. So I urge them to do the one and the other.[21]

With this kind of injunction, who could resist the invitation?

The book caused uproar in the public school system and sensation outside it. It was attacked and praised in equal measure, thus entrapping the widest possible public. It was banned in public schools up and down the country, thus ensuring in a very few months that all schoolboys had read it. Correspondence on the controversy ran for ten weeks in the *Spectator* and six in the *Nation*. Sales were prodigious – it went through seven impressions in the first six months; but the backlash on the family was crippling. Alec was spared most of it by having then departed for war, only to be quickly captured as a German prisoner. The Waughs were excommunicated from the Sherborne fold and for Arthur, who treated the school as a religion, the cruellest blow came when his son's name was expunged from the roll of old boys. It was many years before the rift was healed.

Alec's writing career continued at a pace – he wrote his second novel (which Arthur suppressed, for equally unsuitable content) again in a matter of weeks, and through the 1920s was keeping close to the then publishing dictum of a novel a year. None of these proved lucrative on the scale of the *Loom*, and he was forced to take his income from a job with his father at Chapman and Hall. Despite his manifest attraction to and interest in women, his first marriage in 1919 to Barbara, the daughter of the short story writer, W.W.Jacobs, was a disaster. With typical frankness (especially in sexual matters) he announced in his first set of memoirs "I had been nicknamed Tank at Sandhurst, yet I could not make my wife a woman".[22] They separated two years later and the marriage was annulled in 1923.

It was his second marriage that brought him to the village. After a number of failed relationships, he married in October 1932 Joan Chirnside, the adopted daughter of a wealthy Australian estate owner. The couple decided to live partly in Alec's Chelsea flat and the rest of the time in the country. His cricketing contacts with Kent led to the discovery of a house to let on Sir John Prestige's estate at Bourne Park – an elegant Georgian home that went by the name of Oswalds. The decision to take it was made easier by a further hidden attraction – just eight years before it had also been home to an eminent novelist. Like Stratford to Marie Corelli, the attraction was powerful: would some of the stardust rub off on him?

They took it over, furnished, as a running concern, complete with a staff that consisted of chauffeur-gardener and gardener's boy, cook, parlour maid, housemaid and kitchen maid. The eminent novelist had managed with less. As a modern marriage, they shared the expenses – Alec took charge of the rent of four hundred a year, the heating and the gardener's wages, while Joan looked after the household expenses and the indoor staff.[23] Unlike the eminent novelist, who had kept aloof from the village, Alec immediately settled in at its middle class heart. Apart from the owner of Bourne Park, there were others there he knew already, and the promise of pretty women: "The house nearest to ours was owned by the former Kent cricket captain, L.W.H.Troughton, who had been a prisoner of war with me at Karlsruhe. The rector Canon Burnside had only just retired from the headmastership of St Edmund's, Canterbury. He had three very attractive daughters, two of whom were married to officers in the Buffs. The other was married to a neighbouring farmer who had been an oarsman at Oxford. We could not have had a better introduction into East Kent life".[24]

He made use of these contacts to cement his position in the local sporting hierarchy. The summer of 1933 was a glorious one and outdoor activity was the order of the day. It was not long before he was playing regularly for the village cricket team and for the St Lawrence club at the Kent county ground three miles away.[25] He also joined the Canterbury Golf Club and fell to the game with a new enthusiasm, practising regularly in an effort to improve his handicap. "I would practise in the fields round the house, driving into the paddock off the lawn. I was weak in bunkers, so I had one dug in the garden which I had filled with sand by a local builder".[26] The eminent novelist, who loathed most sporting activity, was by now spinning in his grave. A little later, and after some improvement in technique, Alec was enjoying life out on the links at Sandwich.

The idea of sharing country life (which Alec had never experienced before) with time in London proved a false move. He so enjoyed the new experience that he soon gave up the Chelsea flat and moved his library and pictures down to Oswalds. There was writing work to be done and the new house was well fitted for the task. "I was used to writing in country inns and beach hotels and I did not see why Oswalds should not prove the equivalent of those settings".[27] There were, however, some adjustments to be made. The study of the eminent novelist had been turned into a small library, and between that and the drawing room was a gun room which Alec converted to his own study. Early in the year he discovered that he was to become a father in July, but that complication did not forestall his eagerness to write.

Living in the country was for him as big a change as he had ever known before, but with the constant society of local friends and the weekend guests down from London he soon settled into it. And relaxed too, in what he was later to call "a tranquil summer".

> 1933, a great vintage year for claret, was a memorable summer. Day after day the sun shone on the county that has been called the garden of England. Joan sat under a copper beech, contentedly awaiting her confinement, while I worked on a family chronicle that was to be called *The Balliols,* about five children who had grown up in Hampstead during the early years of the twentieth century.[28]

He wrote through that summer at his usual breakneck speed and had finished, a quarter of a million words, by Christmas. *The Balliols* is a family epic rather in the style of *The Forsyte Saga*. It is based very closely on the two generations of the Waugh family, beginning with Edward Balliol, the managing director of a wine firm, building the family home in Hampstead, as Arthur Waugh had done in 1907. His sister, Stella, becomes a militant suffragette and entices his daughter, Lucy, into the movement: Lucy loses her nerve in a hunger strike and takes food, thus betraying her colleagues and, overwhelmed by the burden of guilt, marries and escapes to Malaya. Her sister Ruth likewise surrenders to the blandishments of Victor Tavenham, Lord Huntercoombe, and goes to live with him on his country estate (shades of Bourne Park). Her brother Hugh (Alec) leaves public school to fight in the war and is badly injured, casts around for some purpose in life, turns to drink and dies in a car crash. His brother Francis (Evelyn) falls for the new world of commerce and becomes a successful business man, but he too is diverted from work by sexual affairs. The youngest daughter, Helen, "rudderless on the tides of post-war freedom"[29] almost succumbs to a seducer but saves herself just in time. She wanders back to the old family home to find it being dismantled.

As usual with Alec Waugh, the book has its *longueurs* – philosophical passages of character motivation, large chunks on the *zeitgeist* of each era – none of them particularly profound; but it is saved, as usual, by the thrust of the narrative, moving rapidly from scene to scene, arresting the reader with its basic themes of love and ambition. The very first paragraphs show how significant a breakpoint in his life this year in the village was for Alec.

> I wrote this book in 1933. I had not meant it to be a novel. That year I became thirty-five, and though it is absurd, patently, to say on any one morning "I have now lived half my life", it is impossible not to regard one's thirty-fifth birthday as a landmark; as an excuse for stocktaking; for looking back and looking forward; for comparing the world as one found it with the world as it has become.[30]

There are references aplenty to what was going on currently in Waugh's own life. Ruth decides to have her baby on the estate at Tavenham just as Joan awaits her confinement on the Bourne estate. And the description of Tavenham runs Bourne Park close.

> ...it would be with a true feeling of homecoming that he would see the broad avenue of chestnuts stretching behind the red-fronted, white-windowed house: a recognition that it was there that he belonged.[31]

Edward Balliol takes up golf and there follow some detailed instructions on how to negotiate the links at Sandwich.

> For the summer he takes rooms in Sandwich. The links
> are intolerably crowded. But if you start from the first
> tee at Prince's at about twelve, you can be certain of a
> quiet round... Even on a windless day he takes wood at
> the short third; and even with wood and a wind behind
> him he never carries the cross bunker at the fifth. But he
> usually gets down from the edge of the green in two.[32]

And if space is thus given to the author's new love, golf, equal
allowance must be made for his first love, cricket. In July 1919, Alec
and his father had been to see the last day of the traditional Kent v
Surrey match at the Rectory Field, Blackheath and were surprised
to note that of the twenty two players in the equivalent match in
1914 as many as fourteen were still there playing, including Alec's
friend Lionel Troughton who now lived next door.[33] The narrator
of *The Balliols* uses the 1914 match, and the image of Blythe (the
best known player to be killed in the war) to point up the shadow
that the European crisis was now about to cast upon the life of the
nation.

> On the following Saturday I went to Blackheath to watch
> the last day of the Kent and Surrey match. So much had
> happened during those four days that as I watched Colin
> Blythe run up to the wicket with that slow tripping
> run and the left arm curled behind his back, I thought,
> "Shall I ever watch another first-class cricket match?"[34]

The only shadow to be cast upon that "tranquil" summer of 1933
was the death of another well-known cricketer, for Lionel Troughton
himself died at the end of August after an illness of some months.
Hundreds attended the funeral at the little village church, but it
was nonetheless an impressively simple service, for Troughton had
requested no mourning, no flowers. Alec undaunted turned up with
a spray of magnolias.[35]

The Balliols was the best book he had written since the *Loom* and received the appropriate reward in high sales and unanimously enthusiastic reviews. He gave up novel writing for a time, so it remained the best book (and his latest novel) until he hit the jackpot in 1956 with *Island in the Sun*, the book and the film combined earning him a fortune. His brother Evelyn mischievously remarked that after this success he never drew another sober breath – an exaggeration, of course, but one that highlights his love of the good life.[36]

All his life he lived a nomadic existence, travelling mostly in the Far East, America and the Caribbean, the great survivor of the literary world, continuing to write (now mostly short stories and non-fiction) wherever he went. He died in Florida in 1981: thirty five was not the midpoint of his life after all.

He was always conscious of this insatiable wanderlust and how it contrasted with the more static world of Kentish culture.

> I fancy that Kent is unlike any other English county. It is a county where you belong or don't. According to which side of the Medway you are born, you are a Man of Kent or a Kentish Man. Kent is a great cricketing county. Its 'family' side is called 'The Band of Brothers', but you cannot become a member just through owning a house in Kent. You have to be born there. That did not worry me. A traveller like myself has always known himself to be a sojourner.[37]

He stayed permanently in the village for little more than a year, for his wife was called away to a family crisis in Australia and the spell was broken.[38] But for one moment in that glorious summer of 1933, as his new book took wing and he watched his pregnant wife, patient under the beech trees, there seemed just an outside chance that he might stay. As he wrote the last word of *The Balliols*, he felt proud enough of the time and the place it was written, and, of course, its connection with the eminent novelist, to subscribe at the end the simple but telling phrase – *Oswalds*, 1933.

CHAPTER 5

An Ancient Mariner

Few writers have ever been as rootless as Conrad, exiled from homeland, from identity, even from language.

Gillian Tindall[1]

Early afternoon on a warm August day in the mid 1950s. My father cycles on ahead shepherding me through the busy city traffic – or what appeared to be busy then but would now be seen as tame and drowsy. We negotiate safely the built-up areas and with a sigh of relief make our way out onto the New Dover Road, which in half a mile will join the Old Dover Road, or Watling Street as our ancestors were wont to call it. Though the traffic is sparser here (and nothing like the fast dual carriageway of today) we are on an arterial road and have to keep our wits about us, falling swiftly into single file whenever a car passes. It is holiday time and we are out on a bicycling jaunt with no set purpose other than to enjoy the blissful late summer sun and gently explore the country the other side of Canterbury, heading nowhere in particular. We have come eight miles already and I am just beginning to droop.

A little way past Bridge we decide to get off this dust-filled road, and halt to consult the map. Just a few yards further on is a right-hand turn down to a small village with at one end a cross on a black rectangle (indicating Church with Tower) and at the other the magic word "Inn". We shall investigate the church – always the central focus of these country perambulations – and seek long overdue refreshment at the pub. We swing round off the main road and free-wheel down the hill between a tall avenue of golden beeches shimmering in the honeyed sun.[2] We are at once in another world, a secret hidden one whose only access is this unfrequented lane which seems to whisper "this is private ground" while the trees beckon us on to explore.

At the junction at the bottom of the hill, where the white wooden signpost stands to attention on its triangle of green, we meet the perfect village and immediately dismount at the unexpected wonder of it all. On our right through the trees is an elegant small Georgian house set in sweetly enclosed grounds, and just beyond that the little flint and stone church we have come to see. To our left is the main sweep of the village street with a jumble of cottages down one side, all different shapes and sizes, looking across to mainly open fields on the other. The main road now seems light years away, along with the rest of civilisation. We wonder how we never found this place before, and for me especially, more sensitive then to village beauty, the novelty is overwhelming. We have not been here before because in truth this is a hidden land, a country of the mind, its frontiers patrolled by an ever-watchful nature. Those who fall on it by chance have earned their passport through.

We lean our bikes up against the flintstone wall and enter the churchyard through the old covered lychgate. Inside, the church is dark and sparsely furnished, a sense of cold high stone walls leading up to a gaunt wooden barrelled roof. I buy a paper guide to read the story of the place later in the quiet of home; for now, we don't want detailed history, just to take everything in. On a plinth midway up one wall, beside the pulpit and facing the congregation, we notice a small stone statue of what appears a medieval preacher, reading from prayer book or bible lying flat across his hands. He bears a priest's cap on his head which leans gently towards the right, and an expression of weariness on his bearded face which the sculptor no doubt intended as an expression of holiness. The figure strikes us strangely for it is rare to find statues in any Anglican church smaller than a cathedral. We note the name and dates beneath the plinth – a holy man connected with the site, no doubt – but they mean nothing to either of us.

We make our way out of the churchyard and wander in the sunlight up the village street admiring the row of cottages to our right with their disparate rooflines, now high, now low. On the left, standing alone on its well mown bowling-green lawn, is a small single-storey building of more recent date, with a rather elaborate Tudor-style porch planted, as if by an afterthought, across its entrance; it must be the village hall. I mount the steps up to the overhanging porch and blink in the sudden darkness to which my eyes take time to get accustomed. And then, glancing up above the entrance door, a sudden shock. Out of the gloom there appears a large head in left profile, with long nose and jaw and pointed bearded chin. It is an exotic face, like that of an ancient Spanish gentleman – Cervantes perhaps – until I see the collar of his only too modern suit. The effect of this great head in profile is overpowering and, for a child, not a little frightening. I call my father over to come and look.

Standing back a step to let the daylight in, it now becomes clear what this unexpected apparition is all about. It is part of a large and elaborate plaque, intricately carved in wood, a work of art one would not expect to find at the entrance to a very ordinary village hall.The head is framed by a circle of letters standing in a square. In the top two corners are a sun and a star, in the bottom two a sailing ship and a lighthouse: the man has something to do with stars and the sea. I slowly decipher the words carved round the head, but this creates even more puzzlement. JOSEPH TEADOR KONRAD KORZENIOWSKI. I am perplexed by the strange and unknown surname; some obscure foreigner connected with the village, but why deserving of such a magnificent plaque? Then at last I notice the two further panels of text on either side of this dominant head, and slowly the penny drops.

The text to the left reads

> To Joseph Conrad, in affectionate memory of the great
> writer who spent part of his life at Oswalds, in this
> village, this porch has been erected by numerous friends
> and admirers throughout the world.

A shock of surprise and delight, no less than the earlier one, to discover that a great writer (as the text said) had actually lived here in this perfect village. The place was no longer just beautiful – it carried significance of a very special kind. The mood is heightened further by the text to the right.

> "Indeed, as a matter of fact, he is not very far from us where
> we sit. But there are men, and women too, whose stars
> mark them for loneliness no man can approach. You mean,
> because they are great? Because they are incomparable."
>
> Suspense [3]

Cryptic, intriguing but rather loose and rambling a quotation for a vehicle conveying greatness. Why was it here and why, apparently, drawn from dialogue? It was only much later that I came to understand that this was an extract from his last novel and the words were here at the entrance to the village hall because they were actually written here, in this village, in the elegant Georgian house we had passed just down the road

My father knew of Conrad as a Pole who, according to popular belief, wrote English of a style that outclassed the English themselves. I knew him from recent struggles to come to grips with *Nostromo*, always without success. But now he was elevated in my eyes by the legend on this astonishing plaque, by the knowledge that he had lived and written here in this special place.

I don't know what happened more that day. Did we drink at the pub after all, or was it past closing time? Did we make it to other villages close by or, overwhelmed by our discovery, merely cycle home? It was some years before we returned again and by then we had probably, like the rest of humanity, graduated to a car and lost the atmospheric of that first open-air arrival. But the place and the experience remained with me in dreams and awake as a lasting signal of their importance. Place had power and writing had power – where they met was a magical land.

I sensed all this intuitively that afternoon as a part of the strange excitement. I had fallen in love with this village, and not just for its simple physical beauty. But as I stood there on that day looking out from the steps of the porch, unbeknownst to me across the way in Ivy Cottage lived another writer who had had the same experience forty years before and was now in middle age fast falling out of love with it. Just a few years before he had sat at his writing desk in the garden-hut of that house across from where I stood and abrogated all those things I now felt. His castigation was complete, right down to the porch and the plaque that had so awakened my imagination.

> Half-hidden by trees and (in those days) remote in its valley, the little street with its scattered houses, its squat-towered church and its slate-roofed Victorian pub was still comparatively 'undiscovered'. A celebrated Jacobean divine had ended his days in the rectory; in the closing years of my childhood, an eminent novelist inhabited the dower-house, a pleasant early-nineteenth-century building near the church; these were the village's only claim to fame. But even in my earliest childhood the bourgeois invasion had begun – my family, indeed, formed part of the vanguard – and nowadays the number of cottages inhabited by land-workers is in a small minority. The lanes and hedges, today, have become scrupulously tidy; the grass in the churchyard is punctually cut; the cottages have sprouted new wings, carefully disguised by expensive 'weathered' tiles; the dower-house is to be

pulled down; and the eminent novelist is commemorated by a bogus-Tudor porch tacked on to the parish Hall. The village, in fact, is fast becoming a garden-suburb.[4]

Time changes all but renews itself for each new generation. Place adheres despite the superficial rearrangement. The dower-house was spared, but the rectory pulled down in its stead.

Joseph Conrad (or Jozef Korzeniowski as he then was) was born on 3 December 1857 in the town of Berdichev in the Ukraine, which had been Polish since the sixteenth century but was then a part of Russia, the pickings of the third partition of Poland of 1795. His father, Apollo, was deeply religious and patriotic, with a melancholy, mystical belief in the eventual restoration of the fatherland and an avid hatred for the Russian state. His mother likewise was a political activist who shared her husband's views from the left wing of Polish nationalism. The first years of Conrad's life were marked by instability as his father cast round for the means to support his family. He abandoned small farming to invest in a publishing house and concentrate on his writing – he had already a reputation for journalistic poetry on social and political themes, and had published translations of works by Shakespeare and Dickens, Alfred de Vigny and Victor Hugo. The future writer knew from an early age the world of putting pen to paper.

In the insurrectionary atmosphere leading up to the 1863 rising, the Russian authorities became suspicious of Apollo's clandestine activities, closed down his printing press, arrested and imprisoned him. He was convicted and sent into exile with his family three hundred miles east of Moscow to a climate and situation that led to a slow deterioration in his wife's health. She died three years later of consumption when she was thirty three and Conrad only seven. Conrad, who himself suffered from various ailments at this time, spent the next four years closely corralled with his sorrowing father who tended his son's illnesses and likewise his education. For some time the pair followed a peripatetic existence, finally landing up in Cracow where Apollo's own tubercular condition was reaching a terminal stage. The child now almost alone in the world was smothered by the weight of his father's illness and deep depression. In an article written some forty years later, Conrad recalled the final days by his father's bedside.

> I would be permitted to tiptoe into the sick room to say good-night to the figure prone on the bed, which often could not acknowledge my presence but by a slow movement of eyes, put my lips dutifully to the nerveless hand lying on the coverlet, and tiptoe out again. Then I would go to bed, in a room at the end of a corridor, and often, not always, cry myself into a good, sound sleep.[5]

His father died some days later. Conrad's uneasy rootless childhood had come to an end. He was an orphan at eleven.

In the ensuing years he was cared for by various members of the family, finally and most notably by his maternal uncle, Tadeusz Bobrowski, who became his guardian and mentor, smoothed the path for his working career and kept up the constant struggle during his nephew's adolescent years to curb the natural Conradian tendency to financial extravagance, a propensity which survived to the end of his writing life. As an orphan he had to make his own way in the world, having consciously rejected his father's legacy of political protest and self-sacrifice which had cost the family so dear. Fuelled by novels of romantic adventure, his mind turned to the sea as the mainspring of his ambition, a career of perpetual travel which mirrored the only life he had experienced so far.

His uncle, an established gentleman farmer, stood out for some time against these childhood fantasies, which seemed to offer a life of unremitting hardship and insecurity, but finally gave way. In 1874, at the age of 16, Conrad left Poland for Marseille where he was to spend the next four years building the foundations of his career as merchant seaman. In the course of the next year he made two trips with a French company to Martinique, first as an observing passenger and then as a fully-fledged apprentice. On return to Marseille, he spent the first six months of 1876 enjoying to the full the bohemian life there, overspending his uncle's allowance, and unconsciously storing up colourful material for his future writing. In July of that year he made his final trip to Martinique with the same company, but this time as steward, and succeeded in setting foot on South American soil, making a short landfall in Venezuela which was to provide him with some of the inspiration and background scenery for the Republic of Costaguana in *Nostromo*.

For the next year or so, Conrad's movements remain unrecorded; he may have been involved in gun-running along the Spanish coast in connection with the Third Carlist War, but this episode is still shrouded in mystery. What is certain is that he lost his job by alienating his French employer and returned to his earlier life in Marseille of total self-indulgence, which seems to have led to a complete loss of self-control and to emotional collapse. It culminated early in 1878 in a visit to Monte Carlo where he blued all his half-yearly allowance at the casino, and returned to Marseille penniless, depressed and without prospects; he attempted to shoot himself which signalled the final cry for help. His uncle responded at once, hot-foot from Kiev, and in a few days managed to turn his nephew's life around. They devised a plan for him to enter the British merchant marine in pursuit of a serious career, taking his seaman's examinations until he became a qualified captain. His hold on English, his fourth language after Polish, French and Russian, could only have been fragmentary at this time, but this fresh start launched him into an entirely English world and the start of his life as an honorary Englishman. When he began to write, it could have been in any of three languages, but by then there was no question of making a conscious choice. His uncle's decision to place him on British ships was in the end to English literature's gain.

For the next fifteen years Conrad built his professional career in the merchant navy, studiously picking up his seaman's qualifications as he went. His first ship took him from Marseille to the Sea of Azov, and then back to England where in early June he had his first glimpse of the white cliffs of the Kent coast, near to which he was to spend so much of his writing life. He later recalled that the North Downs in which he lived were "thick with the memories of my sea life".[6] Two days later he docked at Lowestoft and there, on 18 June 1878, set foot for the very first time on English soil. In all his wanderings from childhood on, he had never had a home, nor perhaps was ever really to find one. Yet without knowing it, on this day he had found a fair substitute for one. Seven years later, after many such returns to the white cliffs of Dover, he was to tell a Polish friend settled in Cardiff "When speaking, writing or thinking in English the word Home always means for me the hospitable shores of Great Britain".[7]

He started small on a family-run schooner plying between Lowestoft and Newcastle, but after a few months graduated to a more exciting life on tall ships bound for Australia, which became his usual destination for the next three years. From 1881 to 1886 he worked on various ships sailing to India and the far east, and the latter year marked two important milestones in his career: in August he became a naturalized British subject, and in November he passed his final examination and received his master's certificate. He was now set up for a long career captaining British ships anywhere in the world. The only problem was that he had achieved his qualifications as the great days of sail were drawing to a close, soon to be overtaken by the new technology of steam which demanded different skills and fewer men.

For the next three years, work took him mainly to the far east, and the Dutch East Indies in particular. In the latter half of 1887 he sailed as chief mate on the *Vidar* from Singapore to Borneo, a richly invigorating trip which furnished him with impressionistic material for four of his books — *Almayer's Folly, An Outcast of the Islands, The Rescue* and *Lord Jim* — which were to build his early reputation as sea-writer of the adventurous east. He next took the opportunity of a longer appointment in the Belgian Congo to which, after lengthy negotiations, he set sail in the spring of 1890. Between August and September of that year he served as first mate and temporary master of the Congo River steamship the *Roi des Belges*. Like most Europeans, he quickly succumbed there to fever and dysentery and the end of October found him in a hammock in hapless state being carried back to base. Partly through the illness and partly through disagreement with his less than enthusiastic employers, his contract was terminated and he returned to England both chastened and ill. In all, he had spent just four months in the Congo, but it had been a new turning point in his career. It had given him the physical and psychological material that was to be woven so deftly into *Heart of Darkness*, his novella, fired off in seven weeks in 1898-9, now generally accepted as a key work of literary modernism; but it gave him also an undercurrent of ill-health from which he was never totally to recover. The pain of creative writing, which he was to bemoan for the rest of his life, had at its heart an underlying propensity to physical and mental breakdown.

He spent most of the following year recuperating in London, undergoing hospital treatment and, in the summer, a period of convalescence in Champel near Geneva. He was still casting round for a new sailing appointment which came by surprise in November 1891 with an invitation to sail as first mate on the *Torrens*, plying between London and Australia. He remained with the ship for two years completing the same passage several times, finally returning to England towards the end of 1893. Though he still for some years kept a weather eye open for a new post, the *Torrens* was the last ship he was to sail in as a professional seaman. For by now he had another string to his bow, not yet taken seriously enough to be considered a rival career. It was symbolised by his meeting on his last voyage on the *Torrens* with John Galsworthy who was travelling on holiday between Adelaide and Cape Town. Though neither man was yet a novelist, they became friends on the journey and a lasting relationship was established. And Conrad had in his pocket the draft of his first novel, *Almayer's Folly*.

He had started to write it in London in the autumn of 1889 in between his travels in the Malay archipelago, on which the book draws, and his posting to the Congo. One of the few who knew of its existence was his aunt and frequent correspondent, Marguerite Poradowska of Brussels, who was herself fast becoming a successful novelist and had the experience to offer encouragement as a role model. In September 1891, he took lodgings at 17 Gillingham Street behind Victoria Station which became his fixed London address until his marriage five years later. The narrow brick terraced house on the south side of the street was his first writing home, the guardian of his early books from where the first groans of the creative process were swiftly heard. In 1894, in the throes of completing his first book, he wrote to his aunt: "I am in the midst of struggling with Chapter XI; a struggle to the death, you know! If I let go, I am lost!" [8] A few months later, on his second book, *An Outcast of the Islands*, the laments to his aunt were still flowing thick and fast: "Yes, it is true. One works hardest when accomplishing nothing. For three days, I've been seated before a blank page – and the page has stayed blank except for a 'IV' at the top. I am really on the wrong path." [9] The groans were to continue in this vein until the very last word on the very last book.

Almayer's Folly was published in April 1895 and received a good press. Conrad, however, was still a seaman on the look out for ships and not a fully focussed writer in search of the next book, but nevertheless he was now encouraged to continue with the pen by Edward Garnett, the publisher's reader and unofficial mentor for the next forty years to many new writers, most younger than Conrad. Garnett persuaded him, not by holding out the prospect of a sparkling literary career but by a simpler expedient, as Conrad much later recalled: "When, after finishing *Almayer's Folly*, I hesitated at the parting of the ways, not at all from literary ambition but because of the strong hold my old life had still on me, I admit that it was Edward Garnett who tipped the balance. His words were: 'You have the style, you have the temperament. Why not write another?'

You will observe that he said nothing about the pursuit of literature. He simply said:– 'Why not write another?'" [10]

This was Garnett's standard down-to-earth approach to writers in need of encouragement – simple, concrete, practical. It always paid off. The two men slid easily into a close relationship, and Conrad had found in the younger man a new surrogate father, at least so far as professional literary matters were concerned. Garnett has left us with a fetching picture of Conrad in his room in Gillingham Street when he first visited him there early in 1895.

> I was introduced to Conrad's snug bachelor quarters where, having placed me in an easy chair, Conrad retired behind a mysterious screen and left me to study the cosiness of the small firelit room, a row of French novels, the framed photograph of an aristocratic lady and an engraving of a benevolent, imposing man on the mantleshelf. On a little table by the screen lay a pile of neat manuscript sheets. I remained conscious of these manuscript sheets when Conrad reappeared and plunged into talk... .[11]

The manuscript in question was *An Outcast of the Islands*, his second novel published in March of the following year. Three weeks later Conrad wrapped up his bachelor life for good and, at the age of 38, married Jessie George to whom he had very recently proposed in cack-handed fashion on the steps of the National Gallery. After a lengthy honeymoon in Brittany, intersected by writing and illness, they eventually came to settle in Stanford-le-Hope, a small town out on the Essex mudflats, near to his closest English friends, the Hopes. There over the course of the next year he completed his first masterpiece, *The Nigger of the Narcissus*, whose experimental narrative and "literary impressionism" did not go unnoticed by the critics when published towards the close of 1897. But while the cultivated literary world embraced his genius, the work made little impression on the ordinary book-buying public, a pattern that was to be followed by all his books for the next seventeen years. The irony was that once, after the runaway success of *Chance*, his books began to sell, the literary genius had run away also.

Apart from the critical success of *The Nigger*, life on the Essex marshes proved a barren time for his writing. He spent most of 1898 struggling with *The Rescuer* (published more than twenty years later as *The Rescue*), a book he had started two years before. He was badly in debt and the fact that he had already been paid for both book and serial publication did not increase his enthusiasm for the writing. In fact, this period represents the first instance of a Conrad near-collapse, when writer's block, combined with financial and family worries (his first son Borys was born at this time "yelled like an Apache" and proved "a ghastly nuisance")[12] reduced him to a nervous wreck, unfit for anything but bed. All through the summer he was torn between completing the book he had been paid for and starting something fresh, even wondering whether he had done right to abandon the sea for writing: "Why the devil did I ever begin".[13] In moments of respite he saw "how ill, mentally, I have been these last four months. The fear of this horror coming back to me makes me shiver. As it is it has destroyed already the little belief in myself I used to have. I am appalled at the absurdity of my situation – at the folly of my hopes, at the blindness that had kept me up in my gropings. Most appalled to feel that all the doors behind me are shut and that I must remain where I have come blundering in the dark".[14]

Then quite suddenly his condition improved. Objectively, the problems remained much the same, but his spirit was relieved of the burden. The change of heart was closely tied to a change of house. In early September he met at Garnett's house, the Cearne, on the Kent-Surrey border the young writer Ford Hueffer (later Ford Madox Ford) and the two soon resolved upon what was to become the strangest collaboration in literary history. What Conrad stood to gain from such a partnership has puzzled many generations of literary critics (though he was careful to keep his own writing quite separate from the joint projects), but one immediate gain was Pent Farm. This was a compact eighteenth century red brick farmhouse with a long sloping roof standing in the midst of farm buildings in the parish of Postling, about three miles from the Kent coast at Hythe and five from Folkestone. Hueffer and his family had lived there until the previous March when they had moved to be close to the Garnetts at the Cearne. It had thus been empty for most of the summer (the artist Walter Crane had rented it for a couple of months towards the end) and Hueffer now offered it to Conrad as a sublet.

He accepted with alacrity. Although rather isolated, the open rolling countryside in which it stood was a more than welcome change from the bleak flats of the Essex marshes. After three months there, Conrad was still revelling in his good fortune and wrote to a Polish relative just before Christmas to describe this very English setting.

> As you will see, we have come to live here; this is also a farmhouse, somewhat smaller but more convenient and, what is most important, it is situated on higher ground. I found that I could not work in our old place. It is better here although I have nothing to boast about. We are only five kilometres from the sea. The railway station is 3 kilometres and Canterbury 1½ [he means 20] kilometres away.... Behind the house are the hills (Kentish Downs) which slope in zigzag fashion down to the sea, like the battlements of a big fortress... On the other side of the little garden stretches out quiet and waste land intersected by hedges and here and there stands an oak or a group of young ash trees. Three little villages are hidden among the hillocks and only the steeples of their churches can be seen. The colouring of the country presents brown and pale yellow tints – and in between, in the distance one can see the meadows, as green as emeralds. And not a sound is to be heard

but the laboured panting of the engines of the London-Dover express trains.[15]

These were the hills which a decade later Jocelyn Brooke would look up to as the mystical barriers to the forbidden territory, the country of the mind, that lay beyond.

There is little doubt that Conrad too was affected by the mysteries of this landscape for he was now entering upon the most productive period of his career. In Stanford-le-Hope he had been aloof from village life and the mainly labouring population. Here, apart from Postling just down the road, there was no village as such, but he had more or less on his doorstep three literary friends who made up for the distance from intellectual London – the young American writer, Stephen Crane at Brede across the Sussex border, Henry James at Rye, and H.G.Wells at Sandgate, whose children's parties were attended by the Brooke family, but sadly not by Jocelyn who was too young.[16] Conrad "loved his house and took pride in it as if he had built it".[17] It led him, probably under Hueffer's influence, into an interest in the history of that part of Kent and its traditions of farming, sailing and smuggling. Here he was at his most social; rarely a weekend went by without visitors – Hueffer, Galsworthy, Garnett, Cunninghame Graham, the Hopes from Essex and many others.

But most important of all was the effect upon his writing. The new sociability was a sign of a more relaxed mind and did not interfere with his weekday concentration when visitors were not around. Soon after his arrival he sent a teasing note to Hueffer who still had nominal responsibility for the building: "We are very happy here from which you may guess we haven't yet set fire to the house".[18] At the same time he wrote to Garnett: "We are here – over a week now and the place is a success... I feel hopeful about my own work. Completely changed".[19] The current millstone round his neck no longer posed a threat of any substance: "I get on dreamily with the *Rescue*, dreamily dreaming how fine it could be..." [20] He was soon relaxed enough to put it aside without guilt and embark on fresh literary adventures of a more substantial kind. In fact, over the next seven years at The Pent he wrote almost all his finest work – *Heart of Darkness, Lord Jim, Nostromo, The Secret Agent* – the core of his achievement.

Two months after the move, in the middle of December, he turned by choice from the peace of the Kent countryside back to the nightmare world of eight years before in the Belgian Congo and started to write what was to become *Heart of Darkness*, planned originally, like many of his novels at this time, as just a 20,000 word story, but developing into a short novella almost twice as long. On the surface a work calling into question the "civilising" role of Europeans in Africa, it raises deeper questions of man's place in nature, and the relationship between morality and the natural world. With it Conrad had found his mature, highly complex, artistic voice, brilliantly sustaining the African sensation of nightmare. The writing went relatively smoothly and the work was completed by February 1899 shortly after the first instalment appeared in *Blackwood's Magazine*. It was not until the close of 1902 that it appeared in book form, in the volume *Youth*, its bold originality well recognised by the more discerning critics like Edward Garnett.

Meanwhile, he was working in fits and starts on *Lord Jim* which too had started life in 1898 as a short story but had mushroomed over time to a full-length novel of 130,000 words. Constantly he predicted he was close to finishing but the work, tantalisingly, just grew and grew. He had two new starts on it in 1899, but the last consistent burst was saved for the spring and early summer of 1900 when he wrote the last third of the text of what was to become his most popular book among the general public so far. He finished it on 12 July. Completion of a major work by Conrad most often occurred in a frenetic burst of nervous energy ending in the small hours of the morning, and was most often followed by a letter describing in fine detail the physical circumstances of the event. His report to Galsworthy on this occasion, painting a vivid picture of a writer's life in the small Kent farmhouse, has become justly famous.

The end of L.J. has been pulled off with a steady drag of 21 hours. I sent wife and child out of the house (to London) and sat down at 9 am, with a desperate resolve to be done with it. Now and then I took a walk round the house out at one door in at the other. Ten-minute meals. A great hush. Cigarette ends growing into a mound similar to a cairn over a dead hero. Moon rose over the barn looked in at the window and climbed out of sight. Dawn broke, brightened. I put the lamp out and went on, with the morning breeze blowing the sheets of MS all over the room. Sun rose. I wrote the last word and went into the dining room. Six o'clock. I shared a piece of cold chicken with Escamillo (who was very miserable and in want of sympathy having missed the child dreadfully all day). Felt very well only sleepy; had a bath at seven and at 8.30 was on my way to London.[21]

The initial reviews of the book when it came out three months later were highly enthusiastic, though it did not on that account sell particularly well. But Conrad was more concerned about reviewers he trusted like Garnett, who this time strongly criticised the last third of the book. Conrad took the criticism to heart with a typically histrionic declaration of despair over all his recent work. " For what is fundamentally wrong with the book – the cause of the effect – is want of power... I mean the want of *illuminating* imagination. I wanted to obtain a sort of lurid light out of the very events... I've been satanically ambitious, but there's nothing of a devil in me, worse luck. The *Outcast* is a heap of sand, the *Nigger* a splash of water, *Jim* a lump of clay. A stone, I suppose will be my next gift to the impatient mankind." [22] In fact, *Nostromo*, his greatest masterpiece, turned out a bar of silver.

Nostromo is unique as a Conrad novel, both in its conception and in its writing. Whereas most of his narratives, particularly the

126

sea-based novels that formed the body of his work up till then, are founded on an historical event (often taken from his own life) and the prevailing atmosphere built on his own detailed experience, this carefully constructed account of a South American republic as it comes into collision with the modern capitalist world is almost entirely imagined. For directly experienced atmosphere it can draw only on his brief landfall on the South American continent back in 1876; the rest is mainly built on his reading. But not completely so. He had also the benefit of his close friendship with Cunninghame Graham, the Scottish aristocrat and socialist MP who had spent ten years of his young life in South America. Conrad invited him over to The Pent where Graham set him on a course of reading (most notably two memoirs from the 1860s on Venezuela and Paraguay)[23] which furnished him with background on the exotic topography of the continent and its dramatically violent revolutionary politics. In addition Graham offered his own considered perspectives on the political background and fed him with colourful personal anecdotes. With this promising practical help, Conrad was able to build the simple incident of the seaman who stole the hoard of silver into this immense account of an entirely imagined country, rich in every aspect of its physical, political, social, religious, and cultural life.

Nostromo marks a critical turning point in Conrad's writing career as he moved from the seafaring stories of his early works to the great political novels of *The Secret Agent* and *Under Western Eyes*, what he was later to call "a subtle change in the nature of the inspiration".[24] As a creative work of art, its range and depth is simply mind-blowing – an intricate mosaic of political events entwined round an astonishing cast list of thirteen central characters, sixteen secondary ones and numerous minor parts, not to mention the vast chorus of social, political and economic groups from soldiers and dockers and railway workers to landowners, politicians and bureaucrats. This deftly created microcosm, utterly convincing in its authenticity, is set against an equally convincing wider background of contemporary movements of capitalist expansion and economic imperialism, marked in particular by the new imperialism of the United States which was emerging at that time. For Conrad was well fitted to handle these larger political and economic themes by his personal experience as the son of a highly politicised family in Poland and his profession of twenty years carrying the goods of the new global capitalists from one end of the earth to the other.

Conrad's supreme handling of this vast world of affairs is matched equally by his probing forays into the souls of his characters, developing the tension between inner identity and social interaction, between the inner world of the moral imagination and the outer world of material fact. His characters invest a moral significance in worldly tasks (Charles Gould develops the silver mine both to avenge his father's ill fortune and to create the economic power that will provide political stability) but the attraction of purely material interests in the end overwhelms the moral crusade. In the process relationships are destroyed.

As if this were not enough, Conrad uses the novel to experiment with new structures and techniques which mark out its pioneering status in modernist fiction. The prose is richer and denser than he has worked before, giving the world it describes its essential authenticity. This is particularly true of the central development of the book – the building of the picture of the town of Sulaco and the meetings in the Casa Gould – so naturally drawn in such unforced detail that the reader is sucked deep in to this human landscape and becomes an inhabitant himself before he is scarcely aware of it. Even more enticing is the author's handling of time in the narrative, which does not follow a strict chronological path but, instead of mixing the timeframe with broad and predictable previews and flashbacks, deals in more subtle movements of time that fit so naturally they are hardly noticed. The effect is to emphasise the nature of the events rather than their mere chronological course, and is a technique which as one critic has described it "confers exceptional temporal solidity on the novel – in Conrad's fiction even time acquires amplitude".[25]

One key aspect of Conrad's fictional writing is his use of many voices to build up a description of the same reality, reflecting his view that objective truth is different from each individual human perspective. In *Nostromo* the technique is applied with considerable mastery, the action unrolling seamlessly in the distinctive voices of the various characters without in any way disrupting the narrative line. In this way, the author exposes the limitations of the interpretation of an event or assessment of a character from a single viewpoint, and enriches our understanding of the fullness and complexity of any given moment in time. Conrad's subtle manipulation of time sequences and use of multiple narrators, now standard techniques in modern fiction, were novel and puzzling to the majority of critics and readers in 1904. Reviewers of this ground-breaking book either ignored its novel structures or condemned them head-on as artistic mistakes. What in time were to be recognised by all as its essential qualities and strengths were dismissed out of hand.

No greater contrast could be found between the content of a book and the physical circumstances under which it was written. The sweeping descriptions of the tropical splendours of the exotic Occidental Province of the Republic of Costaguana, with its ancient capital of Sulaco, in its "inviolable sanctuary" amidst "the solemn hush of the deep Golfo Placido",[26] were all written from a tiny farmhouse close to the far from tropical coast of southern Kent, at a table before a window boasting a very far from exotic English view: "Before my window I can see the buildings of the farm, and on leaning out and looking to the right, I see the valley of the Stour, the source of which is so to speak behind the third hedge from the farmyard." [27] The book is packed with thousands of extras from all walks of life, all shouting loudly through the turmoil of revolution and counter-revolution; the farm stands in an isolated spot, away from the nearest tiny village, and the only visitors to break the enveloping deathly silence are Conrad's few literary friends. "We live like a family of anchorites. From time to time a pious pilgrim belonging to la grande fraternité des lettres comes to pay a visit to the celebrated Joseph Conrad – and to obtain his blessing. Sometimes he gets it and sometimes he does not, for the hermit is severe and dyspeptic..." [28]

The hermit, however, was not always confined to his cell. Sometimes he could be seen running along the quiet lane outside the house pushing his young son Borys in a homemade wheel cart doubling as a motorcar.[29] And one day a week the family would make the winding hilly journey by horse and dog-cart into Hythe to do the household shopping. The expeditions followed a time-honoured pattern. The horse would be stabled at the White Hart Inn, and the master of the house would settle himself in the bar-parlour, chatting with the locals over a whisky and soda, while Jessie and Borys went shopping. Sometimes he would cross the road to the antique shop run by Mr Ninnes (a venue for gift shopping for the rest of his life) and browse happily till the female tasks were completed. Then the whole family would lunch together with the landlady in her own private parlour before returning home.[30]

But even when in anchorite mode, the family was not always so entirely peaceful as its master had suggested. At times the domestic groans that went up were a goodly match for those of a South American revolution. For in the period of almost two years he was working on the book, Conrad fell prey to his regular illness, with the usual bouts of gout and depression, the latter brought on by the slow progress of his writing and his financial and other domestic worries. For in this period too his wife Jessie developed the problem with her knees that were to dog her for the rest of their married life, and Borys, then their only son, was a regular prey to childhood illness, sometimes life-threatening. Furthermore, the writer's financial position was generally dire, buried under a weight of debt, mostly owed to J.B.Pinker, his kindly literary agent who acted as unofficial personal banker; this was mainly the result of his extravagant failure to manage his money, a defect that went right the way back to his youth in Marseille when his Polish uncle had been the one to bail him out. Much of the time his writing thus became a mere process for generating income, running fast but never quite catching up with his debts. It is noteworthy that many of the great novels of this period started life as short stories, works that could be written quickly without pain and turned promptly into cash. But as the work developed and imagination took wing, the story became a novella, then a standard size novel, and finally ended up a long novel.

Such was the process that marked the development of *Nostromo*. In the autumn of 1902 the ideas for the work began to buzz about his head, inspired by the central incident of the stolen silver which he came across by chance in a book by an American sailor he had been leafing through outside a second-hand bookshop.[31] But it was a time he was feeling unwell, too weak to pursue the inspiration immediately. He wrote to Galsworthy late in October: "Only, with my head full of a story, I have not been able to write a single word – except the title which shall be I think: NOSTROMO...".[32] Up till Christmas he worked on *The Rescue*, the book he had been paid for six years before and which was to remain embedded on his conscience for many years yet to come. But he was dissatisfied with the writing and immediately after Christmas, as a light relief from the wearisome book, started on *Nostromo*, a story of 35000 words which he planned to finish by the end of January.[33] It took in fact a further year and a half.

By the beginning of February he was working on the story as hard as he could, but it had now become a novel and the finishing date had crept out to the end of June, following a request from Harpers for a serial of 85000 words.[34] It was money rather than the requirements of artistic expression that had led to this expansion. He told Galsworthy: "I rather think that with the inducement offered I could manage to keep at it." He thought of writing some of it in Winchelsea, close to his friend Ford Hueffer: "I would be afraid of getting stale here as it happened more than once during the Lord Jim trouble. And this thing is worth while taking precautions. It may – with the English book rights – figure up to a thousand pounds, or thereabouts."[35] But nearly all of it was in fact written at The Pent, apart from a stay in London and the very final words composed in his old stamping ground of Stanford-le-Hope. In March he suffered a fresh attack of gout, further bouts of which were to plague his writing throughout 1903. But he was now so deep in the new work that he rejected out of hand a commission for a new short story: "I can't scatter my thought here and there. Now I am engrossed in *Nostromo* I ought to stick to it without further change of plan. To try *another* story at high pressure would be fatal to both".[36] He was gaining confidence in the product: "*Nostromo* shall be a first rate story".[37]

He now cast around for books that would provide firm foundations for this largely imagined work. He asked Hueffer to find him a life of Garibaldi to back the development of Giorgio Viola, the old Garibaldino who features so strongly in the early pages: "Oh! for some book that would give me picturesque locutions idioms, swear words – suggestive phrases on Italy. Giorgio shall take a good space in the book. And then the girls [*his daughters*] too!".[38] In early May, with 15000 words written, he asked Cunninghame Graham (as we have seen) to call at The Pent to help further with books and background, a meeting that was to bear rich fruit in the final text.[39] His ambition for the work was now expanding in great strides, but despite heavy labour he had not yet got beyond the introductory pages: "Nostromo grows: grows against the grain by dint of distasteful toil – but it cannot be said to progress. The pile of pages is bigger certainly by three or four every day; but the story has not yet even begun".[40] By early July, with 23000 under his belt, the traditional Conrad lament went up, half self-deprecating, half truly meant: "I am having an infernal time of it with my silly stuff. It is silly – and I am a fool and the feeling discourages me utterly. However!" [41] He was feeling most pointedly the lack of personal background which had bolstered all his previous work. He wrote to Cunninghame Graham: "I am dying over that cursed Nostromo thing. All my memories of Central America seem to slip away. I just had a glimpse 25 years ago – a short glance. That is not enough pour bâtir un roman dessus. And yet one must live".[42]

By the end of August, he had accumulated 42000 and thought he was halfway through; in fact, this was only a quarter of the completed work. But the three parts of the novel had by then all been planned in detail and much of the remainder written in rough. He felt a growing confidence in the quality of the work, particularly now that a chink of light could be seen at the end of the tunnel, and while he continued of necessity to decry his writing to other authors, to Pinker, his agent, he could declare his true feelings: "I have never worked so hard before – with so much anxiety. But the result is good. You know I take no credit to myself for what I do – and so I may judge my own performance. There is no mistake about this. You may take up a strong position when you offer it here. It is a very genuine Conrad. At the same time it is more of a novel pure and simple than anything I've done since Almayer's Folly".[43]

The autumn brought further attacks of gout and the depression that always followed, not assisted by the arrival of pressing bills which perforce he handed on to Pinker. But his confidence in the power of the book bore him up: "I would be worried out of my wits with these things if the great work were not going on steadily". He had completed the second part and was now deep in the opening pages of the third with the dramatic rescue of the Occidental Province from the hands of the revolutionaries. "I don't send you P IId yet. I simply can't spare time to look it over; the drama of the P IIId filling my mind".[44] By early November, he aimed to be finished by Christmas but the work was getting on top of him; he asked Pinker: "Are you very sick of me? I assure you I am half off my chump sometimes with the pressure of the thing".[45] He was even more expressive in a letter to H G Wells: "I my dear Wells am absolutely out of my mind with the worry and apprehension of my work. I go on as one would cycle over a precipice along a 14-inch plank. If I falter I am lost".[46]

Towards the end of November, looking back on a year of recurrent attacks of gout and seemingly irretrievable debt, the power of the book to lift him up began to falter. He summed up the position in a letter to J M Barrie which, though adopting the self-deprecatory tone that was normal when addressing other authors, gives hints beneath the thick layer of irony of his genuine weariness with the work and his sense that it would be a failure, way beyond the wits of his general readership.

> Your good letter found me in bed, and though I've crawled out of it to-day I remain still recumbent and am writing this on a pad with a horrid fountain pen. Another week lost out of the few left to me for the silly book I am writing now – if the thing can be called a book at all. I am afraid it shall be more in the nature of printed matter. A certain amount of cheap sincerity there is in it, some shadow of intention too (which no one will see), and even an "artistic!" purpose – but all this makes for failure, since I've never felt that I had my subject in the palm of my hand. I've been always catching at it all along; and I shall be just catching at it to the end. That state of feeling leads one to sheer twaddle. I've already suspected that there was a lot of twaddle in the thing; and, since I've heard, the other day, that Harpers' people are very pleased with the part they have got, I am perfectly sure there is. I am trying to persuade myself that the other two parts may fill them with dismay. But I doubt it. I doubt it very much: I am too full of dismay myself.[47]

He rushed to get on with the work before the Christmas break – "I am working desperately to catch up the gout delay" – and was at the same time winding himself up over details of the planned book publication: "And I *will not* put up with the American spelling in the *English* edition. I would rather – and I will too – fling the thing into the fire. Till I am sure of that they shan't get a page more out of me. Let it be clearly understood".[48] On Boxing Day, as he wrote his thank you letters, he summed up the year (the year of his greatest book) in typical melodramatic fashion: "Of myself I have a dread to speak. It has been a most disastrous year for my work. If I had written each page with my blood I could not feel more exhausted at the end of this twelvemonth. And the tale of pages is not yet complete!".[49]

As the year before, the Christmas break seemed to refresh him and he started work again straight after with prospects looking good. In the middle of January he took his family and his work up to London for a change of air. He had intended staying for just a week or so, but early on disaster struck: Jessie fell in the street and wrenched both her knees, aggravating an old injury to one of them. She could not be moved, so they were forced to stay on for two months, Conrad's worries mounting with the incoming doctors' bills which he was in no position to pay. But despite all this, the change of air gave a new impetus to his work. With the end of *Nostromo* in sight, he began to relax on it; he started to rewrite and expand Part 2 and develop further his ideas for the final part; at the same time, he filtered other new work into his schedule (in part a financial necessity for his bank had just failed) – a play based on his short story *Tomorrow* and a series of reminiscences, lightly dictated to his secretary, that were to become *The Mirror of the Sea*: "I've discovered that I can dictate that sort of bosh without effort at the rate of 3000 words in four hours". These were delaying tactics; it was as if he did not want to let go of the book that had filled his life for more than a year. In February he told Wells of his current routine: "So in the day *Nostromo* and from 11 pm to 1 am dictation".[50]

Returning to The Pent in mid-March, he decided to apply the new found skills of dictation to the final part of *Nostromo* – "What the stuff is like God only knows".[51] The answer was – good enough for serial publication, but not for the final book which had to be worked on extensively, and even then betrays signs of a thinner prose than that of the earlier sections. By early May, as he sent off the first batch of Part 3 to Pinker, his confidence in the final result was increasing: "I verily believe that N. has elements of success in book form. I've never written anything with so much *action* in it. The thing is not half bad upon my word".[52] In late June he was still struggling on – "I work desperately but slow – much too slow for the situation... I am not myself and shall not be myself till I am born again after Nostromo is finished".[53]

The book was completed in the usual semi-delirious marathon of work through the last weeks of August 1904. For the final month he wrote practically day and night, going to bed at three and starting again at nine in the morning with what he called "the tenacity of despair".[54] He had planned to complete it at The Pent but just as the last pages were turning he rushed off for a three day visit to his old friend Hope back in Essex, and the book was finished there. As with *Lord Jim*, he passed on a blow by blow account of the final dramatic hours to John Galsworthy, including the last minute intervention of a dentist and perhaps other more spiritual forces.

> Finished! Finished on the 30th in Hope's house in Stanford in Essex, where I had to take off my brain that seemed to turn to water. For a solid Fortnight I've been sitting up. And all the time horrible toothache. On the 27th had to wire for dentist (couldn't leave the work) who came at 2 and dragged at the infernal thing which seemed rooted in my very soul. The horror came away at last, leaving however one root in the gum. Then he grubbed for *that* till I leapt out of the chair. Thereupon old Walton [*his dentist from Folkestone*] said: I don't think your nerves will stand any more of this.
> I went back to my MS. at six pm. At 11.30 something happened – what it is I don't know. I was writing, and raised my eyes to look at the clock. The next thing I know I was sitting (not lying) sitting on the concrete outside the door. When I crawled in I found it was nearly one. I managed to get upstairs and said to Jessie: We must be off to-morrow.[55]

It was, as he later explained to Ford Hueffer, some kind of breakdown: "two blank hours during which I must have got out and sat down –

(not fallen) on the concrete outside the door".[56] There then followed an altogether surreal account of the dreamlike journey to Essex, where he was put to bed only to start again immediately the next morning.

> That night I slept. Worked all day. In the evening dear Mrs Hope (who is not used to that sort of thing) gave me four candles and on I went. Finished at 3. Took me another half-hour to check the numbering of the pages...[57]

The book had taken 20 months from the day he first put pen to paper but almost half the final text had been written in five intensive months, from the end of March to the end of August. He now returned to the bosom of his family and the cooler countryside of Kent. "My sojourn on the continent of Latin America, famed for its hospitality, lasted for about two years. On my return I found... my family all well, my wife heartily glad to learn that the fuss was all over, and our small boy considerably grown during my absence." [58]

The immediate elation of finishing proved transient; because his ambition had been set so high, the execution fell inevitably short of the conception, a source of unease and worrying disappointment. But also a signal of major achievement.

> What the book is like I don't know. I don't suppose it'll damage me; but I know that it is open to much intelligent criticism. For the other sort I don't care. Personally I am not satisfied. It is something – but not the thing I tried for. There is no exultation, none of that temporary sense of achievement which is so soothing. Even the mere feeling of relief, at having done with it, is wanting. The strain has been too great; had lasted too long.[59]

When the book came out in October, the look of it was a new source of anxiety: "I am disgusted at the slovenliness, meanness of the book's get-up – the horrid misprints, the crooked lines, the dropped punctuation marks. By Jove a fourth of the pages slants! I've never seen anything like this!" [60] A week or so later, he was feeling more optimistic, buoyed up by the response from his friends: "I am afraid Nostromo had a bad sendoff. I receive magnificent letters from unexpected quarters; I know well enough that the book is no mean feat – but what about the public?" [61]

The book did not receive the general public applause for which Conrad had hoped, nor the sales that might have relieved his immediate burden of debt. To add to this disappointment, it did not receive from the critics the expected recognition for its intellectual content and artistic innovation. Most of the reviews were slight, seeing nothing more than a dramatic adventure story, and some who went deeper criticised the shapelessness of narrative and prolixity of style. As with *Heart of Darkness*, only Edward Garnett saw and understood the book's real theme. [62] For Conrad, ever in search of a combination of popular success and critical acclaim, the result was, disappointingly, much the same as before.

He wrote one more major work at Pent Farm – *The Secret Agent* – whose reviews in the autumn of 1907, though mixed, were more understanding and led him to concede that it had been at least an honourable failure. [63] The intensity and quality of his inspiration, now at the height of his powers, had of necessity anchored him in these years to the little farm which gave him what he most needed for writing – isolation and peace. But in 1906 he began to make more frequent trips to London, and that year and the following embarked on two lengthy working holidays in Montpellier in the south of France. He was clearly in need of a change of scene.

But then when was he not in such need? His young life in Poland and career at sea had been a constant history of short-term movement, creating a restlessness that remained with him for the whole of his life. As Gillian Tindall has commented: "Conrad, so publicised as the travelling novelist *par excellence*, was a chronic exile quite peculiarly unable to relate adequately to any place on earth, at his best in a storm at sea..." [64] For company at The Pent he had his writing friends close by – Wells, Henry James, Ford Hueffer. There is little indication that he mixed with the villagers of Postling just down the lane. In fact, he appears to have regarded the Kentish peasantry as an alien race, slow-moving, ignorant, malicious towards foreigners. His short story, *Amy Foster*, written at The Pent, seems likely to reflect his personal view, albeit in exaggerated form. In this, a Polish emigrant to America washed up by a shipwreck on the Kent coast is treated with suspicion and ruthlessness by the local population, who fear the unfamiliar and unknown, while he in turn is destroyed by the resultant loneliness and isolation. [65] Perhaps surprising, in light of this, that he remained at The Pent, though propitious for his writing, for as long as nine years.

The immediate cause of his next move was a build-up of unpaid rent to add to his usual money troubles – he needed somewhere cheaper. Matters bubbled up to a head in August 1907 when he wrote to Pinker from Switzerland in desperation: "I must get away from the Pent". [66] They moved as a family back to familiar ground north of the Thames, to Someries "a jolly old Farmhouse" [67] two and a half miles from Luton. He had been looking for a cheaper house, but had been seduced by size and proximity to London into renting one even more expensive. His old extravagant impulses were still very much alive.

They left the farmhouse and Kent on 10 September. Despite the present discomforts there and the burning need for change, he left in the nostalgic knowledge that he had written his best stuff here. He wrote to a friend on the day of departure as though to acknowledge the point: "These are the last words I shall write in the old house". [68]

They arrived at Someries on the day *The Secret Agent* was published. He continued there with the writing of *Under Western Eyes*, his last great novel started at The Pent, but it soon stalled. The house proved unsuitable; perhaps no house would have suited the writer in his current mood – "probably it does not matter in the least where one lives". [69] They remained there for just a year and a half.

After less than a year in the new abode, Conrad longed to return to Kent where his writing had run so freely. He bemoaned his lot to Galsworthy: "I am awfully done up and want a change. If we could take a cottage somewhere in Kent for 3-4 weeks it would be nice. At the same time we could look out for something permanent down that way. Of course that would not mean stopping writing – quite the contrary. It's here that the pen is clogged. I have a positive horror of this place, and wake up each morning with a dread of the day before me".[70] In September 1908 they spent three weeks near to the Hueffers again, this time at Aldington on the northern edge of Romney Marsh where the Hueffers were now based. They scouted round for a permanent house there and found a number that were suitable. By the time they returned to Someries it had become "that damned Luton place". He was honest in his recognition: "I've made a fatal move and it's no use persisting in a mistake".[71] He managed finally to persuade Pinker to arrange the finance for a permanent move to Aldington, achieved in February 1909, to a much smaller, but cheaper, cottage in the centre of the village. It had been an emergency move and the new house could not be more than a temporary stop-gap for a writer who needed space and its concomitant peace.

He was delighted to be back in Kent, as he showed in the joyful invitation to his doctor to make his first visit: "As a motorist you have a map of the fair County of Kent. From London to Ashford all is plain sailing. At about 3-4 miles beyond Ashford on the high road to Folkestone you will come to four cross roads. Take the turn to the right indicated by the sign *To Smeeth Station*. From that point I send you the detail of the road (*not* to scale) down to our very door".[72] Although he loved the area, by September he was beginning to feel more keenly the cramped nature of the accommodation, the upper part of a rambling old building: "Here the house is impossible. But what must be must be. The locality is all right; but in these rooms I can't have that absolute quiet, complete silence, without which it seems that now I cannot work to any serious purpose".[73] The ground floor was occupied by his landlord, a pork butcher, and one especially aggravating factor was the proximity of the slaughterhouse from which could be regularly heard the squealing of stuck pigs![74]

For the previous few years, his anxiety over the writing, his finances and family illness had been building up to a nervous breakdown and the inevitable explosion came early in 1910, precipitated by a major row with Pinker. Gout and depression took him to bed for some weeks and for a good time after that he remained in semi-convalescent state. In June he told Stephen Reynolds who had had a similar breakdown seven years before: "I have been beastly ill and it seems I was not far from dying. If so I may tell you that the border country seems to have no special terrors for the traveller himself however unkindly and gruesome it may appear to the watchers".[75] But by this time, he had moved from the cottage in Aldington ("it has become odious to me after this illness") to "a farmhouse with biggish rooms and $1^1/2$ acres of orchard standing in the fields and surrounded by 750 acres of unpreserved woods where I am at liberty to roam... It's a very attractive place".[76] Indeed Capel House, the seventeenth century farmhouse in the village of Orlestone, partly surrounded by a moat, was arguably the prettiest of Conrad's houses and, according to his son Borys, "undoubtedly the happiest of the Conrad homes".[77] There they were back on old and loved territory, just eight miles from The Pent where they had lived for nine years. They were to live here for a further nine.

Two years later, the writer Richard Curle, last of the young acolytes with whom Conrad surrounded himself at this period, came to visit for the first time. As to the house, he agreed with Borys.

> It was a typical Kentish farmhouse, standing away by itself [*the Jutish topography*] in the midst of flat fields; and in its very isolation, infused with homeliness, there was something almost symbolic to me of Conrad's aloof genius and friendly personality. How often on subsequent summer afternoons Conrad and I have sat in

deck chairs on the rough lawn above its old and weedy moat, enjoying the solitude and the sun. I can see him now, waving his hand at the oak woods beyond and saying, "How I hate the feeling these woods give me of being shut in!" In a sense my happiest recollections of Conrad are bound up with Capel House. There was an informality about life there, a warm comfort, which were never quite caught again...[78]

But he had not stayed at The Pent.

Under Western Eyes was completed at Capel House the year after they moved in, but this was the last of the series of great novels that had begun with *Nostromo*. By contrast, here also he completed *Chance*, the novel that had hovered about his writing desk for more than a decade. It was the book that was finally to bring Conrad to popular fame; within a fortnight of publication in January 1914 it had gone into its fifth impression. The knock-on effect was remarkable; his earlier novels were reprinted and at last made big sales, and soon his manuscripts were being bought for much larger sums than had ever been earned by the original books. He was at last free of money worries and could live at Capel House the life of an English country gentleman, the role for which his genteel Polish ancestry and liberal spending habits had well prepared him. But with popular success and relative affluence, his strong imaginative creativity seems to have deserted him. The financial incentive to write all hours had gone, and he was fast approaching his sixtieth year. He took the easy way out and mined the old seams – the works, like *The Rescue*, he had started but never completed. A few more books trickled through the presses, but there were to be no more *Nostromos*.

Though Conrad had lived an emotionally rootless life, and had never gone in active search of a home, he now, on this return to his most favoured part of Kent, seems to have found the nearest thing to one. In the summer of 1914 he returned to Poland for a visit, his first trip abroad for seven years, and was nearly trapped there by the outbreak of the First World War. The following year he wrote about the journey, drawing movingly on memories of his childhood in Cracow and his father's death. But he wrote movingly too about his departure from England, leaving behind the simple glories of the Kent countryside, his feelings for which become equated with his patriotic feelings for his adopted country.

> As we left the door of our house nestling in, perhaps, the most peaceful nook of Kent, the sky, after weeks of perfectly brazen serenity, veiled its blue depths and started to weep fine tears for the refreshment of the parched fields. A pearly blurr settled over them; a light sifted of all glare, of everything unkindly and searching that dwells in the splendour of unveiled skies. All unconscious of going towards the very scenes of war I carried off in my eye this tiny fragment of Great Britain: a few fields, a wooded rise, a clump of trees or two, with a short stretch of road and here and there a gleam of red wall and tiled roof above the darkening hedges wrapped up in soft mist and peace. And I felt that all this had a very strong hold on me as the embodiment of a beneficent and gentle spirit; that it was dear to me not as an inheritance but as an acquisition, as a conquest in the sense in which a woman is conquered – by love, which is a sort of surrender.[79]

He had come a long distance from the alien castaway of *Amy Foster*. In some measure, he now loved and belonged.

He would probably have stayed on at Capel House to the end of his days, so much did he and the family love it there. But in December 1917 his landlord died and his son decided to take the house back into occupation. Much of the next year, between finishing work on

The Rescue and starting on *Suspense*, was spent charging round the local countryside in a car, sometimes driven by Borys, in search of a suitable new home. When forced finally to relinquish Capel House in the spring of 1919, they took temporary shelter in Spring Grove, a large seventeenth century manor house on the outskirts of Wye.

He did not like the new house, even though it was the first to permit him his own private study which did not, as in the other houses, double as a drawing room; it seemed too large and pretentious for the family's needs and led to a constant stream of visitors, mostly Borys' friends. He wrote to Garnett: "I must remind you of your promise to come and see us in this house (which is odious). But perhaps sitting smoking together we could manage to forget where we are".[80] But when the landlord wrote to ask him, then confined to his bed with gout, how they had settled in, he produced a typical piece of Conradian courteous diplomacy underlaid by a barb of true feeling for only the eagle-eyed to spot: "I can assure you that everybody is very happy in your charming house. I haven't been outside the fences since I saw you, but if one must be a prisoner this certainly is a very charming spot to be imprisoned in".[81]

He could, however, bear the deficiencies of Spring Grove in the knowledge it was rented for only six months, and by the time of moving in he had found, and was already negotiating for, a permanent home that was suitable. He and Jessie had come across it in February 1919 while being driven round the countryside by Borys; Jessie and Borys fell in love with it at first sight, but Conrad himself was doubtful about the setting: he liked his houses on hilltops with good views. But these objections overcome, he had started negotiations the following day, although rather worried about the cost: "It goes awfully against the grain to pay £250 for a year's rent".[82] The owner who was pushing for this healthy sum was a Colonel Bell of Bourne Park. Soon after the move to Spring Grove, the negotiations began to warm up and Conrad told Pinker of his feelings: "I am better, and intend to go out on Wednesday to see Colonel Bell's agent about a permanent house I have in view:

Oswalds, Bishopsbourne, about 4 miles from Canterbury. It will be a great relief to me to have the future settled in that respect; and certainly the house is wonderfully convenient".[83]

Negotiations dragged on through that summer, mostly on very minor matters, until on 21 August he wrote to Pinker again: "I have signed to-day the agreement for Oswalds – house, 2 cottages, 3 gardens – all complete – £250 a year. Two years certain and then on a year's notice".[84] On Tuesday 7 October he sent his first letter from Bishopsbourne: "We slept in this house last night".[85]

CHAPTER 6

Joseph Conrad

I imagine, I fancy I've observed, that you think a little too much of what you've done. The merits of our achievement (I am speaking of *artists*) should not be dwelt upon mentally too much. Contemplated with persistence they cease to be inspiring.

Joseph Conrad, 1909

As I grow older I think much more about my past work in that and in other ways.

Joseph Conrad, 1920[1]

When Conrad moved in to the village in October 1919 he was joining not just a small community (quite a change since his previous permanent Kent homes had been isolated) but also the Bourne estate, run from the splendiferous Queen Anne house that was to inspire the lyrical flights of Jocelyn Brooke's imagination some thirty years later. For Oswalds had been for some time the dower house of Bourne. It had started life in much humbler guise as a blacksmiths and taken its name from one early incumbent whose covered-over forge in the study there dates back to the beginning of the sixteenth century, a hundred years before any great writers arrived in the village.[2] In the early nineteenth century it had been "developed" into a much grander Georgian house with a stately nine-window façade; Victorian extensions were to follow, with a billiard room and ballroom tacked

16. Arthur Waite, historian of the occult, 1922.

17. Waite's grave.

18. The White Cottage site today.

19. Alec and Joan Waugh at Oswalds, 1933.

20. Charlton Park today.

21. Frog Lane, the grand entrance to the village.

22. The Conrad Hall.

23. The teak plaque above the doorway.

24. The young Conrad, age 25.

25. The Pent where Conrad wrote his major works.

26. Conrad with his son John outside Capel House.

27. Oswalds in the 1920s.

28. Outside Oswalds – John, Borys, Conrad and Pinker.

29. Conrad in April 1923 just before setting off for America.

30. Canterbury High Street in Conrad's day: *left foreground* Goulden's Bookshop and further on the Fleur-de-Lis Hotel which formed his base on shopping days.

31. Off to the cricket! The Conrads aboard Pinker's coach and four.

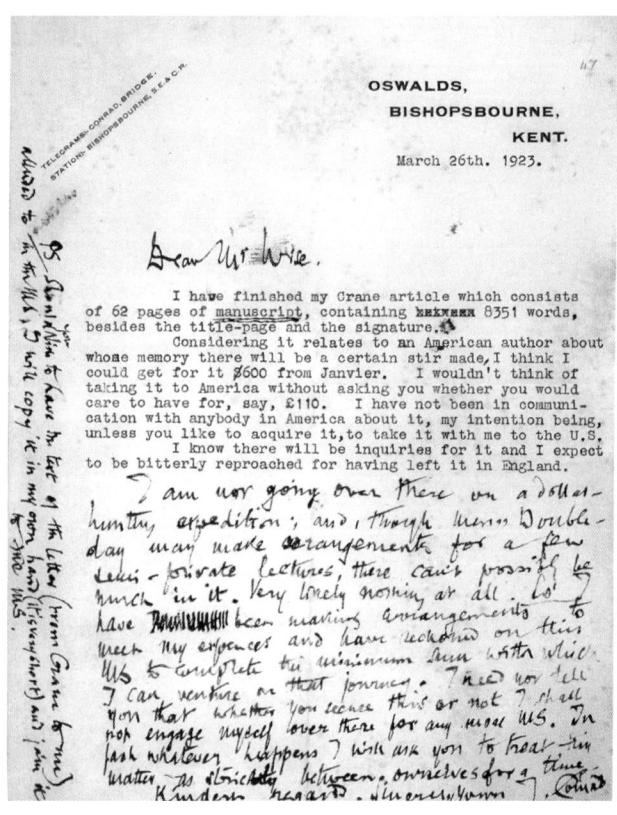

32. Conrad to his collector, Thomas Wise.

on before Conrad's time, later to be pulled down. It was at that time too that the new dynasty of Bourne Park emerged. In 1841 the dower house was leased to a Matthew Bell who hoped that, with one foot in the door, he would be well placed to purchase the whole Bourne estate from Mrs Beckingham, the ageing widow then living in Dover, who was last in the current line of owners.[3] This he did three years later when the old lady died, and by Conrad's time the estate had devolved to his grandson, Colonel Matthew Bell. The junior Bell family had lived themselves for some years in the dower house and as a young child Jocelyn Brooke had been invited to tea-parties with them there.[4] Now at last the Bells took up their full inheritance, moving into Bourne Park and leaving the vacated house to the famous author.

The interior of the building was quite grand, if a little worn. On entering by the front door, Conrad's study was at the end of a short passage to the right; to the left was the door to the dining room. Straight ahead of the entrance hall was a long passage which led down to the one-time ballroom at the rear of the house which Jessie converted into a large drawing-room, conserving the room to the right halfway down the passage as her own private "den", where she could go to rest her crippled leg. The staircase rose to the left of the main passage: Conrad's bedroom stood over the front porch from where he could hear all visitors arrive and leave; Jessie's was next to it above the dining-room with an access door to her husband's room. Conrad's study itself was a pleasant room with book-lined walls, a simple marble fireplace and a large semi-circular bow window, taking up almost all the end wall, and looking out towards the north east and up the hill to the Dover Road. On their arrival the décor of the whole house was somewhat faded and Conrad hired the services of a friend as interior decorator to embellish the public parts of the building, particularly the large drawing room.[5]

Conrad revelled in the Georgian elegance which fitted his image of the country gentleman inviting notables down from London for the weekend; but with it he forfeited much of the cosy intimacy of The Pent or Capel. Whatever Oswalds was, it was certainly not an old Kentish farmhouse. His young friend Richard Curle immediately noted the difference: "In a sense my happiest recollections of Conrad are bound up with Capel House. There was an informality about the life there, a warm comfort, which were never quite caught again in the grander surroundings of Oswalds, where he spent his final years".[6] For Conrad it was just a good-looking, convenient house in the midst of that Kent countryside to which he had for so many years grown accustomed; he could have exchanged it at any time for another if that had been called for. It gave him the space and the peace he needed as a writer, but even these were less vital requirements now, for the writing spark itself was growing dimmer with the years.

What it did give him that the other houses did not was a local urban centre in the shape of the ancient capital of Kent, indeed as some would claim the ancient capital of England, lying just four miles away. Canterbury became a new focus for the Conrad family. It was the place to which Jessie went off on her shopping trips when her knee would carry her; it was the place to which car and chauffeur were directed on Friday afternoons to pick up guests at Canterbury East, and even sometimes Canterbury West; it held a major festival in the August cricket week which drew cricket-mad friends like Pinker, his agent, to the nearby St Lawrence Ground; it was the source of essential provisions from first class retailers, like the long-established booksellers H. J. Goulden Ltd in the High Street who furnished Conrad with his stationery and privately printed for him some of his minor works.[7] The great writer himself would wander around town on his own and sometimes forget (as Richard Curle once found to his cost) that he had come in to pick up a guest at the station.[8] Being close to Canterbury was both a convenience and a life-enhancer.

Moving in to Oswalds that October proved chaotic in the grand tradition of all such Conrad moves. Gale force winds and a rail strike combined to hamper the movement of goods, though the day was partially saved by Borys commandeering a lorry and some voluntary labour from a farmer friend.[9] Jessie as usual on these occasions was in command and Conrad decamped the first weekend to Pinker's stately home in Surrey where he was better out of the way. A week into the move they were still in Conradian chaos, though the master had comfortably secured his own pad on the ground floor: "We are camped in this new house with a few sticks of furniture – and not at home to anybody. But people understand the situation. There are no carpets, no curtains (as yet); the bare boards echo loudly our footsteps in the passages; the nakedness of the walls stares at us from all sides … Luckily my study is more or less completed and may serve for a drawing-room".[10] It was not until January that they had hired their full complement of servants and by the spring the newly designed decoration was all complete.[11]

This very slow proceeding for turning a house into a home was down to another domestic worry that took precedence over even the traumas of moving. It had been arranged for Jessie to go to Liverpool in December for a major operation on her knee by the orthopaedic surgeon Sir Robert Jones who in the course of three years treating her had become a close friend of the family. The worry of the prospective operation overshadowed the whole process of moving and settling in; as Conrad told a friend a week after their arrival "I haven't got the heart to do anything till this horrid suspense of the impending operation is over".[12] It was not an easy time to take in the full novelty of their surroundings and they spent the first two months there in a kind of limbo. In early December they travelled up to Liverpool expecting to stay at least six weeks, but the operation went well and much to their surprise they were home again by Christmas Eve.

The pleasure of homecoming was marred by Conrad's own physical condition. In Liverpool he had been stricken by gout in his wrist and developed a prostate complaint which caused him severe pain, both conditions plaguing him throughout the Christmas holiday. As always, illness led on to a depressive view of his past writing year: he had been taking the easy way out, tidying up existing work rather than embarking on new creation. He summed up the position to a friend: "I've not done a stroke of *profitable* work since last July… It's time to put my literary affairs in order. I confess

I am getting just a little weary of paper and ink and all this business of scribbling".[13]

The war of Jessie's knee trundled on through the first half of 1920. In March she suffered a relapse and was operated on again by Robert Jones in Canterbury, recuperating in a nursing home there for the next three weeks. There were further setbacks and minor operations to follow, but by August she was back on her feet and the prognosis was good, good enough for her to enjoy a holiday with her husband and Pinker on the coast at Deal. By the end of the year she was fit enough to spend a week in London celebrating her hard-won freedom. The relief for Conrad was immense, putting him in one of his (now rare) skittish moods of correspondence. He wrote to his publisher: "she is getting on and contemplates rushing to town (on the 21 of this month) in order to paint it red. I have nothing to do with this enterprise except that I've said I will pay for the paint".[14] He upbraided Pinker for conniving in the enterprise: "I have only heard lately that Mrs C is making use of you as a courier to retain rooms in hotels for her and so on. Infernal cheek – but understand I wash my hands of the Lady and her impudence".[15] On her return, he was equally buoyant in a letter to André Gide: "My wife thought we had fallen out of favour since you came to England without coming to see us. I did my best to reassure her, and she sends you her regards along with a plea not to do it again. That woman has been thoroughly spoiled for me. She spent the past week in London to celebrate her return to perpendicular life. Everybody pampered her so she now thinks of herself as a person of consequence and thus someone on familiar terms with André Gide".[16] For Conrad a major cloud had lifted and he amply deserved his high spirits.

There were other signs too that the family was settling in as formal relations were opened with the neighbouring gentry. The Tattersalls from Charlton Place on the other side of the village called occasionally, and Mrs Tattersall showed particular concern for Jessie's progress.[17] There were cordial relations with the Bells, his landlords, at Bourne Park and the prospect of closer contact over a special concern of Pinker's. His son, Ralph, had been studying agriculture at Wye College and Pinker asked Conrad to try and arrange a training placement for him with the Colonel who, taking over the estate, had now decided to farm it himself. Conrad treated the Colonel's rudimentary plans with a certain detachment: "Bell intends actually to farm the whole estate himself. All the small tenants have had notice apparently for next Michaelmas ... The Colonel being very full of his Great Adventure has been talking to me about it but purely in a conversational manner which struck me as rather grandiose. There apparently is going to be a cattle-farm, a chicken breeding establishment, and so on; and for each of them a specialist is going to be engaged... I have an idea that he may yet make a success of it. It has struck me that he is more able than people give him credit for".[18] The approach paid off and Ralph found his placement, proving a welcome lodger on the smaller Conrad estate on and off for the next two years, and a good companion to Borys too when he was at home.

But the relations with the Bells were not of close intimacy, as Conrad was keen to point out to Pinker that first summer. "The difficulty is that Jessie not being about and the establishment here working very casually it's difficult to ask people to lunch and dinner. But Mrs Bell drops in now and then for a few minutes to see Jessie and I on my side will try to get in touch with the Colonel and get some definite idea of his future arrangements. This, however, may take some little time ... . I must tell you also that, so far, though these people are very friendly and Mrs Bell is very nice to Borys and his young friends we are in no sense on a footing of intimacy with Bourne Park".[19]

Nor, so it seemed, with the rest of the village. Unlike Jocelyn Brooke, he was not to be seen of an evening down at the Lion's Head, the pub at the end of the main street. He got on well with individual villagers, like the local blacksmith for whom he had a high regard, but this more often in the course of some business to transact.[20] He gave donations to the local cricket club and to the flower show but then took no further interest in them; he would buy tickets for all the local entertainments, then invariably give them away.[21] He tended to keep to the confines of house and garden and not go walkabout in the village or its nearby woods and fields, and on the whole stayed aloof from village affairs. Though Richard Curle, his would-be Boswell, saw only a fraction of his daily life, the picture he paints, if over-dramatised, is broadly true.

> Although Conrad often had to go to London on business, he was very much a hermit as far as Bishopsbourne, his own village, was concerned. He entered into its life through contributing to its charities and entertainments, but he was scarcely known by sight to most of the villagers; and I suspect that they regarded him as some odd sort of writing foreigner who had fallen amongst them from the skies. I doubt whether any of them had ever even heard of any of his books, but they all knew he was famous for some reason or other, and they all had that kind of curiosity about him one might have for a man with two heads or no legs.[22]

This is hardly surprising. As a writer, he had always prized his peace and his privacy and a trail of casual visitors through his house on a weekday was the last thing he could have borne. In general, weekends were reserved for socialising with close family, literary and cultivated friends. By the summer of 1920 the new house was fully up and running and the stream of visitors was a certain sign that he had finally settled in. In addition to the regular visits of old friends from the world of letters – Pinker, Garnett, Galsworthy, Jean-Aubry, Curle – there were sudden appearances of even more prestigious visitors to add to the list of newcomers to the village. On 18 July T.E Lawrence (a strong admirer of Conrad's work) turned up with Cunninghame Graham; and Lord Northcliffe, who had himself sought out the visit, arrived the following day from his country retreat in Broadstairs. Some years later, Lawrence recalled the meeting and the demeanour of his host: "What I shall always remember is his lame walk, with the stick to help him, and that sudden upturning of the lined face, with its eager eyes under their membrane of eyelid. They drooped over the eye-socket and the sun shone red through them, as we walked up and down the garden." [23]

Conrad enjoyed the company of Lawrence but was wary of the press baron whom he had never met: "Col. Lawrence was delightful yesterday and I'm sure Northcliffe won't be today". [24] But the few hours with Northcliffe went off well, the start of a genuine family friendship cemented by a follow-up letter that reached the heights of Conradian courtesy: "Your visit has lightened the anxious murkiness of our life here. Never has time passed so quickly! Your passage amongst us seems now to have been like one of those delightful and evanescent dreams one remembers for a long time". [25] Conrad told Pinker with some surprise: "Northcliffe yesterday was geniality itself – a sort of 'dear fellow'. Wonders will never cease!". [26] From now on, when Conrad needed a home for some ephemeral article, the *Daily Mail* stood ready and waiting.

Conrad loved visitors, whether high or low, and all the niceties of the performance of host. The courtesy that might be overdone in formal letters came naturally to him in face to face encounters, particularly with close friends. Curle has itemised the great pains he took to produce the perfect welcome.

> He loved to entertain his friends in a style he thought worthy of them – and Conrad's friends were, in his eyes, worthy of everything. When some old friend would be coming down to lunch his eagerness that things should be just right was delicious. What was there for lunch, what wine would so-and-so prefer, had the car been ordered for the station, what suit should he himself wear, was everything in apple-pie order? And then, when he heard the car draw up outside, how he would hurry, or alas, often hobble, out into the hall to be the first to greet the arrival with out-stretched hands and words of welcome. [27]

Weekends of visits followed a predictable course. With a single guest he would sit up talking late into the night, captivating the listener as the fire burnt down. Next morning he would be prompt down to breakfast, full of boisterous energy and humour. Sunday lunches were his forte: "When, for instance, he presided at the head of his table, with his friends around him, he seemed to grow happier in their congenial company... Conrad was never finer than at such moments. His warmth embraced everyone in the room and radiated into its farthest corners. Those Sunday luncheons of his, when the guests were of his own choosing, saw him expand like some rich tropical flower".[28]

In these early years of the 1920s, Conrad liked his new house well enough but did not like its situation – he often complained it was down in a hole.[29] Strangely, what he disliked about its setting was just that aspect of the village that appeals to most people, its position nestling in the gentle folds of the North Downs. But Conrad enjoyed a good view like the one from The Pent, where he could see across the hills to three village churches. He would regularly ask to be driven out of the village up to Langham Park Farm (the venue for Jocelyn Brooke's childhood walks) or over to the top of the Downs near Lower Hardres, from both of which he could enjoy a panoramic view of Pegwell Bay and the North Foreland. He would not easily be deprived of the view of his sea.[30]

But he was not a countryman in the traditional sense and did not see the village with anything of a countryman's eye. Not for him the long daily walks of Jocelyn Brooke, quietly botanising while he sorted the ideas for the next chapter. Conrad had an extreme disinclination for exercise and was strongly opposed to the principle of walking for walking's sake. Any walking he did took place in the three pretty walled gardens to the rear of the house, which opened from one to the other and stretched right into Bourne Park – and then it was only a warm summer afternoon that would entice him out.[31] More regular contemplation of nature took place from the security of his study window.

Every morning, when he had finished breakfast, Conrad would go directly to his study. If the night had been a good one… then he was always in excellent spirits at that hour, and the first thing he would do would be to walk over to the window to watch the birds hopping about his lawn. He knew nothing whatever about ornithology – Conrad's interests revolved entirely around human beings and their lives – but he derived a sort of humorous pleasure both from birds and from dogs. He liked seeing the birds hunting for their morning meal…[32]

It probably had less to do with the particular attraction of the birds than with anything to postpone the fateful hour of putting pen to paper.

Conrad's study at Oswalds was a small unpretentious room, but with a homely lived-in feel. There were some family photographs on the mantelpiece, a few pictures of ships on the walls, but the main feature was the shelf upon shelf of books, the natural wallpaper of any writer's workplace.[33] By this time, the days had long gone for burning the midnight oil in extravagant three-day writing marathons, like those he had performed at The Pent. At Oswalds he seldom wrote or dictated other than in the morning, and 350 words a day he now considered a fair average output. He was never particularly anxious to begin, but once he had shut himself up with his secretary, Miss Hallowes, he became completely inaccessible. She lived with the family in the house and was an indispensable part of his working method, for the gout now seemed to be lodged almost permanently in his wrist, precluding long stints of manuscript writing, which he reserved for letters to close friends. He would sit in his big armchair facing the window in his study and, leaning over towards the table, would dictate slowly with long pauses.[34] Although he had become used to the art of dictating, the resultant first draft was inevitably looser in expression than the written drafts of the past, and so copious revision (as with the final part of *Nostromo*) was required, a technique in which he now excelled.

In the early days at Oswalds he was working in this way on the revision of *The Rescue*, the book he had contracted to write more than twenty years before. He completed it towards the end of February 1920 and it was published that June. This was a high point of the first year and the book received a good press, although the author had long given up any pretensions to its quality. As he told Hugh Walpole (on the day of the Lawrence visit) in response to a word of criticism: "Of course, mon cher, it is not very good. I did my best work long ago!" [35] Nevertheless, the publication of a new book by Conrad was a major media event now he had become an acclaimed writer, and it brought him flat up against the demands of the popular press, a world far removed from his own. The resultant confrontation could lead to frustration and humour, bordering on farce. He told his publisher, J.M.Dent, of a typical brush with the *Evening Standard* in which the author managed to maintain his public poise while surreptitiously twisting a few tails into the bargain.

> On returning home yesterday I found an absurd wire from the Evening Standard asking me to say whether that forthcoming book of mine had in it any "message for the young". Could anything be more silly than such an inquiry and, especially, to a man like me who had never flapped any "messages" in the face of the world? I was sorely tempted to answer that it all depended whether the "young" in question was an ass or not. But I controlled my feelings and wired a reply to the effect: that "in a work exclusively artistic in aim to appeal to emotions there should be something for everybody, young or old, who was at all susceptible to aesthetic impressions." I don't know what else I could have said and remained polite at the same time. [36]

The *Standard*, ever grateful for a quote, reproduced the reply almost *verbatim*.

But *The Rescue* was not a fresh work; it had been serialised the previous year. Though he toyed off and on with the early pages of his long Mediterranean novel, *Suspense*, the grind of original writing seemed now beyond him and the first two years at Oswalds were spent on the less demanding task of tidying up his earlier work – revising the texts of his planned Collected Edition, writing carefully thought-out prefaces to all his major novels, turning *The Secret Agent* into a play, gathering together with Curle his past miscellaneous essays into the volume that was to become *Notes on Life and Letters*, published in February 1921. This was mostly hack work, drawing on his past labours, but he was anxious to defend those pieces, like the prefaces, which had some claim to originality: the publishers "must not look on them as minor contributions. They have their importance – if any writings have any importance. They are short mainly because they are deeply meditated. It would have been no trouble to write a dozen pages of twaddle".[37]

Yet in spite of this defensive reflex, he recognised readily enough that he was growing old and tired, his creative powers on the wane. As he told John Quinn, the American collector of his manuscripts, he had now earned the right to something of a rest.

> There's nothing I dread more than an impotent old age, and I hope that experience will be spared to me. But if so, then my time cannot be very long now; and you with your knowledge of life know well that a man unsuccessful (in the market) for 20 years can not attain a brilliant position at the end of his time. All I can leave to my people will be my copyrights – which are worth something now. But this is a precarious provision at the best. Meantime I must keep in at work. But I've had two hard lives – each in its way – physically and mentally and I feel the need of easing down a bit. I assure you that through all my writing life I have never had the time to "look round" so to speak. When I went

away from the desk it was to be laid up. Such were my holidays.[38]

So part of his current ambition was to make as much money as he could out of his existing work with the minimum of exertion, recognising that the effort of much new work might be beyond him. And in that process his two main collectors of Conradiana, John Quinn and his recent usurper in England, Thomas Wise, played an important role. Conrad never himself understood the power that the collecting bug (particularly the principle of the "complete" collection) could exercise over people, but once he had become a celebrated author he quickly learned how it could be turned to his own advantage. As early as 1911, when his fame was beginning to accelerate in America, he had sold the manuscript of *Under Western Eyes* to Quinn, the wealthy New York lawyer, and entered into an informal arrangement that he should have first refusal of any more manuscripts that might turn up.[39] And with the Conrad finances still under serious strain, many more did turn up, as ancient boxes lying for years undisturbed in dusty attics became a source of sudden interest.

Wise came upon the scene in 1918 when Conrad, in desperate need of money for a pressing purpose, sold him the typed first draft of *The Arrow of Gold* and a partial manuscript of *The Rescue*.[40] Later Conrad rather speciously excused himself for breaking the old monopoly by claiming to have assumed that Quinn would not be interested in typed documents that had been dictated, and in any case he now had a complete set of both Conrad's written and pre-war manuscripts.[41] The friendship with Quinn duly cooled, but the sales to Wise continued unabated. Whenever a new work was being set for print Conrad kept a careful eye upon the whereabouts of the first typed draft with his manuscript amendments and the first clean copy, both of which he sold on, taking special care to reassure Wise that no further copies had been made. It was a most lucrative and dependable cottage industry; Wise bought everything he was offered without a quibble over price.

In fact, during the barren creative years at Oswalds, the creation of manuscripts for their own sakes seems to have become a special priority. In June 1921 Conrad received a copy of a play by the Polish writer Bruno Winawer, who asked if he could find a translator for it in London. Partly for amusement (he reassured Pinker he was still pounding out 600 words a day of proper work) Conrad took the job on himself and in less than two weeks had a completed text. Before even the final amendments had been made, however, he was offering the manuscript and clean copy to Wise ("work of for me unusual character") for the princely sum of a hundred pounds.[42] With Wise he was so confident of a sale that he could offer almost any crumbs that dropped from his writing table. In May 1920 he offered him a telegram in a typical po-faced letter that reads like a parody of bibliographical scholarship: "*Three MS pages* consisting of a message cabled to the Polish Government Committee of the State Loan to be raised in U.S. being an appeal for subscriptions to Poles and Americans. It is hardly literature but, at any rate, is a public act of mine and very likely to be the only specimen of Conrad's cable style".[43] Another specimen, in fact, of Conrad twisting tails.

Though the early years at Oswalds were taken up with these peripheral ventures that made money but were not new creation, guilt about the "proper" work he should have been doing lay close to the forefront of his mind. In recent times he had at last worked his way through the long-planned projects that had sat on the backburner for so many years, books like *The Rescue* and *The Arrow of Gold*. Now there was only one left – the great Mediterranean novel set in the period of Napoleon's downfall and answering to the working title of *Suspense*. Conrad had long been attracted to the Napoleonic era and the germ for *Suspense* seems to date from the reading he did about the fighting in 1808 around Capri when on holiday there in 1905, but it was not until 1912 that he planned the Elba novel with the aim of publication in 1914 to coincide with the centenary of Napoleon's exile.[44] But, as with other such projects, the years drifted by with nothing done.

The first month settling in at Oswalds "the Napoleonic novel" stood next in line but, as he told his publisher, a start could not be made with Jessie's operation pending: "I have not begun it yet for the state of suspense about the date and indeed the success of the operation hanging over our heads stands in the way of the intense concentration which I need for the beginning of a book. But I am thinking of it every day and the moments thus passed in self-communion cannot be called idle. Something of them will remain and will find its place when the actual work begins".[45] By March 1920, with the operation out of the way, he was still "rather busy contemplating and, as it were, walking round a rather big subject",[46] but in May a new impetus seemed to galvanise him. He told Pinker he was now tackling "the Elba novel" in earnest and meant to continue on a daily basis, but the process of starting a major work was no easier because it had been done before: "A desire of industry is growing on me. I may yet do credit to your bringing up. What I am asking myself is – : why I should suffer from such a state of funk before that book? I have tried my hand at a novel or two already, as you may remember. Then why..?"[47]

His resolve to start was strengthened by some formal work away from home and, just as important, shared with friends. On 7 June he went up to London in the company of Curle and Hugh Walpole (who had both stayed for the weekend) and had a jolly lunch with them at Frascatis. The afternoon was spent in research at the British Museum, working on some books that Jean-Aubry had suggested to him the previous year – a profitable afternoon in which he had picked up "a few hints and suggestions that were helpful". Such was his confidence he had even come up with his first working title for the book "The Isle of Rest". But still prospects did not look good. On arrival home he was immediately struck down with an attack of gout that lasted for a week.[48] The suddenness of the attack seemed to rob him of the confidence that was building up in the new book. Could it be made as good as *The Rescue*, about to be published? He told Pinker of his worries over the breadth of the subject: "The only matter of great concern left just now is to keep up to the standard with the next one, for that will have a tremendous advantage in its subject. That is from the public point of view. From my own private point of view I don't know that a great subject is an advantage. It increases one's sense of responsibility and awakens all that mistrust of oneself that has been my companion through all these literary years. Mine, my dear Pinker, is the only instance within my knowledge of practice not giving self-confidence".[49]

But this admission marked the end of hesitation. In the last week of June he got down to work for the first time and had a chapter in typescript by the end of July. By the middle of August, just before setting off on the holiday to Deal, he was already in the midst of the third.[50] But the three weeks relaxing by the sea seem to have killed off all prospect of work on the novel for the time being; by October he was messing around with the composition of a speculative film script based on one of his short stories.[51] By November he was actually noting the beauties of nature around him, a sure sign he wasn't working: "We have had a most glorious dry weather since 1st September. The last few days there was frost in the morning, all the slope of the Park being white till about 10 o'clock".[52] He was ill for the last two months of the year and fresh starts on the book proved false starts. The new impetus of June had now faded out altogether; his writing life had always been plagued by stop-starts of this kind, but never had his drive been so low. He offered his usual end year lament to Garnett: "I have done nothing – can do nothing – don't want to do anything. One lives too long".[53]

Yet 1921 began on a more hopeful note. He had decided to take Jessie, with her new mobility, away to Corsica – for the sake of both their healths, but also to soak up information and atmosphere for the Mediterranean novel. It promised another fresh start, but he was a little nervous of having to rub shoulders with the English sporting set on holiday: "Perhaps I will be able to do some work in Corsica. All the vendettas have been settled or have died out and it is very quiet there, I am told. On the other hand no golf courses have been laid out yet and no invasion from the dismal tribe with clubs is to be feared –

for this year at least".[54] He would have been less than amused by his literary successor at Oswalds, who so gloried in the links at Sandwich. But on arrival in Ajaccio the omens were less than auspicious: "The weather is bad – and no mistake. Cold. Wet. Horrors. A lot of rather smart people are staying in this beastly hotel … . An atmosphere of intense good form pervades the place. Low tones – polite smiles – kind inquiries – small groups. The only disreputable looking person is the unavoidable Clergyman of the C of E who looks as tho' he must have had a few adventures in his time…".[55] Matters picked up later with a few lively tourist drives about the island, and six weeks in he was starting work on the novel again. Though the holiday was cut short to sort out a financial mess at home, it had nevertheless proved its worth: "I have done a lot of reading and have picked up some good stuff for the novel. From that point of view the journey has not been all loss".[56]

It was a month after the arrival home that he started work on the novel again, proudly assuring Pinker he had accumulated 1500 words in the first four days. At the same time, he confided his deeper concerns to Galsworthy: "I can't get my teeth into the novel – I am altogether in the dark as to what it is about – I am depressed and exasperated at the same time…". Yet he continued nonetheless and by the end of May had picked up momentum: "The novel is moving on and I am now doing the last chapter of Part One, feeling an increased confidence that the thing will be pulled off with some success".[57] This was the first note of optimism since starting the book and it kept him working on through the spring and summer of 1921 and into the heat of July – "I am working all the morning and gasping most of the afternoon". By August he had almost enough corrected text to suggest serialisation as early as November, with the promise of immediate cash and the benefit of being tied in to someone else's strict timetable that might not be evaded.[58]

Summer, however, and the onset of the visitor season brought with it its own distractions. Bertrand Russell, a firm Conrad admirer, then on holiday in Kent, came over to pay his respects at Oswalds.

Conrad enjoyed teasing the great philosopher who had presented him with his latest work, *The Analysis of Mind*: "It is very possible that I havent understood your pages – but the good try I have had was a delightful experience. I suppose you are enough of a philosopher not to have expected more from a common mortal". And Conrad was deeply touched when in November Russell named his first child John Conrad after him. He sent him a letter of congratulation charged with the gentlest Conradian irony: "Jessie must have sent yesterday our congratulations and words of welcome to the 'comparative stranger' who has come to stay with you (and take charge of his household as you will soon discover) ... My affection goes out to you both, to him who is without speech and thought as yet and to you who have spoken to men profoundly with effect and authority about the nature of the mind".[59]

Now that Conrad was fully settled in at Oswalds, he had developed a routine of going into Canterbury once or twice a week, rather in the manner of the old shopping trips to Hythe but in these more affluent days proudly driven in a swish motor-car. When his younger son John was home from school, he would accompany him, and always on the same route: straight up the avenue of beech trees to the Dover Road, through the village of Bridge, left at the Gate Inn and down the Old Dover Road past the cricket ground. Arriving in town, the car would continue along Watling Street, then via Beer Cart Lane and Stour Street into Jewry Lane, and so to the back yard of the Fleur-de-Lis Inn, the poor relation of the County Hotel next door and the very same place that the minor members of the cast of *A Canterbury Tale* were to be housed in the autumn of 1943. This became the Conrad base – the car was parked, and he went off to the tobacconists for his supply of Caporal cigarettes, thence to the chemists and sometimes the wine merchants or ironmongers. At least once a week he would drop into Gouldens, the well-known stationery and book shop in the High Street, where Gontran Goulden, the proprietor, would lead him into his office to show him any books of interest or discuss a pamphlet he was printing for him there. About 12.30 he would return to the private bar at the Fleur-de-Lis for a whisky and soda before the trip home, laden with parcels. He would always give time to chat to the shopkeepers and in a sense knew his way around Canterbury rather better than around his own village.[60]

This came in handy in his preparations for the highlight of the social round that summer – the advent of the Pinker family for Canterbury Cricket Week at the beginning of August. The Pinker family was cricket mad; Conrad was not. In fact, his views on cricket were wholly in tune with those on golf. His son John tells the story of two retired colonels who over tea at Oswalds regaled Conrad with details of every cricket match they had ever attended until he, at the end of his tether, broke in: "I am totally unable to comprehend why a man hitting a ball with a piece of wood can produce a state of near lunacy in people who one would assume were otherwise apparently sane".[61] This was one major feature of the cultural life of his adopted country he was not prepared to embrace.

But for Pinker, his closest friend, exceptions had to be made. Cricket Week, started in 1842, had by Conrad's time become a major event to rival Ascot and Goodwood in the national sporting calendar, and the show of fashion on Ladies' Day, always the Thursday, was a sight to compete with the ladies' promenade at Lord's during the Eton and Harrow or Varsity matches. To mark properly the distinction of the occasion, Pinker decided to invoke another passion of his – four-in-hand driving – at which he was expert. The plan was for him to drive his coach and four up from Surrey and make a magisterial entry to the St Lawrence Ground on one or two of the days. Conrad with his usual courtesy took the greatest of care in the preparations, arranging for the Pinker servants to be put up at the pub in Bridge and fed and watered at Oswalds. He took the most scrupulous pains in arranging the picnic lunches on match days, providing also for a large party from Bourne Park. Jessie was not well enough to provide the food from home, so "I intend to make arrangements with either the County Hotel or the Fleur de Lys to get them ready during the week, for the number of people that are coming for each day's match. Or perhaps there may be a marquee on the spot where we might make arrangements." But he was nervous of local provision: "I am afraid that those lunches won't be tip-top, for Canterbury is not up to much... At any rate I intend to use all my powers of persuasion and fascination to get those Canterbury people to turn out decent things".[62]

Pinker was not to be put off. He took the long drive up from Surrey on the Thursday, rested the horses on the Friday in the newly cleansed stables at Oswalds, and with Conrad and the family made his grand entrance to the St Lawrence Ground on the Saturday morning before start of play. They parked on the bank at the Nackington Road end from where they could command a magnificent view of the pitch and the pavilion. Canterbury Cricket Week was a major tourist attraction and represented the quintessence of Englishness. *The Times* had made the point back in 1910.

> It has been said with some measure of truth that Kent cricket is different from other cricket, and Canterbury is different from other Kent cricket. Certainly there is nothing more delightful. If one wished to show an intelligent (*sic*) foreigner something essentially English and quite unlike anything he could see in his own country, one could not do better than take him to the St. Lawrence Ground.[63]

There was one intelligent foreigner on the ground that day who was distinctly under-whelmed. Conrad sat through the morning's play without a word, thoroughly bored. It was, in fact, a thrilling morning for Kent supporters as their team demolished Hampshire for 68 in an hour and a half, Frank Woolley taking 6 for 28 and Tich Freeman 4 for 18. No doubt the exuberance of the spectators around him confirmed Conrad's view of the perverse nature of their obsession. When, after lunch in the open air, the picnic basket had to be carried back to the car, he made good his escape and spent the afternoon in the more civilised atmosphere of home.[64]

All members of the party turned up for the remaining match days, leaving Conrad at home, though he was persuaded to attend on a cheerless Ladies' Day on the grounds it was a social occasion. He was fortunate in missing Pinker's horse-drawn arrival at the ground on the Tuesday which just happened to coincide with the completion of a half-century for Kent by Woolley, but Borys was present to record the event for posterity.

> Just as we turned into the entrance gates, Frank Woolley
> – a famous cricketer of that time – had just completed
> a century [*only 50, in fact*], and the resultant cheering
> and blowing of motor car horns in acknowledgement of
> this achievement frightened the horses, in consequence
> of which we made a rapid and spectacular circuit of the
> Cricket Ground before Pinker was able to get them
> under control. The spectators greatly appreciated the
> additional entertainment thus involuntarily provided.[65]

This was not the Polish writer's scene, but he put on a brave face. He wrote to Pinker a few days after with a somewhat reserved enthusiasm: "We are delighted to hear that from all your points of view the 'Journey to Kent' was a success. That being so there is nothing to spoil its charming memory for us".[66]

When peace descended on the household that September, he found it hard to get back to his writing. He told Richard Curle: "I am trying desperately to get on with the novel and feel rather worried about it".[67] Much of this was the pressure of facing a possible November deadline for the start of serialisation; he was aiming for 300 pages of typescript by the end of October, but the book was expanding all the time and he feared being left stranded in a timetable not of his making.[68] He felt unwell throughout the autumn and was distracted by everything around him: "I wish I could exclude all sounds and sights from my life and devote myself for the next 25 days to that novel which has not even a name. The sun, the wind, the little birds, the electric pump, everything seems to get in the way. It's like trying to fight off a cloud of gnats".[69] The "whole days with nothing done"[70] were the source of constant depression which in its turn made working impossible.

As in the past when stuck with a major project whose size was getting beyond him, he now took refuge in the idea for a short story to provide some distraction and light relief while still affording the opportunity for "proper" work. In October 1921 he started work on *The Rover*, an off-shoot of *Suspense* in that it was set in the Mediterranean, albeit some 15 years earlier at the beginning of the nineteenth century. The choice of setting shows just how much Conrad was now caught in his literary inspiration by the lure of the past, particularly those formative years in Marseille when his adult life was just beginning. The book followed a typically Conradian pattern, starting as a 30,000-word short story and ending nine months later as an 80,000-word novel. In December Conrad planned to finish it early in 1922, in time for Pinker to take with him on a business trip to the United States, but illness and delay intervened, so Pinker took with him instead the existing batch of *Suspense* in the hope of landing a serialisation contract.[71] Little came of the trip, however, for Pinker died suddenly and unexpectedly in New York at the beginning of February, a severe blow to Conrad who lost both a personal friend and the man who had organised his business and financial affairs for more than twenty years.

The gap was soon filled, however, by Pinker's son Eric who picked up with fitting competence all the strings of his father's office, foremost among which was the careful management of the temperamental convolutions of his leading client down in the wilds of Kent. For the writing of *The Rover* followed the usual cycle of ups and downs. Conrad spent the first three weeks of January 1922 in bed with influenza and gout, only to be followed by the deep shock of Pinker's death – "my affairs too are nearing their end – in a manner of speaking".[72] By March he had recovered from the immediate shock and was working hard, dictating all morning and correcting in the afternoon, and feeling all the better for it.[73] He was laid up again in early April but by the end of the month had a new batch of chapters ready for Eric Pinker: "Herewith Chaps. 4.5.6 of the Rover. I am going on with him and there will be no reason for either of us to be ashamed of the thing when it's done".[74] A few days later he was in bed again. Then more writing, and a further collapse before the end of May. Many of his previous books had followed this exhausting path, but now at the age of 64 he felt less able to cope with the pressure. He told Edward Garnett: "I will make you a signal about joining company for a few days directly The Rover has ceased to rove — and be damned to him. You have no idea how that fellow and a lot of other crazy creatures that got into my head have also got on my nerves. I have never known anything like this before. I have been infinitely depressed about a piece of work, but never so exasperated with anything I have had to do".[75]

These were the final stirrings before the storm in which he finished all his books — four weeks of intensive effort throughout June as all the threads came together and he raced for the finishing line. He told Eric Pinker at the beginning of June: "I am going on at my best gait. It isn't like greased lightning you know. But what a relief it is to feel the whole thing there in one's hand with only one or two more squeezes to get everything that there is in it".[76] He told Richard Curle at the end of June with the work completed: "You may imagine in what mental state I am. The whole thing came on me at the last as through a broken dam. A month of constant tension of thought".[77] Two weeks later as he gathered the revised pages together, he began to feel some optimism for the future of the book: "Now the thing is finished my misgivings have left me. The story will make a good volume. Perhaps a remarkable one." [78]

There was now a surprising delay of eighteen months before publication while lengthy negotiations for serialisation kept failing, perhaps through the loss of all the deft handling that Pinker senior had brought to Conrad's affairs. It came out eventually on 3 December 1923, the author's sixty-sixth birthday, the last novel he was to see published in his lifetime. The public response surpassed expectation: the first print-run of 40,000 sold out immediately and the book hit its third impression before the month and the year was out. The reception was a remarkable turn-round from that given to his earlier books. Now there was popular acclaim among the general readership while many of the serious reviews were critical and dismissive, calling it "downright bad", pale and lifeless.[79] There was a feeling that Conrad, in narrative and prose style, was just going through the old motions. As the critic Desmond MacCarthy wrote later: "*The Rover* was greatly enjoyed and not a little carped at – respectfully of course... I enjoyed it immensely myself; yet when a friend said to me casually, 'I have just finished listening to a performance on the Conrad', I saw what he meant".[80] The reversal of roles between public and critics must have been galling; it was not as though he had set out to write a popular novel. His once brilliant creative powers were coming to their rest.

With the completion of *The Rover* in June 1922 there was no longer excuse for evading work on *Suspense*, which he had not looked at since the previous December. He determined to start in again after a month's break, but by August he was still assuring friends he must get down to it soon.[81] October found him anxiously guilty over the little tinkering he had done: "I don't know what the matter is. Since I finished my novel *The Rover* in July I've not written one line that is worth anything. I am uncertain and directionless, like a ship whose crew has gone to land leaving all her sails in disarray".[82] He posited to Eric Pinker the excuse that would buy him more time: "it is a considerable piece of work which can not be hurried on recklessly; and I know you would not want me to do that".[83]

There was the usual run of major distractions to furnish a more substantial justification. First, there were the domestic worries, including the problem of his own declining powers. He told Galsworthy: "Ever since finishing the *Rescue* (2 years or more ago) I have had, in one way or another, a pretty bad time. The reaction from the war, anxiety about Jessie, the growing sense of my own deficiencies, and even, lately, a special sort of worry, of which I do not want to speak on paper, have combined to make anything but a bed of roses for my aching bones. My very soul is aching all over. My fault of course".[84] The special worry was Borys who had run up a string of debts which took a lot of time and money to disentangle and pay off. The blow to Conrad's finances was severe, but as nothing to the blow to confidence in his son, which worried him the more.[85] Harder to bear too because Borys' shortcomings were mirror images of his own extravagant misbehaviour as a youth, a tendency that had not been entirely eradicated in adult life.

A more pleasant surprise occurred that autumn when, after years of touting his adaptation of *The Secret Agent* around London's theatreland, a producer at last came forward with an offer to put the play on. Conrad attended rehearsals and gave his personal directions to the actors, in whom he reposed a less than perfect confidence. The excitement of this new species of creative venture and fears for the outcome took up all his nervous energy. By the week of the first night in November he had worked himself up into a froth of worry and low expectation: "I am deeply depressed. Those people will never be able to understand the play – or even learn it passably – before Thursday... I'm hardly in a fit state of mind (or body)... owing to the unusual mental irritability I'm suffering from because of that accursed play".[86] The first night at The Ambassadors in fact went off well, with Jessie in her box fêted by all and sundry while Conrad, who could not face the likely disaster, cowered nervously back at their suite in the Curzon Hotel.[87] The press was baffled by the play and most early notices were harsh; poor houses followed and it was taken off after little more than a week. After which, other press critics turned on their colleagues for damning the enterprise and a heated debate ensued on the quality of theatrical criticism in general. Superficially Conrad took it all with studied equanimity ("I was not cast down")[88] but privately resented the producer for taking it off so early – "I feel that all this affair is perfectly asinine".[89] He was not in the frame of mind to return promptly to serious writing.

To add to these distractions he was beginning to think of moving house once more. He had accepted Oswalds despite its setting down "in a hole" mainly for its size and elegance, but he had never been as enthusiastic over it as Jessie who found it much easier than Capel to get around in. It was never a homely house, and Conrad often used to refer to it in Corbusier parlance as a "machine à vivre".[90] It had been badly looked after by a succession of previous owners and its atmosphere of faded gentility hid a number of serious practical problems of which the Conrad family soon became aware. There was trouble with the water tank banging in the roof, and later with the electric plant that needed renewing – the latter repairs requiring the evacuation of the family in September 1920, which they turned into the successful holiday at Deal. Most dramatic of all was the occasion when Conrad one day stamped his foot in temper in the front hall and went straight through the rotting floorboards. Further investigation showed that the Nailbourne, which back in the eighteenth century had been diverted to a north-easterly path round the house, had still retained part of its original flow under Conrad's front door.[91] Thus was the famous author struck down by the power of Jocelyn Brooke's "woe-waters".

All these repairs, which Conrad insisted upon, led to a certain amount of friction with the owner, Colonel Bell. The house was in any case expensive to run, so it was little surprise that on the third anniversary of his arrival there he took advantage of the break in the tenancy agreement to consider giving notice to the owner. At his age and in his state of health, it seemed a big step even for a perennial wanderer: "I am half-unwilling to leave this house, but this is mostly the dread of the move, I think".[92] At the end of September he took the plunge, and told Richard Curle – "I've given a year's notice to Bell!! Am scared now".[93] But by Christmas it had become a *fait accompli*, and he seemed almost to be looking forward to it. He told an American friend coming over on a visit: "You will not find us in this house as I have given notice which expires next September, only, it is true; but if no tenant turns up before that date we shall shut up the establishment about May and lead for a time a rather homeless life".[94]

Towards the end of 1922 there came from his American publisher, F.N.Doubleday, an invitation to visit the United States where his career in recent years had taken off abruptly, just as it had earlier in England. He was reluctant at first, but when it emerged that this was not to be the traditional whistlestop lecture tour but a more gentle encounter with his American readers he began to warm to the idea. Plans were soon fixed for a stay of three weeks the following May at Doubleday's apartment on West 58th Street and his palatial house at Oyster Bay, Long Island, all under his publisher's personal protection.[95]

This could have been seen as yet another distraction from his main task in life, work on the long Napoleonic novel that had again hung fire through most of 1922. But this time the psychology operated in the reverse direction. With a large slice of the novel complete, he now saw the opportunity to polish it all off before setting sail for the New World. Shrugging off his usual Christmas debilities, he started work with a will on the first day of the new year and managed to keep at it solidly for the next three months.[96] But the process of writing was slower and more like hard work than even his worst moments in the past; at the beginning of February he told Curle: "I am working – but nothing like the rate I ought to keep up to make things look better. And yet I am hard at it all the time... I find life rather a trial just now". He was more explicit with his cousin in Poland: "My work progresses very slowly. I spend entire days sitting at my desk and by evening I feel so tired that I no longer understand what I am reading".[97]

By early March he had finished the then Part III of *Suspense* when he heard that Doubleday had arranged the publication of *The Rover* for the end of the year. Since the two books could not be published simultaneously, this news now relieved him from the pressure of working against the clock, and he looked forward to completing the novel that October and publishing in the autumn of 1924. He put the book aside to write the introduction to a biography of Stephen Crane, hoping to take it up again in two months on his return from the States.[98] But he never really picked it up again; these first three months of 1923 represent his last concerted effort of work upon the novel. Even at this late date, however, he saw it as a crucial part of his *oeuvre*. He described this latest push towards completion in bullish terms to Eric Pinker: "I have worked under a certain stress. I did not want to get out of touch with the novel. I was and am anxious about it. My reputation hangs on its quality. It is a big piece of work – the biggest since "Western Eyes" ".[99]

This was undoubtedly true. If *The Rover* were the only novel completed at Oswalds, it was what it had started out being, a work as slight as a short story. By contrast, *Suspense* was a novel more on the lines of *Nostromo* – a tense narrative of action acting as the vehicle for vast movements, in politics, in society, in culture. It concerns the arrival in Genoa of a young Englishman, Cosmo Latham, who comes from a landed family in Yorkshire which after the revolution gave shelter to the family of a marquis, an émigré diplomat later repatriated in France. Once in Genoa Cosmo meets and falls in love with the marquis' daughter who (in a surreptitious twist of the plot) happens to be his half-sister and is now unhappily married to a rich self-made man. Genoa itself is on a state of alert with rumours of movement by Napoleon on Elba, and swarms with spies acting on both sides, the revolutionaries and the restored monarchies. The book ends *in medias res* with Cosmo, captured by the revolutionaries whom he partly supports, drifting out to sea to confront God knows what further adventure and fate.

The "suspense" in question is that of the whole of Europe waiting to see what move Napoleon might make – the restored monarchies fearful of losing their power once more, the revolutionaries praying for restoration of republicanism and freedom. The marquis makes the point early on: "uneasy suspense is the prevailing sentiment all round the basin of the Mediterranean. The fate of nations still hangs in the balance".[100] In a letter home, Cosmo writes: "you can form no idea of the state of suspense in which all classes live here, from the highest to the lowest, as to what may happen next".[101] This is the same problem confronting the reader of this work that hangs suspended in mid air – impossible to tell whether the 300 pages of relatively slow development is just the initial fragment of a very long novel, or whether they represent perhaps three-quarters of a text awaiting a sudden climactic dénouement.

The themes that emerge from the narrative, still waiting further development, are in every way as vast as those of *Nostromo* – the legacy of Napoleon in political and social movements throughout Europe, in particular the Italian movement for independence; the socio-cultural changes inspired by the French Revolution; the contrast between the societies of England, France and Italy; and in personal psychological terms, the love between the half-siblings, Cosmo and Adèle. The prose is clear and simple, abandoning the rich tapestries of Conrad's stylistic past, and the narrative builds slowly, yet still holding the reader in its grip. But overall the book lacks the bite of his old masterpieces, the scepticism and the all-pervading irony: the major themes are slow-moving and self-consciously introduced where in *Nostromo* they would emerge naturally from a single scene or punchy piece of dialogue. Set-piece descriptive scenes scarcely reach below the surface of things: the evening reception given by Adèle cannot approach the power and symbolism of *Nostromo* with the meetings in the Casa Gould.

Conrad himself knew only too well that the vast scope of the book was beyond his steadily waning powers: "It's like a chase in a nightmare, weird and exhausting." [102] Thus effectively he gave up that chase in the spring of 1923, though he continued to worry guiltily about it until his very last days. The unfinished work was published in 1925 and received as something of a curiosity; and it supplied a text for the Conrad memorial in the parish hall of the village in which it was written.

Just before the trip to America he felt reluctant to go ("the journey does not appeal to me")[103] but it turned out a triumph. He had hoped to keep his arrival low key, but when he reached New York on 1 May was inevitably swamped by an eagerly welcoming press – "To be aimed at by forty cameras held by forty men that look as if they came

174

out of the slums is a nerve-shattering experience".[104] But the press reception was of the most genial kind. A great deal was made of the fact that Conrad had eschewed the lecture circuit, in which literary visitors had traditionally grubbed for every dollar they could lay hands on, and was making no money from a tour designed purely to meet and talk one-to-one with individual Americans. This was part of the Doubleday strategy – to turn Conrad's age and relative frailness (he could never have coped with a lecture tour even had he been adept at public speaking) to advantage in the hope that this generous public image would bear fruit in sales and money later on. It was a strategy well-judged. Towards the end of his stay, Doubleday offered him a guarantee of £4,000 a year (perhaps almost two million in today's money) for the next three years, and as much more as possible on top.[105]

He was nervous of public speaking, particularly of the impression given by his still-Polish accent, so only one set-piece engagement was laid on. It was at the New York mansion of Mrs Curtiss James, one of the leading, and richest, lights of American society, and he was to talk and give readings from *Victory*. It turned out a brilliant success as he told his French friend, Jean-Aubry: "Thursday evening at 9.30 I spoke, and read a few extracts from Victory before a very brilliant audience in the grand hall of the house of Mrs Curtiss James. About two hundred people – the top of the basket of the literary and fashionable circles. They were fighting for invitations – so I'm told. Ah well, my dear fellow, I've been a success almost without any preparation. They laughed, they snuffled into their handkerchiefs (Lena's death), there was much applause. I closed the book at a quarter to eleven and there was a moment of silence before the tempest, which I also found quite moving".[106] He capped the evening by declining any payment, which was "greatly appreciated".[107]

Apart from a visit to Boston and a tour by car, he spent much of his stay at the Doubledays, receiving journalists and literary figures. He was overwhelmed by the typical American enthusiasm and hospitality, and made many new acquaintances who would fill his subsequent correspondence. But just a fortnight in he was beginning to feel anxious to get home and, even more surprising, get back to work which was, he told Pinker, "the only thing that matters really". He was missing Jessie, as he told her too: "My thoughts are constantly with you all. In the midst of new scenes my mind remains fixed on your dear person at Oswalds".[108]

He arrived home in mid-June only to go down immediately with an attack of gout (probably the reaction to the exertions of his trip) which again invaded his wrists and prevented him holding a pen. Despite his best intentions, therefore, it was a summer of occasional work, checking the proofs of *The Rover*, for example, while all the time worrying with guilt over *Suspense*.[109] On 9 July he announced "I have plunged into Suspense", but the enthusiasm was short-lived. A month later he told Jean-Aubry: "I am sorry to tell you that *The Suspense* is not going well. That book has given me some bad moments".[110]

July was hot – a time for sitting in the garden and forgetting work. He invited a friend for a day visit: "All we can offer is a sort of sit-in-the-garden and dream (if not exactly doze) day".[111] He painted a picture of that garden life for the eleven year old daughter of a friend laid up after an accident: "Did the heat worry you much? Perhaps you have a nice airy room? I have to tell you that here the very gardens (we have three) felt hot and stuffy. My chauffeur's puppy would not play: Mrs. Conrad's chickens did nothing but stand in the shade and yawn: the flowers drooped their heads and no bird would touch a crumb on the lawn. And some of them were very good crumbs too. At 2 P.M. on Thursday last I watched from my chair a wagtail crossing our so-called tennis-court. He could hardly put one foot before the other; he was positively dragging his tail after him. I suppose no such sight was ever seen since the creation of wagtails".[112]

American visitors picked up on his recent trip had to follow the more exacting itinerary of the tourist. He reported back on them to Doubleday's wife, Florence, in a short-lived soap-opera entitled "The Oswaldians". While Conrad dozed in the garden, his secretary was told off to take them round the sights. "In the afternoon Miss

Hallowes took them over to Canterbury for a visit to the Cathedral. I don't know what their appreciation of Gothic architecture may be but I know that they were very much amused by the verger who took them round. He, I believe, was Gothic too." [113]

The autumn brought less happy times. They had planned to leave the house that October, but no new tenant turned up and they themselves had found nowhere to go, so they decided to stay on for one more year. Jessie's knee flared up once more and a further operation was predicted. Conrad himself was laid up with a new attack of gout from which he took longer than normal to recover. [114] Ominously, there were problems with his heart, he told Curle: "I had Fox to come and see me, and the fact of the matter is that the action of the heart is not satisfactory. 'Flabby heart,' he calls it in his horrid way. As a matter of fact the organ is tired... and now it betrays its condition by fluttering and missing about every fourth beat." [115]

Little wonder then that he could not get down to the novel, which grew more intimidating the longer he kept away from it. He embraced every chance to postpone the evil day by writing something less taxing, like the article on geography and exploration that Curle had found for him in late October. [116] His gratitude to Curle when the article was written showed just how poor were the prospects for the great novel that still lay on his desk: "And now it's done let me thank you, my dear fellow, for shoving the thing in my way. It's obvious that for some time I have not been fit to grapple with the novel, and it was a great moral comfort to have some work to do which I was capable of doing". [117]

Now even a minor article proved worthy of the valedictory description of its last moments of composition, like the rumbustious accounts he had given of *Lord Jim* and *Nostromo* as the sun came up to greet the final pages. He sent the good news to Curle, from his desk looking out on the end of a winter's afternoon, but now the words were pale and tinged with shadows. "I am sure you will be fraternally pleased to hear that I have this moment – 4.20 p.m. – finished my 'Geographical' introduction, the light of day dying out of the window as line succeeded line on the last page".[118] And a few weeks later, passing on a copy of the newly minted *Rover* to Arnold Bennett, he used the same metaphor to explain the reason for the gift: "It is because I feel (why conceal it?) that twilight lies already on these pages".[119]

CHAPTER 7

A Photographical Microscopist and a Political Cricketer

From Marsh and Weald their hay forks left,
To Bourne the rustics hied,
From Romney, Cranbrook, Tenterden,
And Durent's verdant side.

Surry Triumphant:
Or the Kentish-Men's Defeat (1773)[1]

Joseph Conrad had been brought up in Poland as a Roman Catholic but in maturity never actively practised his religion. He never went to church and upbraided any relative who tried to persuade his children to go: it would only drive them in the opposite direction.[2] On the other hand, he never renounced the faith. At Bishopsbourne, he was on nodding terms with the Rector, the Reverend Walter Ashton-Gwatkin and his wife, Frances – "the Old Birds" as he called them[3] – but rather closer to their son Frank, not because he was a vicar's son but because he wrote successful novels while doubling as a Japanese expert in the Far Eastern Department of the Foreign Office.[4]

The Church of St Mary stood right next door to Oswalds but as far as we know Conrad never entered it – except on one well-documented occasion. After tea one afternoon he called his son John to accompany him on a mystery walk.

'Come. It is not far.' We walked to the drive gate and turned right! I had expected that we'd go straight on to the forge but no, my father went through the churchyard gate and stopped to wait for me by the church door. I opened it and stood aside to let him pass in but he took my arm saying 'No. We go in together', then laid his hat and stick on the bench and entered and turned towards the altar. He stopped me with a slight pressure on my arm, bowed respectfully but did not make the Sign of the Cross. After a few moments we moved on, stopping to look at the memorials and stained glass, entered the sanctuary and went up to the altar, paused for a minute or so, bowed and took two paces backward before turning to retrace our steps to the door which we closed, quietly, behind us. Not a word was spoken while we were in the church. I was curious to know why he had not crossed himself, because my aunt, also a Roman Catholic, always did and I expected JC to do the same. As we continued our walk round the church I asked him why he had not done so. 'My boy, when you are aloft taking in canvas in a gale there is no one between you and death but the Good Lord, and you cross yourself many times in the course of a voyage – I think He will pardon me – to make the sign now would be pointless – there is no need.'
We carried on, pausing now and then to look at some tombstone and then, as though thinking aloud he said, 'Profanity is the preserve of the devil'. Then as we passed through the lychgate he said 'Don't assume that

because I do not go to church that I do not believe, I do;
all true seamen do in their hearts.' [5]

This surprise visit to the church by the pair of them may have signalled
a slight change at that time in Conrad's attitude to religion – his sense,
perhaps, that the sands were running out. On that day, they did not
see the little statue of the mysterious preacher that my father and I
were to puzzle over thirty years later, for that still stood in a niche at
the entrance to the rectory until the latter was demolished.[6] But they
could not have missed the flat tombstone in the shade of the north
wall, just inches from the path; it belonged to a rector some half a
century before the Reverend Gwatkin came on the scene, and he had
a story, and a fame, all his own.

The vicar who came to take charge of the parish in 1863, and settle
with his wife in the rectory made famous over two hundred years
before, was a lively sixty year old with long white hair, slightly
balding on top, a round handsome face and sharp alert eyes which
spoke of someone with an active mind and an imaginative curiosity.
These latter attributes he held in abundance: for he was a scientist
with a nose in a wide range of disciplines, always experimenting,
always inventing. He saw no conflict between the two callings –
clergyman and scientist – even though he arrived at Bishopsbourne
in the post-Darwinian world when the Church had already begun the
battle against the new and threatening scientific orthodoxy. For him,
the world of nature, both high and low, which he scrutinised with
devotion through his microscopes and telescopes, was God's world
too, and he wondered what all the fuss was about.

Like most of the others, he had done his life's work and made
his reputation before coming to the village but, also like them, had
no intention of treating it as a retirement home: there was further
work to do. He had been born Joseph Bancroft Reade[7] in Leeds in
the spring of 1801 to a father who was a Christian activist as well as
a merchant, the author of several religious pamphlets, and a mother

related to the natural theologian, William Paley, whose work had had such an influence on Darwin. The scientist and the theologian were already in his genes. A bright boy at Leeds grammar school, he made his way to Cambridge according to expectation and graduated from there in 1825, taking holy orders the following year. In the year of his graduation, he married his wife Charlotte, the daughter of a Cambridge professor, and the basis for a settled, happy life – job, wife, intellectual pursuits – was already set. But nothing so carefully prepared ever works out smoothly. Their marriage had more than its share of sorrow: their only son died at 14 months, their first daughter twelve years later aged 14, and their last child, another girl, just after reaching 21. They arrived in the village seven years later an ageing and childless couple.

Following his first curacies in Leicestershire and Halifax, he took the bold step of moving down south, finally ending up as proprietor in 1834 of a preparatory school in Peckham where his scientific work began in earnest. London gave him access to the learned societies and the company of like minds, and began to build him a reputation in the fields of microscopy and astronomy. In 1839 he was invited by Dr John Lee of Hartwell and the Royal Astronomical Society to become vicar of the nearby parish of Stone in Buckinghamshire. At the vicarage a small school for about twenty pupils was established and an observatory built in the garden. It was the perfect set-up for a clergyman of scientific disposition and here he spent a fruitful twenty years, taking the services, teaching the students, and pursuing his experiments in numerous fields.

His burning interest at this time was still microscopy, studying the anatomy of plants, minute creatures and the microscopic structure of chalk and flint. His first scientific paper "Observations and experiments on the solar rays that occasion heat", written at Peckham, had been read to the Royal Society in December 1836. In it he proposed the use of two convex lenses adjusted to condense sunlight onto a microscope specimen while defocusing the harmful rays of heat. He was greatly interested in the design of optical devices

182

for the microscope, particularly for illuminating specimens on slides during microscopic examination. In several of his earliest papers he combined his optical interests with his love of chemistry by carrying out micro-incineration experiments on botanised specimens. His paper "Observations of some new organic remains in the flint of chalk", published in 1838, contains the first microscopic illustrations (from drawings) of microfossils, prehistoric marine organisms, then called "Xanthidia", that more than a century later were identified as organisms crucial to the identification of geological strata relating to petroleum. His wide-ranging interest in the chemistry of metal salts led him in 1846 to obtain a patent for inks.

The provision of the small observatory and telescope at Stone enabled him to keep up his interests in astronomy, though his publications in this field were not extensive. Between 1844 and 1850 he contributed a series of observations on comets (a continuing love) to the Royal Astronomical Society, and his enthusiasm for the optical perfection of the microscope was turned also on to the telescope. He designed a "solid eyepiece" for the telescope which was displayed at the Great Exhibition of 1851 and received a medal. Intertwining as ever his multiple areas of expertise, he combined his photographical interests with astronomy to become the first Englishman to take photographs of the moon, presenting them at the Paris Exhibition of 1856.

Reade did not just *take* photographs; he played a part, if only a small one, in the invention of the early photographic process itself. In March 1839, he used an infusion of nut galls to make photographic paper more sensitive, an event in the evolution of photography which, together with the influence of Herschel, led to Fox Talbot's discovery that gallic acid developed the latent image. His early use of gallic acid led to the appearance of Reade (but not of Herschel) in 1854 as a defence witness in a lawsuit *(Talbot v Laroche)* relating to Talbot's calotype patent, and his part in this case brought him attention in the photographic world through the rest of his life.[8] He joined the Photographic Society in 1855 and as vice-president in the late 1860s he often went up to London from Bishopsbourne to chair their meetings.

From the breadth of his scientific interests and the range of his inventions, it is plain that he was not a professional scientist with a single-track purpose, but more of the typical English amateur. While his place in the history of photography, astronomy and microscopy is assured, to modern eyes some of his work in these fields can be faulted for lack of accuracy and thoroughness and his papers and contributions to Society meetings were at times discursive and unclear. It has to be remembered that for all his adult life he was a vicar with a parish to run, and for some of the time a schoolmaster to boot.

He was a relatively old man when he arrived at the old rectory in the late autumn of 1863. Like his most famous predecessor there, he made a gentle impact upon village life, always kind and genial, honest, modest, affable and unassuming. This character comes clearly across in his evidence in the case of *Talbot v Laroche* where at one point he interjected "I hope I shall not be accused of pushing myself unduly forward when I merely answer the questions of friends".[9] With his long white hair, he had a venerable appearance which befitted his years and his gentle manner.

But age did not affect his vitality. Together with his pastoral work, his energetic involvement in scientific matters continued unabated. In particular, at Bishopsbourne he went on working to improve the design of the microscope and there in 1869, just a year before his death, he invented an equilateral prism for microscopic illumination. In 1839 he had been a founding member of the Microscopical Society, in which he became especially active in his final years, being elected president in 1868 and regularly travelling up to London to chair their meetings, in addition to those of the Photographic Society.[10]

While at Bishopsbourne he took a public stand in the political battle between evolution and religion that had been raging ever since Darwin's publication of *The Origin of Species* in 1859 had thrown the Victorian conscience into turmoil. He was one of the signatories to "The Scientists' Declaration" of 1864-5 in which scientists and men learned in other fields declared their belief that the discoveries of science and the teaching of the Bible were wholly reconcilable. For a clergyman who spent his days exploring the wonders of God through microscope and telescope he had perhaps less difficulty than others in squaring the circle.

In the seven years he spent in the village he kept up his astronomy too. While fifty years later, Jocelyn Brooke on special firework nights would be watching from the garden of Forge Cottage his beloved rockets bursting over the Barham Downs, Reade in the 1860s was panning the same horizon from the rectory garden, watching for meteors. In October 1869 two meteors crossed the village in the space of ten days and he wrote of this good fortune in a letter to a friend and fellow member of the Royal Society, working at the Greenwich Observatory, with a quasi-scientific account of the sightings, not scientific enough, however, to obscure the observer's patent excitement. The second one, on 11 October, was rather disappointing. "It was seen here, at Bishopsbourne, from the rectory garden by my niece, Miss Reade, and I find that the point of its observed disappearance behind a large tree on the horizon is about 40 degrees west of north, having 6 degrees of altitude. It had no illuminating power, though the colour was bright yellow, and the magnitude something less than the apparent size of Jupiter."

By contrast, the meteor of 1 October 1869 was spectacular and led its observer on to lyrical heights, for he had actually seen it himself.

> On the evening of the 1st of this month, at about 8h 12m 30s Greenwich meantime, I was the fortunate observer of another meteor of surpassing splendour. Its path was nearly vertical, with a slight easterly deviation, from Algenib to a point about 5 degrees above the horizon and about 60 degrees east of south. It did not bound and rush into extinction like an echo to the grand old Poet's words: 'Thunders impetuous down and smokes along the ground', but slowly and majestically descended, not fell, from its celestial throne 'till it vanished suddenly and noiselessly within mortal ken. The body of the meteor

seemed to increase in size as it approached the earth and gave the observers (myself and the two gardeners) the impression that it was between us and the horizon. It illuminated the whole of the Barham Downs and valley with its bright magnesium light, and for the last three seconds it left a train of intense brilliancy, about four times the length of its major axis, a dazzling blue and red dividing the train in about equal portions. The light of the body, which was egg-shaped and about half the size of a gibbous moon, was extinguished in a moment and the effect was startling. It was slightly in advance of its train before it vanished and the red end of the train was the last to disappear. I was preparing to observe Jupiter with my fine old Tully Newtonian … and our attention was suddenly arrested by this remarkable meteor, which seemed in a moment to convert night into day. Of the many meteors I have observed, this is emphatically the one to be remembered. The time of visibility was about 7 seconds.[11]

Some observing for a 68-year-old-man with just a few seconds to capture the detail; and some firework display, of a brilliancy to which even the youthful Brooke could never have aspired.

The next year, 1870, Reade developed cancer and suffered for a long time in pain at home. He still struggled, however, to perform his duties as President of the Microscopical Society and kept up a regular correspondence with the Secretary – his final and moving letters from Bishopsbourne. He had to pass on the letters he received from other colleagues: "I have hoped to find a day on which I could feel equal to sending a reply, but my weakness and pain do not allow the exertion... my state is the same as it was three or four months ago – only I am weaker and very very thin". As a keen experimental scientist he could keep track of his symptoms and, at the same time, look out for the development of new palliatives. "I am reclining on the sofa as my easiest position. I have a few good points in pulse, appetite and sleep – this latter, however, due partly to opiates which ease the pain". "Have you heard of the Red Gum as a new and good astringent in such a case? Dr. Picard, my friend at Bridge, told me of it".

But he was also a practising clergyman who took succour from friends and family and put his ultimate trust in God. "I still think I had a gracious Providence to be restored again to my family and friends... I do indeed value your prayers and those of many dear friends and I trust it may please the Heavenly Father to send an answer of peace. But peace will be the result in any event". By November that peace could not come fast enough: "the fearful pain of the sciatic nerve and the old pain in the back make me weak indeed and longing for rest. When will that happy day arrive?" The answer was not long in coming as towards the end of the month he developed the jaundice that was to kill him: "I have now the comfort of a water bed but I still suffer severe pain and the hardening of the liver is now followed by yellowness of the skin".[12]

He died at home in the rectory on 12 December. Tributes were paid to his scientific work, but many more to his kindness and modesty. His friends in the Photographic Society recorded: "In the great world of science he has not left a single enemy". One friend of these later years also commented: "He was a dear old man and there must have been few who knew him who did not also love him." An elderly parishioner from a former parish, when told of his death, said merely "Ah! sir, he was a homely man".[13] He was buried four days later close by the north wall of the church at a funeral attended by many scientific dignitaries and members of his family. Matthew Bell was there, of course, as owner and representative of Bourne Park. Charlotte, Reade's widow, moved out of the village and survived him a further twelve years, choosing herself to be buried in the churchyard at Stone together with their two young daughters, the source of such joy and such sorrow. So he lies alone today under an almost illegible stone slab, passed by without recognition by Joseph Conrad and countless others since.

The *Kentish Gazette* summed up his relationship with the village and its rustic inhabitants – he "lived so quietly and unobtrusively that many may have been constantly near him without knowing how great a man he was … A man who, versed in the deepest mysteries of science, could adapt himself to the capacities and requirements of the simple people of a country village".[14] Much the same could be said of his illustrious predecessor at the old rectory to whom we must shortly turn.

The Matthew Bell who attended Reade's funeral was, as we have seen, the first of the new generation of Victorian owners of Bourne. The family he had supplanted were the Auchers (later down the female line the Beckinghams) who had lived in the place for three hundred years. They were descended from the courtier, Sir Anthony Aucher, notorious for his ruthless and corrupt exploitation of Crown offices for his personal aggrandisement. It was out of his ill-gotten gains that he purchased the manor from the see of Canterbury in 1557. He was a significant man in his day – protégé of Thomas Cromwell, Master of Jewels to Henry VIII and Surveyor of Victuals at Boulogne. He was killed in heroic fashion at the siege of Calais in 1558 before the Crown could get all its money back. It was the widow of his descendant, Dame Elizabeth Aucher, who from 1704 to 1707, during the minority of her son, Sir Hewitt, rebuilt the ageing Elizabethan manor house in the new and imposing Queen Anne style with stonework from the ruins of Westenhanger Castle that had been put on general sale in 1701. Sir Hewitt died a bachelor at the age of 40 in 1726 (after first turning on his mother and robbing her of her inheritance – a Chancery case that reached the House of Lords), the estate passing through his sister to her eldest daughter Catherine who was married to Stephen Beckingham of Grays Inn. The first of the Beckingham squires, he died in 1756 when the estate passed to his son, another Stephen.[15] The new owner preferred to live elsewhere and so let the estate to Sir Horatio Mann, a chance transaction that was to bring the estate and the village to the centre of Kent, and indeed English, cricket.

Horatio Mann was a diplomat who spent much of his life in Florence where for some years he was British envoy to Tuscany. Well-known in Italy, especially for his sociability and grand entertaining, his reputation in England stems principally from his close friendship to Horace Walpole and his contribution to the voluminous and classic Walpole correspondence. Since Mann was regularly out of the country, in 1765 he invited his nephew, another Horatio, on reaching his majority to live at Bourne Park, an arrangement which proved so successful that in 1775 the nephew formally took over the tenancy.

The younger Horatio Mann (known as Horace, and later Sir Horace following his knighthood in 1772) was an ebullient figure in eighteenth century society, eccentric, pleasure-loving and, like his uncle, extravagant in entertaining. He always chose the most distinguished guests. At the end of July 1765, soon after he and his newly wed wife, Lucy, had taken charge of Bourne House, he invited the Mozart family, whom he had met in London, to stop off there on the way back to Dover after their year long English sojourn parading the precocious talent of the nine year old Wolfgang. The ostensible reason for their week long stay at Bourne Park was to attend the Canterbury races and assuage Leopold Mozart's passion for the quality of English-bred horses, but there had also been plans for a concert by the two Mozart children in Canterbury. Whether that concert came off or not we have no record, but there is no doubt that at some time during that week (perhaps every night) the grand rooms of the newly built house would echo to the sound of the entrancing impromptu music-making of Wolfgang Amadeus himself.[16]

Horace Mann had been born at Boughton Malherbe in 1744 and was educated at Charterhouse and Peterhouse, Cambridge. His father, a clothier by trade, had landed a most lucrative contract supplying uniforms to the British Army and was able on his death in 1756 to bequeath to his son £100,000 (about ten million today) and the family estate at Linton Park, near Maidstone with its fine house that Horace Walpole thought "stands like the citadel of Kent; the whole county is its garden".[17] Like his uncle, he was involved in political life, becoming MP for Maidstone 1774-84 and for Sandwich 1790-1807. He spoke ably in the House of Commons and was highly critical of Lord North's handling of the American War. On the fall of North in 1782, he was one of those country members who met in the St Alban's tavern in London in the failed attempt to bring about a Fox-Pitt coalition. But politics was not the centre of his life, for he was a man "dedicated to pleasure rather than to business".[18] His life was dominated by something a little more enticing than the counting of Commons votes – the patronage of cricket.

There had been cricket in southern England since at least the beginning of the seventeenth century, a village game played to no standard set of rules and in some places difficult to recognise for the game of today. One of the earliest records of its play in Kent comes from Harbledown near Canterbury in the 1630s where a Puritan minister castigated the act of "profaning the Sabbath by cricket-playing".[19] It took a strong hold in the Canterbury area where bat and trap (a primitive form) was also played, and by the middle of the eighteenth century there was much activity in the neighbourhood of Bishopsbourne. There is an elegant and well-known picture of a match played in 1760 in front of the great house at Kenfield Hall just three miles to the west of the village, and one of the earliest clubs in the county was that of Bridge Hill, under the aegis of Bridgehill House, just the other side of the park at Bourne, a club that in 1751 was meeting for practice every Wednesday afternoon.[20]

As these examples indicate, this was the period in mid-century when the landed gentry and aristocracy began to take up the heretofore village game for rustics, whether to play themselves, to organise and support financially as part of their duty of social patronage, or just to develop as one of the more exciting forms of gambling, a failing to which that social class in those days was particularly prone. None more so than the 21 year old Horace Mann arriving at Bourne Park in 1765, now of an age when he could at last begin to spend his inheritance. Already cricket mad, he saw the game being played at the country houses all around him and determined to outdo the lot of them, particularly the well-established Bridge Hill club just up the road. So his first action on taking over the house was not to rearrange the rooms or build on, but to lay out amidst the trees of the park a new and spacious cricket ground which he swiftly made the centre of cricket in East Kent.[21] The Bourne Club, of which Mann was the moving spirit and for whom he sometimes played, was soon taking on other Kent teams such as Chatham and Dover, and as Bourne "Paddock" established itself it became the venue for more grandiloquent matches, like that between the counties of Surrey and Kent played there in 1773.

Thanks to Mann's money and competitive instincts, Bourne Paddock had more elaborate accommodation than most other grounds of the period. In the early days, spectators had to go across the park to Bridgehill House for their refreshment, but by 1767 there were the usual booths on the ground selling food and drink, including one for gentlemen "in a tent pitched for that purpose, separate from all the other booths". Until 1780, one John Farley held the concession, and then it was opened out so that several publicans from Bridge and Canterbury were allowed to set up booths, though they too had to compete with rivals operating just outside the ground.

Some of these matches were really big affairs. When the foremost club of the country, Hambledon of Hampshire played "England" at Bourne in August 1772, the attendance on the first day was said to have numbered 20,000. A grandstand was built to accommodate the huge crowd expected, tickets for which in later years cost a shilling. But there was no admission charge for the rest of the ground, and the thousands that turned up were ordinary Kentish folk coming from all ends of the county,[22] as confirmed by a poem celebrating the Surrey victory in the 1773 match:

> From Marsh and Weald their hay forks left,
> To Bourne the rustics hied,
> From Romney, Cranbrook, Tenterden,
> And Durent's verdant side.

This was a match in which Mann himself played, and the only evidence of his skills as a cricketer come from this same poem which records his walk to the wicket:

> At last Sir Horace took the field,
> A batter of great might,
> Moved like a lion, he a while,
> Put Surrey in a fright.

In fact he made 22, quite good for the time, and his highest known score that has been recorded; his contemporary fame as a player, therefore, must have rested with innings played before 1772 when individual records begin.

But Mann was an organiser and supplier of funds, rather than a player. There were, after all, plenty of good professional players to be seen at Bourne in this miraculous period, quite as many as at Lord's in a later generation. Most of the finest players in England were there at some time, including the great players of Hambledon, made heroes for posterity by John Nyren's accounts some fifty years later. By the 1780s, the aristocratic patrons of the great village clubs like Hambledon, not content with supporting them financially, began to buy up the best players for their own teams and personal glory, rather in the way foreign tycoons buy up football clubs today. Mann himself was at the forefront of this development. In 1777 the Hambledon batsman James Aylward scored 167 in a match against "England", at that time the highest score ever made. Impressed by the feat, Mann secured his services for the Bourne Club by employing him as his bailiff, a role for which he turned out to be peculiarly unfitted. But as with many such transfers, Aylward never reproduced the form at Bishopsbourne he had showed at Broadhalfpenny Down. By 1786 he had retired to Bridge to keep a pub (the last refuge of the superannuated cricketer in all ages) and was regularly to be seen setting up his booth at the Paddock for all the Kent matches.[23]

Gambling and lavish entertaining were to be Sir Horace Mann's ultimate undoing. Just two years after his arrival at Bourne his uncle was worrying from Florence about his "thoughtless behaviour" in "dissipating the fortune which his father had gained with so much industry".[24] He warned him against betting in sums of hundreds of pounds. Nyren records Mann, at a match on which he had made a particularly heavy bet, walking agitatedly around the boundary "cutting down the daisies with his stick", and cheering every run as if his whole fortune were staked on the game.[25] In the early 1770s when the first big matches were being played at Bourne, his uncle became convinced by reports in the London newspapers that young Horace was "ruining himself at cricket".[26]

As the matches grew grander at Bourne, so did the entertainment there. There was immense rivalry both on and off the field between Mann and the other great Kentish cricketing patron, the Duke of Dorset at Knole. When Hambledon played at Sevenoaks early in July 1782, the Duke gave a great ball and supper at Knole on the second evening of the match; when Hambledon played "England" at Bourne three weeks later, Mann retaliated with an equally elaborate entertainment. In 1786, there was an even more splendid party when Kent played the White Conduit Club (the forerunner of the MCC) at Bourne which attracted, according to the local paper, "the most brilliant company that has been assembled in this part of the county for many years", including the Duke of Dorset, the earls of Winchilsea and Thanet, and virtually all the principal families of East Kent. They watched the match all day shaded by the tree-lined parkland and after a lavish supper danced until six in the morning.[27]

Bourne Park and the village that lay in its shelter were now on the map as they never had been before, but it was a relatively short stay at the apex of fashionable cricket society. It was a mistake for someone of Mann's resources to attempt to compete with a duke in eighteenth century England. The lavish spending continued on a downward path until in 1807 he was formally declared bankrupt. He had abandoned the tenancy of Bourne in 1790, perhaps in an attempt to live more frugally, but also because the cricket world itself was rapidly changing.

The great patrons who for much of the century had kept the rural game alive now turned their attentions and their money towards London with its population growth and its convenience – the long horse-rides between matches would come to an end. Rural cricket in the 1790s was on the decline and the MCC about to emerge to promulgate a standardised game. The old Hambledon days were over: their celebrated batsman John Small appeared at Bourne in 1787 to score, at the age of fifty, 40 and 24 in a match against England. But this was the swansong of a cricketing age. Mann moved to Margate where he established a new club at Dandelion Fields nearby which gave rise to a few more grand matches (and also his bold experiment of cricket on horseback!) before the money finally ran out. He died there in 1814.

The great epoch of cricket at Bourne had lasted just twenty five years. The Bridge Hill club continued up the road to play its less grand village matches; but another fifty years were to pass before such great matches were to be seen again in the neighbourhood of Canterbury when the St Lawrence Ground was established to delight the likes of Joseph Conrad. At Bourne Park in the early nineteenth century peace had at last returned; the crowds, the grandstands, the refreshment booths, it all might never have been. Except that still in the middle of the twentieth century a visitor to the big house would have pointed out to him in the park to the east the old tree under which for those twenty five years the ancient scorer sat, marking the notches on his stick as each run was completed.[28]

CHAPTER 8

A Learned and
Judicious Divine

We Richard Fox by divine providence Bishop of
Winchester, being desirous of ascending to heaven
... and anxious to aid others in a similar ascent, have
founded a certain bee garden which we have named
the College of Corpus Christi wherein scholars like
ingenious bees are day by day to make wax to the
Glory of God and honey to the profit of themselves
and all Christians.

Statutes of Corpus Christi College, Oxford

Michaelmas Term, 1962. A student emerges from his rooms in the
Annexe, opposite Merton Chapel, into the chill October morning
and turns right into Merton Street. Before him stands the imposing
crenellated façade of Corpus Christi College, like a medieval castle,
in those days blackened with soot which to the newcomer gave it a
stern air of foreboding. Driven on by the cold and the hunger, he
rushes to the small open doorway in the lofty main gate and gingerly
puts a foot through and down into the pitted flagstone inside, a trap
for the unwary worn away by four centuries of ancient youthful
feet. In the porter's lodge he riffles through his pigeon-hole but, no
surprise, there is no post for him. These are the first days he has ever
lived in a town and, at moments like this, he feels the pull of life in
the countryside of Kent.

The porch opens out into the impressive expanse of the front quad, spread with its golden sanded gravel, so deep a gold as to elevate the elegant buildings of Oxfordshire stone that hem it in on all sides, and put to shame the dull flagstones that have since replaced it, for cheap and easy maintenance. Before the Pelican sundial that for centuries has given the college its public symbol, our student veers to the left down a corridor clanging with pots and plates and pans, and into a warm and inviting soup of breakfast smells, porridge and bacon and coffee and toast. The scouts serving breakfast bid a cheery good morning as he turns finally into the lofty wood-panelled darkness of the college hall, hung with sombre paintings of worthies of the past, and squeezes into a bench amidst the raucous chatter of the worthies of the future, now alien and unknown to him but from among whom he may one day make a friend or two.

There is plenty of scope in these early days for nostalgia for the known world of home and family, most of all when the dusk begins to fall and the small band of history students make their way out of the Chaplain's rooms after an hour and a half of translating and cogitating Bede. The nervousness of these early encounters is mixed with puzzlement as to the purpose of these twilight sessions – why Bede and why the Chaplain for students entering the school of *modern* history? Some of that uncomfortable strangeness continued into the Hilary term in a year when the snows of Boxing Day were to lie on the ground (in Kent at least) until early May. In college, the pipes froze for many weeks and one woke in the deathly cold of the morning to find thick sheets of ice had formed on the *inside* of bedroom windows where they were to remain for most of the day. Overworked scouts now had to carry pitchers of scalding water up to every room in their charge so the frozen inhabitant could wash and shave in relative comfort.

It occurred to me at that time that, so far as these essential services were concerned, we were living very much in the style of those early inhabitants of the college in the middle of the sixteenth century. The scholars of those days would rise at 4 o'clock, share a penny piece of beef between four of them for lunch, and 10 o'clock at night would find them walking briskly up and down in an effort to get a little heat into their feet before retiring to ice-cold beds.[1] They too must have been frozen to their rooms, and not just in bad winters. But of who those early inhabitants were, I remained in quiet but blissful ignorance. It had not, for example, occurred to me that Richard Hooker, one of Fuller's *Worthies*, was a Corpus worthy also. Indeed, Hooker was then no more than a vague name connected with the Elizabethan settlement, of which one might hope to learn more if one survived the barren wastes of Bede.

It is a strange process how knowledge builds up in adolescence, particularly the way in which books feed off other books to lead the novitiate round the literary maze, where mainstream branches off into the most esoteric corners. It was Carlyle who first whetted my desire to read Boswell where in turn I found Dr Johnson's view of *Walton's Lives*: "He talked of Isaac Walton's Lives, which was one of his most favourite books. Dr. Donne's Life, he said, was the most perfect of them".[2] Coming to the book itself, with its powerfully simple English, I agreed with Dr Johnson's general assessment; but as to his particular view, I found Hooker's life the most captivating, even more than that of Donne. Again it was the English that held one, as much as the nostalgic picture of humble saintliness that Walton set out deliberately to paint. And there again, there was the power of familiar place – not just the Oxford college but somewhere closer to home.

Richard Hooker was born around Easter of the year 1554 (we do not know the date precisely) in the village of Heavitree just outside Exeter, in the first year of Mary's reign when altars were rebuilt, chalices brought out and dusted off and the mass celebrated once more openly and in earnest. By the time he was four and capable of forming a memory, Elizabeth had ascended the throne, and England, at least at a political level, was a Protestant country once more. It might be said he came from a broken home. His father disappeared early to run the Carew estates in Ireland and saw little of his son throughout his life. It is not clear either for how long his mother tended him though he is recorded as expressing great love for her. The vacuum was filled by surrogate fathers who later transmuted into active patrons of his intellectual, academic and ecclesiastical career.

At the age of eight, he moved into the house of his uncle John Hooker in the centre of Exeter where he was nurtured into adolescence. His uncle was an important figure in the local government of the city, then holding the office of First Chamberlain, and the move an important springboard to high class schooling. In 1562 he entered Exeter Latin High School (later Exeter Grammar) where, as the name implies, all teaching and converse was in Latin, and the pupil throve. Though Walton's deliberate hagiography, both as to facts and to character, has been corrected by subsequent generations of historians (he was writing, like Hooker himself, to a political commission in support of the Anglican settlement and had to project an aura of sanctity around his subject), his description of the man at various stages of his life, which has created the abiding image, is still worth quoting, still broadly valid. Here, as a schoolboy

> His complexion (if we may guess by him at the age of forty) was sanguine, with a mixture of choler; and yet his motion was slow even in his youth, and so was his speech, never expressing an earnestness in either of them, but an humble gravity suitable to the aged. And it is observed (so far as inquiry is able to look back at this distance of time) that at his being a school-boy, he was an early questionist, quietly inquisitive. "Why this was, and that was not, to be remembered?" " Why this was granted, and that denied?" This being mixed with a remarkable modesty, and a sweet serene quietness of nature, and with them a quick apprehension of many perplexed parts of learning, imposed then upon him as a scholar, made his master and others to believe him to have an inward blessed divine light, and therefore to consider

him to be a little wonder. For in that, children were less pregnant, less confident, and more malleable, than in this wiser, but not better, age.[3]

For a child so bright, the next step was from school to University. John Hooker was a friend of John Jewel, the devout and scholarly apologist of the reformed church, who under Mary's reign had fled the country for Strasbourg and Zurich, but was appointed Bishop of Salisbury in the early years of Elizabeth when the Marian bishops had all resigned. Jewel took Richard under his wing (the first of his powerful patrons) and when asked to propose a college for the boy naturally suggested Corpus, where he had been a fellow before his expulsion from the country. Thus in 1569, at the age of 15, Richard Hooker went up to Corpus to take a clerk's place under the tutorship of Dr John Rainolds, the renowned Calvinist, later to become President of the college and an important contributor to the authorised version of the Bible, part of the translation of which was completed round his sickbed in his lodgings at Corpus.

By dint of hard work and natural ability, Hooker's academic progress over the next five years was impressive. In the words of Walton, he "had, by a constant unwearied diligence, attained unto a perfection in all the learned languages; by the help of which, an excellent tutor, and his unintermitted studies, he had made the subtlety of all the arts easy and familiar to him, and useful for the discovery of such learning as lay hid from common searchers. So that by these, added to his great reason, and his restless industry added to both, *he did not only know more of causes and effects; but what he knew, he knew better than other men*".[4] He took his first degree in 1574 and his M.A. in 1578; the following year he took holy orders and was elected fellow of Corpus.

In all, he was to remain at Corpus no less than fifteen years before he was thrown pell-mell into the cauldron of Elizabethan ecclesiastical politics. He never achieved high academic office in the university, though he did become *de facto* regius professor of Hebrew as the informal stand-in for a failing incumbent. In his latter years in college, he worked for a doctorate in Divinity but never had time to complete his studies. Nevertheless, it was during his academic career that he built up the powerful contacts that were to help him, not to ecclesiastical preferment, but in support of his life's work as underwriter of the Elizabethan Anglican settlement.

In 1571 John Jewel died and Hooker lost the patron who had contrived his entry into the academic world. Such was the growing intellectual reputation of the young student, however, that he soon came to the attention of Edwin Sandys, then Bishop of London, who had known Jewel well from their shared Marian exile in Germany. A few years later Sandys decided to send his son, another Edwin, to Corpus for the express purpose of being tutored by Hooker. In the volatile bishop, later to become Archbishop of York, Hooker had won an even more influential friend who could pull all the political strings, and was struck as much by the young man's personal piety and conduct as his academic prowess. Walton, predictably, makes much of Hooker's very *un*-student-like qualities:

> And for his behaviour, amongst other testimonies, this still remains of him, that in four years he was but twice absent from the chapel prayers; and that his behaviour there was such as showed an awful reverence of that God which he then worshipped and prayed to; giving all outward testimonies that his affections were set on heavenly things. This was his behaviour towards God; and for that to man, it is observable that he was never known to be angry or passionate, or extreme in any of his desires; never heard to repine or dispute with Providence, but, by a quiet, gentle submission and resignation of his will to the wisdom of his Creator, bore the burthen of the day with patience; never heard to utter an uncomely word; and by this, and a grave behaviour, which is a divine charm, he begot an early reverence unto his person, even from those that at other

> times, and in other companies, took a liberty to cast
> off that strictness of behaviour and discourse that is
> required in a collegiate life... Thus mild, thus innocent
> and exemplary was his behaviour in his College; and thus
> this good man continued till his death; still increasing in
> learning, in patience, and piety.[5]

The period of Hooker's stay at Corpus was one of revolutionary change
in the structure of teaching at Oxford – a move from the lonely scholar
mode of the medieval clerk-student, who looked to the University
for direction, to the new college-based tutorial system. By 1576, all
students were registered to an individual college under the tutelage of
fellows. Teaching was no longer the work of distant public lecturing but
a more intimate process of direct personal interaction; and nowhere
was the system applied with greater fervour than in the new college
of Corpus, founded only fifty years before by the academic zeal of
Bishop Fox. Fox insisted that the college should be open to all classes
(including poor scholars like Hooker), but all his "Bees" had to work:
"the gluttonous and useless drone shall be driven off from the hive lest
he devour the food of the honey making and working bee".[6]

In addition to Edwin Sandys the younger, Hooker now became
tutor to George Cranmer, great-nephew of the archbishop burnt at
Oxford under Mary. Hooker was only a couple of years older than
these two most eminent of his pupils, and all three young men became
close friends in, as Walton puts it, " a friendship made up of religious
principles, which increased daily by a similitude of inclinations to
the same recreations and studies; a friendship elemented in youth,
and in an university, free from self-ends, which the friendships of age
usually are not".[7] Though self-ends were not then in contemplation,
this three-cornered friendship was to play a major role in Hooker's
life and achievement, Sandys and Cranmer providing the political
drive and the money to bring to fruition his *magnum opus*; though they
were also to be the cause of some heart-searching and frustration in
the latter years of his life.

At Oxford, Hooker had always lived in relative poverty; but in 1584 he was offered, probably through the aegis of Edwin Sandys senior, now Archbishop of York, the living of Drayton Beauchamp in Buckinghamshire, to help shore up his finances. There is plenty of evidence that Hooker enjoyed the peace of the English countryside but Walton saw it as the wrong career move: "the good man was drawn from the tranquillity of his college; from that garden of piety, of pleasure, of peace, and a sweet conversation, into the thorny wilderness of a busy world; into those corroding cares that attend a married priest, and a country parsonage".[8]

Hooker held the living for little more than a year, and probably resided in the parish only for a matter of months, from October 1584 to March 1585. Walton mistakenly believed he had gone there on marriage (his marriage in fact took place four years later) and this to Walton's mind was the chief "corroding care". But Walton was right in the sense that this appointment was the first time that Hooker was to be thrust out into the "busy world", the source of pains but also the fulfilment of achievement.

It was in 1581, just a little before Drayton Beauchamp, and probably again through the influence of Archbishop Sandys, that Hooker was invited to preach at St Paul's Cross, the historic little pulpit box in the corner of St Paul's churchyard where sermons had been preached and wrongdoers brought to public penance since the early fourteenth century.[9] Paul's Cross was a somewhat up-market version of the modern-day Speakers' Corner, a national platform for the exposition and discussion of public policy and religious doctrine, and at times the promulgation of national news; Carlyle had called it "a kind of *Times Newspaper*, but edited partly by Heaven itself".[10] The appointment to preach there was issued only to past or present Oxbridge men and was mandatory; they were given a month's notice and were directed to specific lodgings at the house of the so-called "Shunamite" – their fee was forty-five shillings.[11] Since the invitation came from the Bishop of London, most speakers were on the government's current ticket, but in the vibrant religious atmosphere of the sixteenth century no invitee could be relied on with certainty to toe the party line. It was an honour to be invited to speak there, but the resultant public exposure on matters of controversy could generate hostility and, on occasion, instant riot in the churchyard – not, then, a platform for the shrinking violet.

We do not have the text of Hooker's sermon there, but we do know from Walton and others that he seemed to cast doubt on Calvin's doctrine of predestination: "That in God there were two wills: an antecedent and a consequent will: his first will, That all mankind should be saved; but his second will was, That those only should be saved, that did live answerable to that degree of grace which he had offered or afforded them".[12] It was typical of Hooker that his movement away from pure Calvinist teaching should have sprung from his belief in a more benign God, a view which was to lead shortly to more controversial statements in favour of Roman Catholics, in particular his contention that those Catholics from past ages might yet, in spite of their erroneous beliefs, have been saved if they had died with faith in God.

The sermon at Paul's Cross, Hooker's first national public appearance, was well received by the Church establishment and was to lead shortly thereafter in March 1585 to his one major public appointment (albeit as a compromise candidate in a closely fought political battle) – as Master of the Temple, looking after the spiritual needs of the judges and benchers of that society. Since lawyers and politics always walk hand in hand, the Temple pulpit was another important platform for the development of the fraught and controversial church politics of the time. The appointment would have meant a better income than that at Drayton Beauchamp but, according to Walton, the country-loving priest was reluctant to go and live permanently in London: "his wish was rather to gain a better country living, where he might 'see God's blessing spring out of the earth, and be free from noise' (so he expressed the desire of his heart) 'and eat that bread, which he might more properly call his own, in privacy and quietness' ".[13]

But at last he was persuaded to accept the appointment and face the challenge that the Temple now held in store. It is often forgotten, thanks to the pernicious effect of historical hindsight, that the future of the Church of England was all to play for in the early days of Elizabeth's reign. In the reign of Henry VIII, church policy had see-sawed from left to right, as it had done since his death, the stern Protestantism of Edward VI giving way to the rampant Catholicism of Mary. When Elizabeth came to the throne, it soon became clear that Reformation was safe in her hands, but it was a close-run thing. In the celebrated words of the leading historian on the English Reformations: "The Church of England was established by the merest whisker, a margin of three votes: a margin achieved by political chicanery, and by keeping the Church rather more Catholic than had been planned".[14] But established it was in a very few years, in part by the necessary caution of the law-makers at the centre, in part by the turning of blind eyes in the parishes. As time went on, however, there remained the overriding question, which reformation was it to be – mild High Church or root and branch Puritan? It was a question on which the world was eventually to turn to Hooker for an authoritative answer.

By the mid-1580s any threat of a second Catholic restoration had been effectively seen off, to be confirmed by the execution of Mary, Queen of Scots and the defeat of the Armada. Catholicism had gone underground in the houses of the conservative gentry. But there was plenty of scope for a bitter fight among the reformed parties. On one wing were the Puritans, theologically Calvinist and fired by the Pauline epistles with their assurance of predestined election and emphasis on redemption, salvation, justification by faith and "living in the spirit". They believed in the primacy of Scripture as the sole authority for faith and practice, and argued endlessly on the minutiae of the latter. In general they were firm advocates of the Presbyterian, as opposed to the episcopal, form of church polity. Walter Travers, Hooker's bugbear rival at the Temple, was a leading one of these.

On the other wing were what might be called the emergent

Anglicans, seeking further liturgical and theological movement away from Rome while maintaining firm support for an episcopal polity. They stood for an established Church ruled by bishops and headed by the Crown; and the use of the Book of Common Prayer and Bishop's Bible as against the Geneva Bible – the middle ground in biblical interpretation between Rome and Geneva. They preferred the synoptic Gospels to Paul's epistles, but in any case regarded Scripture as the primary, but not the only, source of faith and practice; reason and religious custom were two other important sources of God's revelation. They emphasised the incarnation, passion and resurrection as central theological and liturgical themes, attaching importance to the worship of sacraments and common prayer, not to preaching. They stressed human awe and wonder before the holiness of God and were aesthetically inclined; quite different from the Puritan emphasis on personal sin and God's judgment.[15]

Where stood Richard Hooker in all this? The simple answer is that he was his own man, taking his influences and shaping his views according to his very individual personality. He was a man of charity who saw good in everyone, even the misguided, and abhorred the religious wrangling of his age, even when he found himself caught up in the thick of it. In his early academic career Hooker came under a number of different influences. His family background was firmly Calvinist: his first benefactor, Bishop Jewel of Salisbury, was in his youth an ardent Calvinist, as was his second benefactor, Edwin Sandys; his tutor at Corpus, John Rainolds, had a marked Puritan streak. The college at this time was racked by the contemporary religious controversy of right and left. Hooker in fact was briefly expelled from Corpus in 1580, along with Rainolds and others, for opposing John Barfoote as a candidate for President because of his orthodox, conformist views. Walton glosses over the cause of his expulsion because he did not want to jeopardise his picture of Hooker as the champion of conformity by drawing attention to his youthful nonconformist tendencies.[16]

But the founding spirit of sixteenth century Oxford was that of

Erasmus and Catholic humanism, and the prevailing religious leanings at Corpus at this time, thanks to Bishop Fox and his "Bees", were undoubtedly Catholic. Hooker, with his charitable temperament, was inevitably influenced by this strong residual Catholic presence and from an early stage showed a tolerant attitude to Catholics. His natural inclinations were towards free will rather than Calvin's rigid determinism, to follow the patristic tradition, to balance Scripture with reason. It was these inclinations that were to create the so-called "middle way" set forth in his great work which became the intellectual underpinning of the Anglican settlement. In the words of today's leading expert on Hooker, he was attempting "to define an ethos for the English church that was unambiguously reformed, historically founded, and charitably inclusive".[17] But it was these inclinations also that led Hooker into his earliest controversies – the accusation of being too soft on Catholics.

Hooker's appointment to the Temple had less to do with his personal qualifications for the post than with the convolutions of contemporary church politics, resulting in a trial of strength between Archbishop Whitgift and the Queen's chief minister, Lord Burghley. The post was a strange one, quite independent of the Bishop of London and in the gift of the Queen; it was because of this independence from the church hierarchy that it offered an opportunity for Puritan infiltration. Whitgift's safe candidate was the orthodox Dr Nicholas Bond, one of the Queen's chaplains; that of Burghley was the very learned and spiritual Walter Travers, number two in the Puritan hierarchy behind Thomas Cartwright whose spats with Whitgift in the public prints had formed the leading controversy of the day.

For four years Travers had held the post of Lecturer at the Temple, as deputy to the ageing Master, Richard Alvey, whom he had put somewhat in the shade. His clear aim was to turn the Temple over to Presbyterian theology and liturgical practice, and through his sermons, delivered in the usual emotional Puritan style, had built up a concerted following for his views, particularly among the young lawyers. He had thus strong expectations of succeeding Alvey, but when Bond dropped out of the running on health grounds, Hooker became the orthodox candidate, probably on the suggestion of Edwin Sandys. Although little known outside Oxford, Hooker was the safe candidate and, after much deliberation, proved acceptable to the Queen. Whitgift had won this particular battle with the Puritans, but Hooker's battles were only just beginning.[18]

The thwarting of Travers' ambitions by Hooker's appointment gave an extra bite to his theological onslaught on the new Master. It might have been expected that, with Hooker in post, Travers would simply leave, but at the intervention of the Privy Council, Travers' pension was continued and a compromise worked out in which Hooker was to preach Sunday mornings and Travers in the afternoon. Hooker preached the morning sermon in his usual broad-spirited Anglican vein. Travers used his evening sermon to challenge the orthodoxy of Hooker's teachings, particularly his favourable attitude towards Catholics and his lax interpretation of the Calvinist doctrine of predestination, often picking up Hooker in quibbling Presbyterian mode on words he had spoken just a few hours before. This was to give rise to Fuller's famous saying that at the Temple then "the pulpit spake pure Canterbury in the Morning and Geneva in the afternoon".[19] Like most aphorisms, this was a convenient exaggeration, since the debates between the two were often just small differences of emphasis circling round some firmly shared assumptions. But they were not just about predestination or tolerance of Catholics or minor issues of liturgical practice. Underneath them all lay the central issue of the English Reformation: in the absence of the single authoritative tradition of Rome, to what authority was one to appeal when a difference arose in the interpretation of doctrine? For Hooker the answer was plain: the authority of ecclesiastical law over biblical precedent, and above all the authority of reason, both divine and human, in matters of religious truth.

Controversy poured out of the two pulpits in trenchant style. Both men kept a constant eye on each other's utterances lest either should gain advantage, until the contest between them seemed almost to take precedence over the routine running of the Temple. This was of some annoyance to Hooker as the Master in charge, particularly as Travers, in his subordinate role, failed regularly to consult him when about to refute the Master's latest sermon. The situation was getting out of hand and causing great concern to Whitgift: the Temple was a public forum, and any debate – particularly in front of half the future lawyers of the country – threatened to compromise his drive for uniformity throughout the reformed Church. The Archbishop stepped in, and called a halt to proceedings by prohibiting Travers from preaching more. This was a blow, to Travers' livelihood as much as to his theology, and he appealed against it with a Supplication to the Privy Council, hoping to gain renewed support there from the Earl of Leicester, very much the Puritan's friend. When the petition was eventually refused, Travers' party, hoping to stir up wider support in the country, had it privately printed and circulated widely.

With the controversy now drawn out beyond the Temple into the national debate between Puritans and would-be Anglicans, it became incumbent on Hooker to draw up an Answer, not least to refute the attacks upon himself; which he did "and it proved so full an answer, an answer that had in it so much of clear reason, and writ with so much meekness and majesty of style, that the Bishop began to have him in admiration, and to rejoice that he had appeared in his cause".[20] In his early sermons at the Temple as defended in the *Answer to Travers* we meet for the first time all that was to become so characteristic of his later work: his patient exposition of complex issues, his faith in the tools of rational inquiry and logical demonstration, his charity and forbearance, his wide reading and keen sense of history, and above all his deep devotion to his church. This then was the beginning of Hooker's public fame as national apologist of the Anglican communion and a dummy run for the great work that was to follow.

Not that Hooker was at all a natural controversialist. While Travers' *Supplication* is highly rhetorical and at times quite nasty in tone, Hooker's *Answer* is milder but nonetheless an assiduous refutation of Travers' whole attitude and approach, rather than his detailed theological points. Hooker was appalled by the generally disputatious attitude of his age in religious matters and took every opportunity to bewail the fact, in this document as in others. He was particularly concerned for the negative effects of controversy: "there can come nothing of contention but the mutuall waste of the parties contendinge till a comon enemye daunce in the ashes of them both".[21] The quiet country parson-to-be was personally reluctant to jump with both feet into the political fray: "I take no joye in stryvinge. I have not byn nousled or trayned up in it. I would to Christe they which have att this presente inforced me hereunto had so ruled theire handes in any reasonable tyme that I mighte never have byn constreyned to strike asmuche as in myne owne defence".[22]

But in spite of this, he felt compelled to spring to the Church's defence to ensure that its case was set out fully and transparently before the public. "When I sawe howe master Travers carped att theis thinges onely because they laie not open, I promised att some conveniente tyme to make them clere as lighte both to him and to all others." [23] This was the reasoning that produced not only the *Answer* of 1586 but also the *Laws of Ecclesiastical Polity* of 1593; and which explains the strange paradox that the man who hated ecclesiastical controversy and was temperamentally ill-equipped to handle it should have been thrust into the role of apologist for the Anglican settlement, picking and driving his way through the endless minefields that hemmed it in.

Hooker's arrival in London to embark on a public career was also the occasion of an important development in his private life. When he had first come up to preach at St Paul's Cross, he had been required to lodge at the house of John Churchman in Watling Street, that self-same road that bordered the fringes of our village in Kent. Churchman was a big man in the city of London who reached the height of his power in 1594 when appointed Master of the Merchant Taylors Company. Hooker was made very much at home there, and so it was natural that when appointed Master of the Temple he should once again take up lodgings with the Churchmans in their magnificent city house standing in the shadow of St Paul's. There he became closely acquainted with the Churchmans' daughter, Joan, the couple fell in love and were later married at St Augustine's, Watling Street in February 1588. After the wedding, they continued on in the Churchmans' house, but spent time also in the summer at the family's country retreat in the village of Enfield. Between 1589 and 1593, while still in London, Joan gave birth to five children, a boy who died in infancy, followed by four girls.

It is unfortunate that, just as Walton made a saint out of Hooker, he made for posterity a harridan out of Hooker's wife. She was said to be ugly and ignorant, had been thrust on Hooker by his mother-in-law and, worst of all, gave her new husband hell by her shrewish behaviour. As Walton put it, "*There is a wheel within a wheel*; a secret sacred wheel of Providence (most visible in marriages,) guided by his hand, that *allows not the race to the swift*, nor *bread to the wise*, nor good wives to good men".[24] There is no evidence to justify Walton's remarks as to either Mrs Hooker's personality or her person. The truth is that the Cranmer family, to whom Walton was close, had fallen out with the Churchmans after Hooker's death, and fed him his ill-spirited material. Some of the malignity can be put to the test: to take one example, Churchman was a leading man in the City but Walton describes him as a poor draper. Historians of recent years have leapt to Mrs Hooker's aid, but sadly neither their reputation nor their prose can compete with that of Isaak Walton.

Hooker remained in the Churchmans' house for ten years, six of them while Master of the Temple. His friend Edwin Sandys, who had probably introduced him to the Churchmans in the first place, came to lodge there at the same time. Their close friend George Cranmer was always in and out, as was Dr John Spenser, Cranmer's brother in law and later President of Corpus. With all of these "emergent Anglicans" *in situ*, the house in Watling Street became quite by chance the focus for the movement in defence of the Church against the Puritans. With Sandys, Cranmer and Spenser all strong

33. J.B.Reade, scientist and clergyman.

Bishopbourne Rectory
Nov 25 /70 –

My dear Mr. Hogg
I have now the
Comfort of a Water
bed but I still suffer
severe pain and the
hardening of the liver
is now followed by
yellowness of the skin –
As it will be impossible
to join you at the next
meeting I must ask
you and Mr. Slack

34. Reade to Jabez Hogg.

35. Reade's indecipherable grave.

36. Cricket at Kenfield Hall *c* 1760.

37. Horace Mann, politician and cricketer.

38. Corpus Christi College, Oxford – the front quad in 1880.

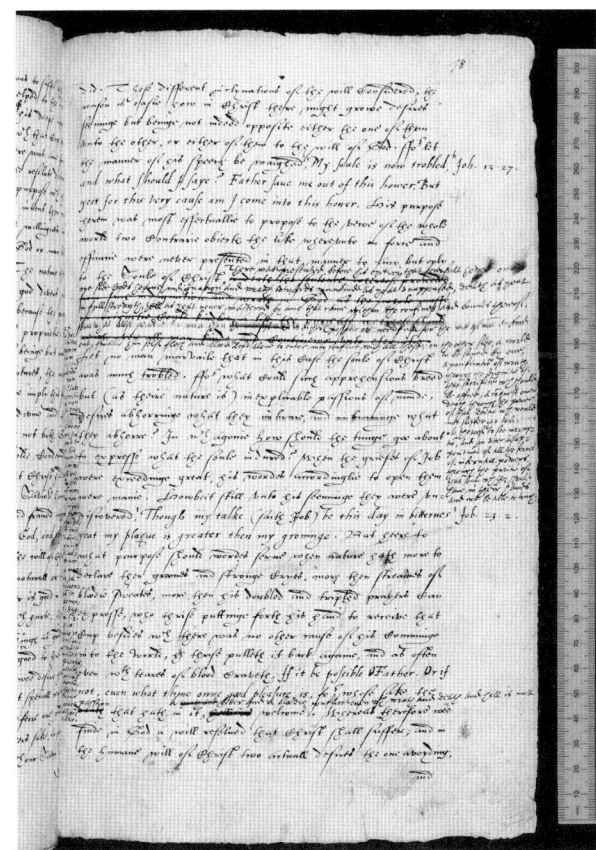

39. A folio from the *Polity*, Book V – the Greek and marginal amendments are in Hooker's hand.

40. Richard Hooker, Elizabethan divine.

41. Bishopsbourne Rectory garden in 1935, *water-colour by Margaret Mallorie.*

42. Bishopsbourne Rectory in 1954, just before demolition.

43. The grand ceiling of the room where Hooker died.

44. The small statue of Hooker in St Mary's Church.

45. The Hooker memorial in St Mary's.

46. Conrad's grave at Canterbury in the 1920s.

47. Ninnie (Emily Ford) *left* and The Owl (May Brooke) at the gate of Ivy Cottage *c* 1950.

48. Brooke the country botanist on one of his walks.

supporters of and informal collaborators with Hooker in his next venture, it became also the powerhouse for the writing of the *Polity*.

With the failure of the petition against his sacking, Walter Travers finally departed the Temple and Hooker's life settled down to a more routine existence. He was kept busy enough with all the pressures of a large administrative job as well as his spiritual teaching. And the Travers syndrome did not entirely go away, the strong dissenting element among the young lawyers striving to keep up the onslaught on all the supposedly heretical aspects of Hooker's teaching. It was this backwash from the debates with Travers which gave Hooker, egged on by Sandys and Cranmer, and possibly informally by Archbishop Whitgift, the seed of inspiration for the *Laws of Ecclesiastical Polity*. As always, Walton puts it the most succinctly.

> After the publication of his Answer to the Petition of Mr. Travers, Mr. Hooker grew daily into great repute with the most learned and wise of the nation; but it had a contrary effect in very many of the Temple, that were zealous for Mr. Travers, and for his Church discipline; insomuch, that though Mr. Travers left the place, yet the seeds of discontent could not be rooted out of that society, by the great reason, and as great meekness, of this humble man: for though the chief Benchers gave him much reverence and encouragement, yet he there met with many neglects and oppositions by those of Mr. Travers judgment; insomuch that it turned to his extreme grief; and, that he might unbeguile and win them, he designed to write a deliberate, sober treatise of the Church's power to make canons for the use of ceremonies, and by law to impose an obedience to them, as upon her children; and this he proposed to do in eight books of the Laws of Ecclesiastical Polity; intending therein to show such arguments as should force an assent from all men, if reason, delivered in

211

sweet language, and void of any provocation, were able
to do it ...[25]

Though the hostility of Travers and his supporters may have been the
immediate occasion for the writing of the book, it was no surprise
that Hooker should have turned to the written word where the spoken
word had seemed to fail him. Unlike the Puritans with their highly
emotional extempore preaching, Hooker's sermons were closely
argued written treatises which he read out solemnly, without much
expression to warm the hearts of his congregations. As Fuller pointed
out: "He may be said to have made good Musick with his fiddle and
stick alone, without any Rosin; having neither Pronunciation nor
gesture to grace his matter". Yet those who listened attentively
and stuck it out were rewarded in the end. "Hooker his Stile was
prolixe but not tedious, and such who would patiently attend and
give him credit at the reading and hearing of his Sentences, had their
expectation over-paid at the close thereof." [26]

Hooker, after all, was an introspective scholar, more comfortable
engaging the religious issues of the day with the pen than the tongue.
He cared deeply about those issues, and since he knew that all
contemporary defences of the Church fell well short of the mark, he
felt a compulsion to address them himself on behalf of the Church
in a more coherent and lasting manner than had been attempted
heretofore. Thus it was that he resolved upon the major work of
his life: the construction of a wide-ranging apologia setting out the
special nature and genius of the Church of England and defending it
against its Puritan enemies.

The project involved a huge amount of reading and research
on manuscripts brought to the house; and it is likely also that the
Archbishop granted him free run of the treasures of the Lambeth
library. He seems to have started work about the spring of 1587, and
managed to continue until 1591 while fulfilling at the same time his
administrative and spiritual duties at the Temple. But he now sought
release from these onerous duties to give him more freedom to

pursue his writing and his studies. Walton has him linking this desire for release to his love of the country, and addressing Archbishop Whitgift thus: "My Lord, when I lost the freedom of my cell, which was my College, yet I found some degree of it in my quiet country parsonage: but I am weary of the noise and oppositions of this place; and indeed God and nature did not intend me for contentions, but for study and quietness".[27]

The Archbishop, in his self-appointed role as hammer of the Puritans, had as great an interest as anyone in buying Hooker the time and peace to complete his work, which promised well to dish those Puritans for good. So in July 1591 Hooker was relieved of the Temple and appointed rector of Boscombe in Wiltshire and prebend of Netheravon, attached to Salisbury Cathedral. Unlike with Drayton Beauchamp, there is no evidence that he ever resided in either parish; so this was not the romantic offer of a writing desk under an apple tree in the cool of a country garden, but merely the wherewithal to continue his studies at his desk in John Churchman's dark house overlooking the dusty, rubbish-strewn streets of the City. It is thus a painful irony that in order to dish the Puritans and defend the Church Hooker had needs indulge in that very pluralism which was one of the major scandals of Church practice of which the Puritans complained.

The precise history of the completion of Hooker's eight books of the *Polity*, three of which were published posthumously, will probably never be known, but it seems to be generally accepted now that the drafts of all eight books were ready by 1593, six years after he started work on them. That was an important year because in the up-coming session of Parliament a Puritan *putsch* was expected in debates on two Government bills designed to tighten the law against Popish recusants, but whose wording might seem to apply to Protestant dissent as well. Sandys who was active in the debates argued openly that one of the measures should apply to the extremist Puritan groups – the Brownists and Barrowists – a proposal that mainstream Puritans regarded as a direct threat to them. Sandys and Cranmer, politicians both, wished to pray Hooker in aid as a means to clinching the debate.

The *Polity* was essentially a work of two halves: the first four books were general, philosophical and theoretical; they would serve the purpose of the general public debate. But the last four formed a detailed account of how the general principles should be put into practice, on some aspects of which Sandys and Cranmer had important reservations, most notably those passages that seemed to favour Catholics overmuch or a social contract above divine right, and at a more functional level Hooker's attempt in Book VI to extend the jurisdiction of church courts into the civil area. Hooker had already touted the work round the City publishing houses to universal rejection, for a work of high theology (especially one in support of the establishment), without polemics or scandal, was seen even at this period to be insufficiently commercial. He was told it could be published only at his own cost; so the wealthier Sandys picked up the tab and agreed to finance publication. With the money came enhanced editorial control, Sandys deciding that only the first four books should be published in the first tranche, and the remaining, more controversial, four left over for further discussion and revision. This was an important moment. Sandys as a close friend of the writer must have discussed the work many times before, but there is no evidence of any formal collaboration up to this point. The eight books Hooker had completed by 1593 were the expression of his own views and beliefs, sometimes ambiguous, sometimes contradictory; now they were to be subject to the political purposes of Sandys and Cranmer in their fight with Puritan dissent, and required essential clarity and orthodoxy to fit that bill. The proposed "revision" was, as we shall see, tantamount to the rewriting of the entire second half of the work, a process that was to lead to argument and contention, and the publication of only one more book in the writer's lifetime.

Thus it was that Books I to IV alone were published in March 1593 in the midst of a Government and Parliamentary outcry against the Puritans, to which Hooker's work provided a useful backcloth of intellectual support. There was no way, of course, that these weighty books would be read in time to influence the Parliamentary debates in detail, but Hooker had written a preface short enough to be read. It was intended as a direct address in the second person to the individual dissenter, an appeal not perhaps containing "such bowels of love",[28] as Walton put it, but at least constructed in Hooker's measured, low-key, occasionally ironic, style. To this preface, Cranmer persuaded Hooker, probably against his better judgment, to add a final part containing a most un-Hooker-like polemical attack upon the more extreme Puritans – the Brownists and Barrowists who were to be added to the scope of the anti-Catholic bill. It was this last part of the preface, more than any other piece of the work, which would have influenced the immediate public debate.

The preface contains some prime examples of Hooker's ability to build a description with sharp, yet not ungentle, irony, as with this account of the extreme Puritans' affectation of doleful solemnity and otherworldliness.

> All their exhortations were to set light of the things in this world, to count riches and honors vanitie, and in token therof, not only to seeke neither, but if men were possessors of both, even to cast away the one and resign the other, that al men might see their unfaigned conversion unto Christ. They were sollicitors of men to fasts, to often meditations of heavenly things, and as it were conferences in secret with God by prayers, not framed according to the frosen maner of the world, but expressing such fervent desires as might even force God to hearken unto them. Where they found men in diet, attire, furniture of house [*Hooker himself scored highly in this class of possession, as we shall see*], or any other way observers of civility and decent order, such they reproved as being carnally and earthly minded.

Every worde otherwise then severely and sadly uttered, seemed to pearce like a sword thorow them.[29]

This more aggressive chapter of the preface, which Cranmer induced Hooker to write, continues in similar vein, but even in his most forthright attacks Hooker maintains his magisterial and crystalline late-Elizabethan prose, studded here and there with out of place images and startling phrases that give sudden impetus to the text. Here he is describing the methods used by the more extreme Puritan leaders, conveniently attributing them only to those in foreign parts, but with an implied read across to their brethren in England.

The meanes whereby they both allured and reteyned so great multitudes were most effectuall; first a woonderfull show of zeale towards God, wherwith they seemed to be even rapt in every thing they spake: secondly an hatred of sinne, and a singular love of integritie, which men did thinke to be much more then ordinary in them, by reason of the custom which they had to fill the eares of the people with invectives against their authorised guides, as well spirituall as civill: thirdly the bountifull reliefe wherwith they eased the broken estate of such needie creatures, as were in that respect the more apt to be drawne away: fourthly, a tender compassion which they were thought to take upon the miseries of the common sort, over whose heads their maner was even to powre down showers of teares, in complayning that no respect was had unto them, that their goods were devoured by wicked cormorants, their persons had in contempt, all liberty both temporall and spirituall taken from them, that it was high time for God now to heare their grones, and to send them deliverance: lastly a cunning slight which they had to stroke and smooth up the mindes of their followers, as well by appropriating

> unto them all the favourable titles, the good wordes, and
> the gracious promises in Scripture, as also by casting the
> contrary alwaies on the heads of such as were severed
> from that retinue.[30]

Note here, in particular, the sudden appearance of "wicked cormorants" and the wonderful image of "stroking and smoothing up" minds.

But when Hooker is left to his own devices, the preface, and indeed the whole book, is more a sympathetic appeal to the individual Puritan to review his beliefs and actions in the light of reason (the foundation of Hooker's system) and the individual arguments set out in the book. He ends the preface on exactly this note, the tone which Walton ascribed to the "bowels of love".

> The best and safest waie for you therefore, my deere
> brethren, is, to call your deedes past to a newe reckoning,
> to reexamine the cause yee have taken in hand, and to
> trie it even point by point, argument by argument, with
> all the diligent exactnes yee can; to lay aside the gall
> of that bitternes wherein your mindes have hitherto
> overabounded, and with meekenes to search the truth.[31]

It has been said more than once that Hooker is the name of a book rather than a man.[32] Given his eminent place in the Anglican canon, it is perhaps strange that he is as a writer almost unknown among the general public. And apart from a small coterie of intensely devoted scholars, who have ground the last ounce out of the most obscure of his works, the book is scarcely read either. Many are the retired clergymen, reposing in the quietude of their country retreats, who hold the book on their shelves but have never dared venture within its covers. It is one of those rare works that is pre-eminently alive in its historical and literary contexts, but no longer active in the world of today.

Had Book I stood alone, without the weight of the seven books that follow, it might certainly be read more widely now, for it is a complete treatise on the philosophy of systems of law and one of the finest theoretical treatments of law and civil society. Hooker sees law as the creative force of his universe, the foundation of order, harmony and reasonableness among all creation. God's supreme law is founded not just on his will, but on reason:

> That law eternall which God himself hath made to himselfe, and therby worketh all things wherof he is the cause and author, that law in the admirable frame wherof shineth with most perfect bewtie the countenance of that wisedome which hath testified concerning her self, *The lord possessed me in the beginning of his way, even before his works of old, I was set up etc*. That law which hath bene the patterne to make, and is the card to guide the world by ... .[33]

Hooker shows how God's law works in nature, where active reason does not enter in, and eventually in the law man makes to regulate society, both political and ecclesiastical, where reason is at the crux of his search for goodness.

In his discussion of the formation of man-made society, Hooker ventures into the territory (dangerous for his age) of popular sovereignty. In his scheme, power comes originally from the community which

> knew that no man might in reason take upon him to determine his owne right, and according to his owne determination proceede in maintenance therof, in as much as every man is towards himselfe and them whom he greatly affecteth partiall; and therfore that strifes and troubles would be endlesse, except they gave their common consent all to be ordered by some whom they

218

should agree upon: without which consent, there were no reason, that one man should take upon him to be Lord or Judge over another; because although there be according to the opinion of some very great and judicious men a kind of naturall right in the noble, wise, and vertuous, to governe them which are of servile disposition; neverthelesse for manifestation of this their right, and mens more peaceable contentment on both sides, the assent of them who are to be governed, seemeth necessarie.[34]

In this social compact, Hooker is not thinking radically of the possibility of the governed withdrawing power from the governors, but merely that once a government is established it must be assumed to have the tacit assent of the people, albeit that differences may arise on individual laws or actions. His later development of these arguments in Book VIII was to take him into more politically fraught waters, and to contribute to the reasons why the last three books were never published in his lifetime.

Behind the intellectual rational philosopher, we catch occasional glimpses in the early books of the personal Hooker and his own private thoughts and prejudices. In Book II, for example, he falls into the writer's temptation of giving a puff to his personal friends, in this case his mentor Bishop Jewel of Salisbury, whom he characterises as "the worthiest Divine that Christendome hath bred for the space of some hundreds of yeres".[35] He shows from time to time his irritation with the modern world and its narrow, shallow approach to life. The opening paragraph to Book I is famous as a critique of the advantages of those who routinely attack established authority, and gives voice to the lament of men in political power in any age who know that those on the outside, whether tabloid press or party opponents, can never know the weight of the internal constraints that shape the responsible decision. Hooker himself had tasted political power and mindless opposition during his stint at the Temple and his frustration rings out like a cry from the heart.

He that goeth about to perswade a multitude, that they are not so well governed as they ought to be, shall never want attentive and favourable hearers; because they know the manifold defects whereunto every kind of regiment is subject, but the secret lets and difficulties, which in publike proceedings are innumerable and inevitable, they have not ordinarily the judgement to consider. And because such as openly reprove supposed disorders of state are taken for principall friends to the common benefite of all, and for men that carry singular freedome of mind; under this faire and plausible coulour whatsoever they utter passeth for good and currant. That which wanteth in the waight of their speech, is supplyed by the aptnes of mens minds to accept and believe it. Whereas on the other side, if we maintaine thinges that are established, we have not onely to strive with a number of heavie prejudices deepely rooted in the hearts of men, who thinke that herein we serve the time, and speake in favour of the present state, because therby we eyther holde or seeke preferment; but also to beare such exceptions as minds so averted before hand usually take against that which they are loath should be powred into them.[36]

At times his attack upon the perceived anti-intellectualism of the age becomes quite sparky. Of the two paths to the discovery of goodness, for example, the modern age can take only the easy way out.

And of discerning goodnes there are but these two wayes; the one the knowledge of the causes whereby it is made such, the other the observation of those signes and tokens, which being annexed alwaies unto goodnes, argue that where they are found, there also goodnes is, although we know not the cause by force whereof it is there. The former of these is the most sure and infallible way, but so hard that all shunne it, and had rather walke as men do in the darke by hap hazard, then tread so long and intricate mazes for knowledge sake. As therefore Physicians are many times forced to leave such methods of curing as themselves know to be the fittest, and being overruled by their patients impatiency are faine to try the best they can, in taking that way of cure, which the cured will yeeld unto: in like sort, considering how the case doth stand with this present age full of tongue and weake of braine, behold we yeeld to the streame therof; into the causes of goodnes we will not make any curious or deepe inquirie...[37]

In the first book, Hooker confronts in a number of places the predilection of the Puritans for attributing all law and church discipline only to what is set down in Scripture. He is particularly scathing on the contention that even the most trivial matters of liturgical practice and ceremonial must have an origin in Scripture, and by that token can never be changed.

...as a man whose wisedome is in waighty affayres admired, would take it in some disdaine to have his counsell solemnely asked about a toye, so the meannesse of some thinges is such that to search the Scripture of God for the ordering of them were to derogate from the reverende authoritie and dignitie of the Scripture, no lesse then they doe by whom Scriptures are in ordinarie talke very idly applyed unto vayne and childish trifles...[38]

Whereas Book I is a wide-ranging treatise on the origins of law, the three remaining books of 1593 pursue these very narrow questions of the dissenters' unthinking reliance on Scripture, but pursue them in a determinedly philosophical manner. Book II declares against the error of the Puritans in holding Scripture to be the only law regulating the whole of man's activities. In Hooker's view, the authority of the Church and of scholars, deploying human reason, is essential for interpreting the Scriptures, whereas under Puritan practice even the most ignorant feel qualified to pronounce with authority on these issues.

> ...it doth not as yet appeare, that an argument of authoritie of man affirmatively is in matters divine nothing woorth. Which opinion being once inserted into the minds of the vulgar sort, what it may growe unto God knoweth. Thus much we see, it hath alreadie made thousandes so headstrong even in grosse and palpable errors, that a man whose capacitie will scarce serve him to utter five wordes in a sensible maner, blusheth not in any doubt concerning matter of scripture to thinke his own bare *Yea*, as good as the *Nay* of all the wise, grave, and learned judgements that are in the whole world. Which insolency must be represt, or it will be the verie bane of Christian religion.[39]

Hooker warns that elevating Scripture beyond what it can perform is ultimately to demean the power of Scripture: "as incredible praises geven unto men do often abate and impaire the credit of their deserved commendation; so we must likewise take great heede, lest in attributing unto scripture more then it can have, the incredibillitie of that do cause even those thinges which indeed it hath most aboundantly to be lesse reverendly esteemed."[40]

In Book III he addresses the even narrower claim that the whole of church governance is laid down in Scripture, and in Scripture alone. According to the Puritans, if elements of church discipline cannot be found in the Bible, they are illegitimate and not to be followed. Hooker refutes this view by drawing a distinction between matters essential to salvation, all of which are contained in Scripture, and things "indifferent", such as the precise form of church governance, liturgical practice and ceremonial. These indifferent matters are resolved by God, through the agency of man's reason. Because they are second order issues, uniformity throughout the Christian church is not necessary; different practices can co-exist happily alongside each other. In this context, Hooker makes a celebrated plea for tolerance between the various branches of Christianity. No man has the right to judge others as to who is the true Christian, and this toleration should reach as far as the Roman Catholics, a proposition which was inevitably to lead Hooker into contention.

Book IV directly addresses the Roman Catholic threat and the claim that the Anglican polity is corrupted by the retention of Popish rites and practices. Here Hooker develops his argument that such matters are subject to the reason of man and always capable of change unless set down by God. The Church has the right to discard Romish or reformed ceremonies according to what best fits its particular circumstances. Where Roman Catholic practices are retained, it is because they are an effective part of the Church's traditions. In rebutting the contention that retaining such practices gives hope and succour to the Roman Catholics, Hooker employs a telling simile: "surely a wise bodies part it were not, to put out his fire, because his fonde and foolish neighbour, from whom he borrowed peradventure wherewith to kindle it, might happily cast him therewith in the teeth, saying, were it not for me thou wouldest freeze, and not be able to heate thy selfe".[41]

The first four books of Hooker's *Polity* (or rather the preface that introduced them) had proved effective in helping to see off the Puritan parliamentary challenge in the spring of 1593. But there was as yet not the slightest hint that this was to become the greatest work of Anglican theology. The booksellers who had refused to underwrite the publication were, as ever, proved right. Of the estimated 1200 copies printed, many of the unused sheets turned up in later editions, implying that only a very few hundred were sold. For all his labours Hooker received just £30.[42]

But none of this was to the point. Hooker was not after money or public applause; his goal was to influence the minds of men, and this he had undoubtedly done in the small circle that comprised the major players in the theological controversies of the day, from Archbishop Whitgift downwards. A wider public for this remarkable English text was still awaited. And there was still a major literary challenge confronting him: the work he thought he had finished was now, by public declaration, only half complete; four more books remained in various stages of completion, and these were the difficult detailed ones that promised not just months and years of revision, but of contentious deliberation as well.

Hooker continued on with his reading, thinking and writing in the Churchmans' house in Watling Street, though 1594 brought plague to London and he and his wife and family were able to escape to the summer house in the wilds of Enfield. This experience of urban plague must have renewed in his heart the old yearning for the countryside where one could live the simple Christian life and write without worry or interruption. The life opportunity was to come to him more quickly than he could ever have imagined. Towards the end of 1594 William Redman was appointed the new Bishop of Norwich. In January 1595, Richard Hooker, whom according to Walton the Queen loved well, received a letter out of the blue nominating him to take over Redman's old parish which boasted a good living wholly suitable for a resident incumbent. Redman had been rector of Bishopsbourne and Barham, two little villages in the rolling wooded downland just south of Canterbury in Kent.

CHAPTER 9

Richard Hooker

I have begun a treatise in which I intend a justification of
the laws of our ecclesiastical polity ... and I shall never
be able to do this, but where I may study, and pray for
God's blessing upon my endeavours, and keep myself
in peace and privacy, and behold God's blessing spring
out of my mother-earth, and eat my own bread without
oppositions ...

Richard Hooker, according to Isaak Walton[1]

It was early in 1595 that Hooker arrived in the village to start his new
life away from the clamours of London. He had spent all his time as
a city dweller – from Exeter to Oxford to London – yet had never
really accustomed himself to the hurly-burly, the noise, the swarms
of people. What he looked for now in this new, unaccustomed
environment was the peace and the time to complete the master
work that still buzzed around in his head, half finished yet still full of
knotty intellectual and political problems to resolve. This was not then
retirement, a chance at last to live just for the day and quietly perform
his pastoral duties to the familiar rhythms of the country seasons. He
had a project and a timetable which tied him to a calendar, if only the
calendar that was to mark out his last remaining days on earth.

But first there was the family to take care of. For this was another
new departure for the man and wife who had spent the last seven years
in the father-in-law's house – the setting up of home together for the

first time, with their four young daughters, Alice aged 4, Cicely 3, Jane 2 and Margaret 1. Their heavy furniture and belongings came by sea and they followed on by sea and road, Hooker normally travelling by boat to Gravesend then overland to Canterbury. The old rectory which greeted them stood on a beautiful site opposite the church; set in open country and on a slight rise, it held a commanding, yet protective, view over the village. It was a substantial house with twelve rooms and various outhouses, including a separate bakehouse, washhouse, stables and barn. It had been built, like the church, in the fourteenth century and in the form of a long house, rather rustic in appearance, with main rooms on the ground floor and attics in the long sloping roof lighted by tiny dormer windows. There were two gable roofs at the extreme end.

It was not to outlast Hooker by much more than two hundred years. By the 19th century only the ground floor of the old building was being used and the rector in 1846 decided on a drastic alteration, creating a completely new upper storey in an uncompromising Georgian style. Some aspects of the ground floor were preserved and the building still retained its feeling of age.[2] In the 1930s, visitors like Alec Waugh would still be shown the room on the ground floor in which Hooker was said to have died, left much as it was with its fine ceiling of moulded beams in black oak; and the window at which he sat to write, looking out on the yew hedge he planted round his garden, 250 foot long, 14 foot high and 7 foot wide.[3] Though from an historical and literary perspective one of the most important rectories in the country, it was torn down in 1955, with scarce any local objection, to make way for a modern building.[4] The yew hedge lasted well into the 20th century but sadly that too has gone.

One thing that does remain is an inventory of Hooker's household goods and chattels, drawn up three weeks after his death, which gives us a little intimate peep inside the house as he lived in it for the next six years. There were four living rooms downstairs, excluding the kitchen and two larders. The main hall, where the family must have eaten, contained two tables and various high-backed benches and a settle of oak. Next came the "greater parler", a sitting-room which boasted "a greate chaire of wallnuttree", a wood rare in England at this time except in houses of the well-to-do, two rich carpets and a dozen "turky" cushions. Such wealth of furnishings reflected the riches of Hooker's father-in-law rather than his own priestly poverty. Two other rooms formed his intellectual workplace. The study housed a square table at which he wrote, seated on a rather rudimentary bench made up of a plank resting across two trestles. Here also was the majority of his library in two book presses (large shelved cupboards) and seven bookshelves. Nearby was the "little parlor" containing a further book press and cupboard, with a "truckle bedstedle" (small bed) in an adjoining room. In imagination one sees Hooker reading into the small hours his theological tomes and going to bed next door so as not to waken the wife. By the time the inventory was taken, his books had been packed away in various chests and hampers and, at a valuation of three hundred pounds, formed the single most valuable item of his estate.

The master bedroom ("the greate chamber") stood over the parlour and held an oak bedstead with a feather bed upon it, and beside it another truckle bed. A small oak cupboard stood under the window with its green serge curtains. There were five other bedrooms similarly furnished but with bright rugs on the floor, one in green, one crimson and one in chequered pattern. The kitchen was well supplied with cupboards, dressers and shelves on which were stacked pots of pewter, iron and brass, copper and brass kettles, dripping pans, frying pans and spits. The two butteries and two larders held the food and the beer. The establishment was run rather like a small holding with five cows, two horses, two pigs and numerous chickens. In their own barn and another at Barham the family held £190 worth of wheat, oats and barley, no doubt the product of the tithe.[5] It was well supplied, therefore, against the next famine.

And famine was not so remote a prospect in the mid-1590s. For although the threat of foreign invasion and the overturning of the religious order had largely evaporated, the country now faced a serious economic downturn with a spate of wet summers and poor harvests, particularly bad in the years 1594-6, and the resultant social unrest in the shape of food riots and increased vagrancy. Intervention in the market by the municipalities did not solve the problems of local food supply. In 1597 the mayor of Canterbury complained that the shortage of grain there was so bad "the poorest folk and a great part of the people being of some small wealth are like to starve".[6] A local ballad of 1594 provides an image of poverty and starvation in its title alone: *The Kentish Miracle or a strange and miraculous work of God's providence showed to a poor distressed widow and her seven small fatherless children who lived by a burnt six-penny loaf of bread and a little water for above seven weeks in the Wild of Kent*. The miraculous burnt loaf was the chance gift of a baker's boy who happened to take pity on her.[7]

Near-famine brought with it the return of plague and most clergymen in England were soon burying more and baptising less. The epidemic hit Canterbury hardest in the late summer of 1595, just a few months after Hooker's arrival, and by July the villagers in the country roundabout were boycotting Canterbury shops for fear of infection.[8] Yet Hooker, who had spent recent summers evacuating his family to Enfield to escape the London plague, now found himself in an altogether different world which, though feeling the pinch of bad harvests, was far removed from the major social upheavals felt in the capital. As he walked out of his rectory of a morning, past the church and down into the village, he could smell a different air from that of London.

In painting the picture of Hooker's new role as country clergyman, Walton continues to over press the saintly image, albeit with warts and all. What the villagers saw was "an obscure, harmless man; a man in poor clothes, his loins usually girt in a coarse gown, or canonical coat; of a mean stature, and stooping, and yet more lowly in the thoughts of his soul: his body worn out, not with age, but study and holy mortifications; his face full of heat pimples, begot by his inactivity and sedentary life". He was both humble and shy, in support of which Walton gives us the celebrated image of his encounters with Sampson Horton, his devoted parish clerk, each man wishing to defer to the other: "God and nature blessed him with so blessed a bashfulness, that as in his younger days his pupils might easily look him out of countenance; so neither then, nor in his age, did he ever willingly look any man in the face; and was of so mild and humble a nature, that his poor parish-clerk and he did never talk but with both their hats on, or both off, at the same time...".[9]

Life soon settled down to the novel duties of the rural parish priest. Hooker had swapped for parishioners the clever and arrogant lawyers of the Temple for the simple peasants of Borne; he could handle both on their own level, but there was no doubting whom he liked best. Elizabeth had been on the throne for almost forty years and Protestantism was now an accepted part of parish life, but despite the increase in preachers the majority of villagers in rural parishes were not attuned to new-fangled doctrines of justification by faith but still held to the simple Catholic beliefs in the efficacy of prayer and good works, albeit now within the context of a thoroughly Prayer Book world. Though an intellectual theologian, Hooker with his liberal doctrinal outlook and charity towards the poor and meek was just the right person to minister to such a congregation. He was an active pastor, always to be seen about the village. In an age when sickness and death were ever present, he was assiduous in attending his parishioners in their own homes: "He was diligent to inquire who of his parish were sick, or any ways distressed, and would often visit them, unsent for; supposing that the fittest time to discover to them those errors, to which health and prosperity had blinded them... . and at his entrance or departure out of any house, he would usually speak to the whole family, and bless them by name".[10]

Sickness and death were no strangers to his home either. In the autumn of their first year at Bishopsbourne, Joan Hooker fell pregnant once more after a (for her unaccustomed) gap of two years. Her son, named Edwin after the Sandys, was baptised at the Churchmans' family church in London in June 1596; but he survived little longer than his brother Richard, dying at the Churchmans' Enfield house in July 1597, barely a year old. In all, Hooker had two sons who died in infancy and four daughters who survived into maturity – in the infant mortality statistics of the sixteenth century there was little doubt which was the weaker sex. He felt the pain of loss keenly, but in a Christian spirit of acceptance. "No," he wrote, "God will have them that shall walk in light, to feel now and then what it is to sit in the shadow of death." And he spoke words from the pulpit that underlined the family sorrow: "Can a mother forget her child? Surely, a mother will hardly forget her child".[11]

At a time when intelligent, university educated priests were still comparatively thin upon the ground, the village was fortunate indeed to have for its instruction one of the foremost theological brains of the age. We do not have record of the sermons he preached in the little church of St Mary in Bishopsbourne, for they (we assume) were simple advocacies tailored to the understanding of his largely peasant congregation, not the closely argued theological texts that have been handed down from his years in the Temple.[12] We have only Walton's word for how his village sermons were conducted. Such was his humility that he never eyeballed his listeners, but "though he was not purblind, yet he was short or weak-sighted: and where he fixed his eyes at the beginning of his sermon, there they continued till it was ended …"[13]

> His use was to preach once every Sunday, and he or his Curate to catechize after the second lesson in the evening prayer. His sermons were neither long nor earnest, but uttered with a great zeal, and an humble voice: his eyes always fixed on one place, to prevent imagination from wandering; insomuch, that he seemed to study as he spake. The design of his sermons (as indeed of all his discourses) was to show reasons for what he spake; and with these reasons such a kind of rhetoric, as did rather convince and persuade than frighten men into piety; studying not so much for matter, (which he never

wanted,) as for apt illustrations to inform and teach his unlearned hearers, by familiar examples, and then make them better by convincing applications; never labouring by hard words, and then by needless distinctions and subdistinctions, to amuse his hearers, and get glory to himself; but glory only to God. Which intention, he would often say, "was as discernible in a preacher as a natural from an artificial beauty".[14]

At the customary time of year, he would lead his parishioners in the age-old ceremony of beating the parish bounds, guiding them out of the churchyard, up the beech-lined lane to Watling Street, along the old road to Dover (not in those days in any fear of traffic), and then turning right along the boundary with Kingston parish and back into the village again. On this annual walk, he seemed, according to Walton, to take on an uncharacteristic gaiety: "in which perambulation he would usually express more pleasant discourse than at other times, and would then always drop some loving and facetious observations to be remembered against the next year, especially by the boys and young people; still inclining them, and all his present parishioners, to meekness, and mutual kindnesses and love...".[15]

On the Sunday before each of the four ember weeks of the year, he would remind his parishioners from the pulpit and encourage them to carry out the traditional fast and devotions on the following Wednesday, Friday and Saturday. Walton gives us an intimate picture of how he himself performed these ember day devotions: "And to what he persuaded others, he added his own example of fasting and prayer; and did usually every Ember-week take from the parish-clerk the key of the church-door, into which place he retired every day, and locked himself up for many hours; and did the like most Fridays and other days of fasting".[16]

But the saintly hermit, incarcerated in his church, is not the only picture of Hooker in these days. With the publication of the first four books of the *Polity*, he was now a theologian of international renown. Walton recounts how the *Polity* was introduced to Pope Clement VIII by Cardinal Allen and Dr Stapleton, two English Catholic clerics, telling him that "though he [*the Pope*] has lately said he never met with an English book, whose writer deserved the name of author; yet there now appeared a wonder to them, and it would be so to his Holiness, if it were in Latin; for a poor obscure English Priest had writ four such books of Laws, and Church polity, and in a style that expressed such a grave and so humble a majesty, with such clear demonstration of reason, that in all their readings they had not met with any that exceeded them". Stapleton read the whole of the first book to the Pope, translating into Latin as he went, at the conclusion of which the Pope is said to have remarked: "There is no learning that this man has not searched into: nothing too hard for his understanding: this man indeed deserves the name of an author: his books will get reverence by age; for there is in them such seeds of eternity, that if the rest be like this, they shall last till the last fire shall consume all learning".[17]

What more can any author ask than to carry in his work the seeds of eternity; and what higher reviewer than the Pope? With puffs like this, it is not surprising that he was not left too long in his new parsonage to fast and pray alone.

> This parsonage of Borne is from Canterbury three miles, and near to the common road that leads from that city to Dover; in which parsonage Mr. Hooker had not been twelve months, but his books, and the innocence and sanctity of his life became so remarkable, that many turned out of the road, and others (scholars especially) went purposely to see the man, whose life and learning were so much admired...[18]

Oxford and London friends would drop in for a weekend in the country; and in particular Edwin Sandys and George Cranmer who still retained their professional role as anxious collaborators in the *magnum opus* that still remained to be finished. It was their continued input, in fact, that contributed most to the delay.

One new theological friend, the soulmate and intellectual recharger of the last years of his life, was local. Adrian Saravia, then 72 and a generation older than Hooker, had recently been appointed a canon of Canterbury cathedral. He was the most prominent Dutch theologian living in England in Tudor times, favoured and supported by Leicester and others in the Elizabethan court and by Archbishop Whitgift himself. Though starting life as a leader in the Calvinist Church in the Netherlands, he had been drawn to England by a growing belief in the episcopal basis of the Church there, and this became the specialist area of theology in which he chose to work. Like Hooker, his name was made by a book – *Of the Diverse Degrees of Ministers of the Gospel* – published in 1591 while Hooker was still at the Temple. It caused a sensation with its claim that God himself had established the role of bishops in the Church and that therefore their authority sprang directly from Him. Saravia was thus playing much the same role as Hooker as one of the great intellectual apologists of the emergent Anglicanism.

On their new found friendship Walton once more waxes lyrical: "in this year of 1595, and in this place of Borne, these two excellent persons began a holy friendship, increasing daily to so high and mutual affections, that their two wills seemed to be but one and the same; and their designs both for the glory of God, and peace of the Church, still assisting and improving each other's virtues, and the desired comforts of a peaceable piety...".[19] But the friendship had a more practical down-to-earth advantage. Both men could with regularity bounce off each other their theological propositions and discuss their latest writing, and Saravia, on the same theological wave-length, was the perfect sounding-board for the principal object of Hooker's final years of life – the amendment and completion of the last four books of his *Polity*.

Books VI to VIII, which covered broad swathes of church politics – in order, ecclesiastical jurisdiction and the use of lay elders; the episcopal system; the relations between church and state – were all ones (especially Books VII and VIII) in which Saravia had a special expertise, and could make a potent contribution. But they were also politically contentious and (as we have seen) the source of some continuing argument between Hooker and his friends Cranmer and Sandys, which was to delay their completion and publication until after Hooker's death. They were thus to prove a source of anxiety throughout his final years, and deal the ultimate blow when he came to realise that he would never live to see them in print.

Book V was quite another kettle of fish. It was to be his explanation and defence of the faith and practice of the Church of England, from the reasons for building churches right down to the purpose and feeling behind the minutest aspects of liturgy and ceremonial. It is his most lasting contribution to the Anglican tradition, the most complete and inspirational *raison d'être* for the Church he loved. If Book I is the bible for the intellectual theologian, Book V is the prayer book for the common worshipper. Church prayer and practice was the part of church polity closest to Hooker's heart; he was not by any means a wholehearted political polemicist, and the joy of Book V was that it contained scarcely any politics, on which friends like Sandys and Cranmer might push their personal points. Hooker could frame and compose it entirely on his own, and it is thus as pure and undiluted an expression of his personal thinking on the subjects he cared most deeply about as we shall ever see. Though a first draft had undoubtedly been written by 1593, he gave the first two years at Bishopsbourne to further work on it and there is no doubt that he wrote much new material from his country window there. As with Proust, his love of the subject matter rather carried him away, and he ultimately gave birth to a completed work many times longer than the initial draft. When published in 1597, this his final contribution from the Kent countryside weighed in with more words than the first four books put together.

He starts with a sigh of resignation as he contemplates the weight of the task before him; now in his country retreat, he has dispensed with the confrontational polemics of the Temple and aims, as befits a person in retirement from the world, at a quietly rational explanation of where the opposition has gone wrong.

> Few there are of so weake capacitie but publique evels they easilie espie; Fewer so patient, as not to complaine, when the greivous inconveniences thereof woorke sensible smart. Howbeit to see wherein the harme which they feele consisteth, the seedes from which it sprang, and the method of curing it, belongeth to a skill, the studie whereof is so full of toyle, and the practise so besett with difficulties, that warie and respective men had rather seeke quietlie theire owne, and wish that the world may goe well, so it be not longe of them, then, with paine and hazard, make themselves advisers for the common good. Wee which thought it at the verie first a signe of colde affection towardes the Church of God, to preferre private ease before the labour of appeasinge publique disturbance, must now, of necessitie, referre eventes to the gracious providence of almightie God, and, in discharge of our dutie towardes him, proceede with the plaine, and unpartiall defense of a common cause. Wherein our endevour is not so much to overthrowe them with whome wee contend, as to yeeld them just and reasonable causes of those thinges, which, for want of due consideration heretofore, they misconceyved. .[20]

In true Hooker style, he starts with the philosophical principles on which the public ordering of church affairs should be based, and then swiftly gets down to practical matters — a defence of the building of churches against those nonconformists "who bite asunder theire owne tounges with verie wrath that they have not as yet the power to pull downe the temples which they never built, and to levell them with the ground".[21] He strongly defended the sumptuous building and decoration of churches in honouring the sublime majesty of God:

"Can wee judge it a thinge seemelie for anie man to goe aboute the buildinge of an howse to the God of heaven with no other appearance, then if his ende were to reare up a kitchen, or a parlor, for his owne use?.... Touchinge God him selfe, hath he anie where revealed that it his delight to dwell beggerlie? and that he taketh no pleasure to be worshiped, savinge onlie in poore cotages?" [22] He ends the discussion peremptorily and with a stroke of the pen writes off the anti-church builders by comparing them with pagans of old.

> Thus much it maie suffice to have written in defense of those Christian oratories, the overthrow and ruine whereof is desired, not now by infidels Pagans or Turkes, but by a speciall refined sect of Christian beleevers pretending them selves exceedinglie greived at our solemnities in erecting Churches, at the names which we suffer them to hold, at theire forme and fashion, at the statelines of them and costlines, at the opinion which we have of them, and at the manifold superstitious abuses whereunto they have bene putt. [23]

Much space is devoted in the early part of Book V to the Puritan emphasis on preaching as the indispensable form of Christian instruction and their attack on the Anglican practice of "bare" reading from the Bible. Here Hooker, as throughout the work, displays his learning by drawing on the history of the growth of the scriptures, betraying much time spent among the riches of the cathedral library in nearby Canterbury. In discussing the reading of the Apocrypha as lessons in church, we are given a rare example of the author's own personal predilection, but humbly balanced, as ever, with the predilections of others.

> Which bookes in case my selfe did thinke, as some others doe, safer and better to be left publiquelie unred, neverthelesse as in other thinges of like nature even so

in this, my privat judgment I should be loth to oppose against the force of theire reverende authoritie, who rather consideringe the divine excellencie of some thinges in all, and of all thinges in certaine of those '*Apocrypha*' which we publiquelie reade, have thought it better to let them stand as a list or marginall border unto the old testament, and, though with divine, yeat as humane compositions to graunt at the least unto certaine of them publique audience in the house of God.[24]

Yet he is robust enough when attacking Puritans like Cartwright who pour scorn upon the Apocrypha.

Yeat as men through too much hast oftentimes forgett the errande whereabout they should goe: So here it appeareth that an eager desire to rake together whatsoever might prejudice or anie way hinder the credit of Apocryphall bookes, hath caused the collectors pen so to runne as it were on wheles, that the minde which should guide it had no leasure to thinke, whether that which might happelie serve to withhold from giving them thauthoritie which belongeth unto sacred scripture, and to cut them of from the canon, would as effectuallie serve to shut them altogether out of the Church, and to withdraw from grauntinge unto them that publique use wherein they are onlie helde as profitable for instruction.[25]

On the principal controversy between preaching and bare reading, Hooker has nothing against preaching as a mainstay of Christian worship: "So worthie a part of divine service we should greatlie wronge, if we did not esteeme preachinge as the blessed ordinance of God, sermons as keyes to the kingdom of heaven, as winges to the soule, as spurres to the good affections of man, unto the sound and healthie as foode, as phisicke unto diseased mindes".[26] But he takes issue with Cartwright's contention that simple reading of Scripture is not necessary in the church; and searches in ironical vein for a word lower than "necessary" on the scale of dispensability. Here Hooker shows off his mastery of English vocabulary as well as his sense of humour: "Shall we therefore to please them chaunge the word 'Necessary', and saie that it hath bene a commendable order, a custome verie expedient, or an ordinance most profitable (whereby they knowe right well that we meane exceedinglie behoofull), to reade the word of God at large in the Church, whether it be as our manner is, or as theires is whome they preferre before us?" [27]

He now turns from preaching to prayer, and we find Hooker once more glorying in the joys of Christian practice with a compellingly lyrical definition.

> Prayers are those caulves of mens lippes; those most gracious and sweet odors; those rich presentes and guiftes which beinge carryed up into heaven doe best testifie our dutifull affection, and are for the purchasinge of all favour at the handes of God the most undoubted meanes we can use. On others what more easilie, and yeat what more fruitefullie bestowed then our prayers? If we give counsell, they are the simpler onlie that neede it; if almes, the poorer onlie are relieved; but by prayer we doe good to all. And whereas everie other dutie besides is but to show it selfe as time and opportunitie require, for this all times are convenient. When we are not able to doe anie other thinges for mens behoofe, when through maliciousnes or unkindnes they vouchafe not to accept any other good at our handes, prayer is that which we alwaies have in our power to bestowe and they never in theires to refuse.[28]

And public prayer is more valuable than private prayer because of its social benefits, and since it is a public spectacle it must be conducted with solemnity and grace, unlike the ragged extempore praying of the nonconformists.

> When we publiquely make our prayers, it cannot be but that we doe it with much more comforte then in privat, for that the thinges we aske publiquely are approved as needfull and good in the judgment of all, we heare them sought for and desired with common consent. Againe, thus much helpe and furtherance is more yeelded, in that if so be our zeale and devotion to Godward be slack, the alacritie and fervor of others serveth as a present spurre... A great parte of the cause, wherefore religious mindes are so inflamed with the love of publique devotion, is that vertue, force and efficacie, which by experience they finde that the verie forme and reverende solemnitie of common prayer dulie ordered hath, to help that imbecillitie and weakenes in us, by meanes whereof we are otherwise of our selves the lesse apt to performe unto God so heavenlie a service, with such affection of harte, and disposition in the powers of our soules as is requisite. To this ende therefore all thinges hereunto apperteininge have bene ever thought convenient to be don with the most sollemnitie and majestie that the wisest could devise. It is not with publique as with privat prayer. In this rather secretie is commended then outward show, whereas that beinge the publique Act of a whole societie requireth accordinglie more care to be had of externall appearance. The verie assemblinge of men therefore unto this service hath bene ever sollemne.[29]

Hooker is celebrated as a major stylist in the English language, even among those who have never read him. The most notable aspect of his style is his period, the long sentence made up of subordinate clauses hanging perilously over the cliff until the suspended main clause finally explodes at the end to provide the resolution. This is a Latin rather than an English construction and fully attests that Hooker was of that generation, possibly the last in England, equally at home in both languages. Though sometimes difficult to the modern eye, the grammatical tensions worked up by this construction intensify the reader's expectations as the sentence builds towards its climax, and the climax as a result increases in persuasive force, both emotionally and intellectually. Probably the best known and most frequently quoted passage in the *Polity* is the sentence in Book I where Hooker surmises what would become of man if nature gave up and all the lights in the universe went out, a passage cited as illustration of the Elizabethan sense of an ordered cosmos.

> Now if nature should intermit her course, and leave altogether, though it were but for a while, the observation of her own lawes: if those principall and mother elements of the world, whereof all things in this lower world are made, should loose the qualities which now they have, if the frame of that heavenly arch erected over our heads should loosen and dissolve it selfe: if celestiall spheres should forget their wonted motions and by irregular volubilitie, turne themselves any way as it might happen: if the prince of the lightes of heaven which now as a Giant doth runne his unwearied course, should as it were through a languishing faintnes begin to stand and to rest himselfe: if the Moone should wander from her beaten way, the times and seasons of the yeare blend themselves by disordered and confused mixture, the winds breath out their last gaspe, the cloudes yeeld no rayne, the earth be defeated of heavenly influence, the fruites of the earth pine away as children at the withered breasts of their mother no longer able to yeeld

them reliefe, what would become of man himselfe, whom these things now do all serve?[30]

Though celebrated as a piece of Elizabethan English, this is somewhat atypical of the Hooker period. Normally his long suspended sentences are built up of closely argued logical relationships, and the deftly interlocking subordinate clauses themselves give power to the intellectual argument. In such cases, Hooker's rhetorical style is part and parcel of his intellectual apparatus.[31]

Hooker uses this style, even where the main clause is not suspended, to build lists – whether of words, ideas, arguments – to produce an effect of accelerating power. The mountain is built to an internal rhythm which gives a poetic feeling of crescendo. A good example to be found in Book V is his listing of the objections of the Puritans to the (relatively) new *Book of Common Prayer*, a matter which is closest to Hooker's heart. The choice of words and the emotional commitment of this passage gives rise to some fine writing, reminiscent of the style of the *Authorized Version* of fourteen years later.

> *Grosse errors and manifest impietie* they graunt we have *taken awaie*. Yeat many thinges in it they say are amisse, many instances they give of thinges in our common prayer not agreeable as they pretend with the word of God. It hath in theire eye too great affinitie with the forme of the Church of Rome; it differeth too much from that which Churches elswhere reformed allowe and observe; our attyre disgraceth it; it is not orderlie read nor gestured as beseemeth; it requireth nothing to be don which a child may not lawfullie do; it hath a number of shorte cuttes or shreddinges which may be better called wishes then prayers; it intermingleth prayinges and readinges in such manner as if Supplicantes should use in proposinge theire sutes unto mortall princes, all the world would judge them mad; it is too longe and by that meane abridgeth

preachinge; it appointeth the people to say after the minister; it spendith time in singing and in readinge the psalmes by corse from side to side; it useth the Lords prayer too oft; the songs of *Magnificat, Benedictus* and *Nunc dimittis* it might verie well spare; it hath the Latanie, the Creed of Athanasius and *Gloria patri*, which are superfluous; it craveth earthlie thinges too much; for deliverance from those evels against which we pray it giveth no thankes; some thinges it asketh unseasonablie when they need not to be prayed for, as deliverance from thunder and tempest when no daunger is nigh; some in too abject and diffident manner, as that God would give us that which we for our unworthines dare not aske; some which ought not to be desired, as the deliverance from suddaine death, riddance from all adversitie, and the extent of savinge mercie towardes all men. These and such like are the imperfections, whereby our forme of common prayer is thought to swarve from the word of God.[32]

The more the objections pile up, the more ludicrous and trivial they appear, until this becomes a list predisposing the reader *in favour of* the form of common prayer. But this 250-word sentence is not just a flight of stylistic fancy; it serves rather as an index to the succeeding chapters of the book, for Hooker now proceeds to take up each one of the objections and demolish them with philosophy, historical precedent or merely withering scorn.

Even on the minutiae of "things indifferent", like the wearing of vestments, he spends time and trouble (and many words) both to demolish hostile arguments and promote favourable ones. In contradiction again of Cartwright's views on the wearing of the surplice as "especially unmeete",[33] Hooker comes out fighting: "as wee thinke not our selves the holier because we use it, so neither should they with whome no such thinge is in use thinke us therefore unholie, because we submitt our selves unto that, which in a matter so indifferent the wisdom of authoritie and lawe hath thought comlie. To solemne actions of roialtie and justice theire suteable ornamentes are a bewtie. Are they onlie in religion a staine?" [34] In other words, if dressing up is good enough for kings and judges, why not for vicars too?

But the surplice is not just comely; it represents positive values – our love and reverence for God. "The wise man which feared God from his harte, and honoured the service that was don unto him, could not mention so much as the garmentes of holines but with effectuall signification of most singular reverence and love. Were it not better that the love which men beare to God should make the least thinges that are imployed in his service amiable, than that theire over scrupulous dislike of so meane a thinge as a vestment should from the verie service of God withdrawe theire hartes and affections?" [35] There is so much advantage to be gained from "that Church-attyre which with us for the most parte is usuall in publique prayer; our ecclesiasticall lawes so appointinge, as well because it hath bene of reasonable continewance, and by speciall choice was taken out of the number of those holie garmentes, which (over and besides theire mysticall reference) served for comlines under the lawe, and is in the number of those ceremonies, which may with choice and discretion be used to that purpose in the Church of Christ; as also for that it suteth so fitlie with that lightsome affection of joye, wherein God delighteth when his Sainctes praise him...". [36]

Having disposed of the question of the surplice, he is even more peremptory in handling the more minute questions of stance and gesture at divine service – the questions when to kneel, when to sit, when to stand, whether the priest should face the congregation or not. Now that the mass, altars, rood lofts and images had all gone in the process of reform, these finer points of worship were all that was left for the more zealous reformers to press; but while all these were "things indifferent", they, rather than the political doctrines handed down from on high, were the issues on which the several Reformations of the Tudor period were fought out and ultimately decided at parish level. The presence of an altar or a communion table in your parish church told you more clearly than anything else whether Catholics or Protestants were in local charge. By the 1590s, the physical battles over altars, crosses and statues of Our Lady were very much a thing of the past and what was left of these controversies could well be regarded as unworthy of debate.

> ...the next question whereinto wee are drawne is, whether it be a thinge allowable or no that the minister should say service in the chancell, or tourne his face at any tyme from the people, or before service ended remove from the place where it was begun. By them which trouble us with these doubtes we would more willinglie be resolved of a greater doubt, whether it be not a kinde of takinge Gods name in vaine to debase religion with such frivolous disputes, a sinne to bestowe time and labour about them. Thinges of so meane regarde and qualitie, although necessarie to be ordered, are notwithstandinge verie unsavourie when they com to be disputed of; because disputation presupposeth some difficultie in the matter which is argued, whereas in thinges of this nature they must be either verie simple or verie froward who neede to be taught by disputation what is meete. When we make profession of oure faith wee stand; when we acknowledge our sinnes, or seeke unto God for favour, we fall downe, because the gesture of constancie becometh us best in the one, in the other the behavior of humilitie.[37]

The complaints he responds to become more and more refined. Cartwright had objected to the congregation repeating prayers after the minister whereby "the time is unprofitablie wasted, and a confused noise of the people one speakinge after an other caused".[38] Hooker rejects the arguments and then dismisses the objectors as beneath concern: "The reasons which we have alleaged induce us to thinke it still *a good worke* which they in theire pensive care for the well bestowinge of time accompt *wast*. As for unpleasantnes of sound if it happen, the good of mens soules doth either deceive our eares that we note it not, or arme them with patience to indure it. Wee are not so nice as to cast away a sharp knife because the edge of it maie sometimes grate. And such suttle opinions as few but Utopians are likelie to fall into, we in this clymate doe not greatelie feare".[39]

When confronting the nonconformist objection to the frequent use of Psalms in the Anglican service and, in particular, the arch-crime of setting them to music, Hooker offers up a sigh of despair: "I am not able to expresse how much it doth grive me, that thinges of principall excellencie should be thus bitten at, by men whom God hath indued with graces both of witt and learning for better purposes".[40] But here he turns the tables on the Puritans by moving from a negative demolition of their arguments to a forthright espousal of divine service as practised in the Church of England, an open rejoicing in the wonder of the Psalms, of the music to accompany them (in which Hooker had a special expertise),[41] and in the joy of priest and people as they, in mutual harmony, offer up their prayers to God. These are some of the most inspired passages in all eight books of the *Polity*, couched in the most perfect English.

First, Hooker on the Psalms.

> What is there necessarie for man to knowe which the psalmes are not able to teach? They are to beginners an easie and familiar introduction, a mightie augmentation of all vertue and knowledge in such as are entered before, a stronge confirmation to the most perfect amongst others. Heroicall magnanimitie, exquisite justice, grave moderation, exacte wisdom, repentance unfained, unwearied patience, the mysteries of God, the sufferinges of Christ, the terrors of wrath, the comfortes of grace, the workes of providence over this

world and the promised joyes of that world which is to
come, all good necessarilie to be either knowne or don
or had, this one celestiall fountaine yeldeth. Let there
be any griefe or disease incident into the soule of man,
anie wounde or sicknes named, for which there is not in
this treasure house a present comfortable remedie at all
tymes readie to be found. Hereof it is that we covet to
make the psalmes especiallie familiar unto all. This is
the verie cause why we iterate the psalmes oftner then
any other parte of scripture besides, the cause wherefore
wee inure the people together with theire minister and
not the minister alone to reade them as other partes of
scripture he doth.[42]

Next, Hooker on music.

Touchinge musicall harmonie whether by instrument
or by voice, it beinge but of high and low in soundes a
due proportionable disposition, such notwithstandinge is
the force thereof and so pleasinge effectes it hath even in
that verie parte of man which is most divine, that some
have bene thereby induced to thinke that the soule it
selfe by nature is, or hath in it harmonie. A thinge which
delighteth all ages and beseemeth all states; a thinge as
seasonable in griefe as in joy; as decent beinge added unto
actions of greatest waight and solemnitie, as beinge used
when men most sequester them selves from action. The
reason hereof is an admirable facilitie which musique hath
to expresse and represent to the minde more inwardlie
then any other sensible meane the verie standinge risinge
and fallinge, the verie stepes and inflections everie
way, the turnes and varieties of all passions whereunto
the minde is subject: yea so to imitate them, that
whither it resemble unto us the same state wherein our

246

mindes alreadie are or a cleane contrarie, wee are not more contentedlie by the one confirmed then changed and led away by thother. In harmonie the verie image and character even of vertue and vice is perceived, the minde delighted with theire resemblances and brought by havinge them often iterated into a love of the thinges them selves. For which cause there is nothinge more contagious and pestilent then some kindes of harmonie; then some nothinge more stronge and potent unto good. And that there is such a difference of one kinde from another wee neede no proofe but our own experience, in as much as we are at the hearinge of some more inclyned unto sorrowe and heavines; of some, more mollified and softned in minde; one kinde apter to staie and settle us, another to move and stirre our affections; there is that draweth to a mervelous grave and sober mediocritie, there is also that carryeth as it were into ecstasies, fillinge the minde with an heavenlie joy and for the time in a maner severinge it from the bodie. So that although we lay altogether aside the consideration of dittie or matter, the verie harmonie of soundes beinge framed in due sorte and carryed from the eare to the spirituall faculties of our soules is by a native puissance and efficacie greatlie availeable to bringe to a perfect temper whatsoever is there troubled, apt as well to quicken the spirites as to allaye that which is too eger, soveraigne against melancholie and despaire, forcible to drawe forth teares of devotion if the minde be such as can yeld them, able both to move and to moderate all affections.[43]

Last, Hooker on the Psalms set to music.

a thinge whereunto Gods people of old did resort with hope and thirst that thereby especiallie theire soules might be edified; a thinge which filleth the minde with comefort and heavenly delight, stirreth up flagrant desires and affections correspondent unto that which the wordes conteine, allaieth all kinde of base and earthly cogitations, banisheth and driveth awaie those evell secret suggestions which our invisible enimie is alwaies apt to minister, watreth the harte to the ende it may fructifie, maketh the vertuous in troble full of magnanimitie and corage, serveth as a most approved remedie against all dolefull and heavie accidentes which befall men in this present life, to conclude, so fitlie accordeth with thapostles own exhortation *Speake to your selves in psalmes and hymnes and spirituall songs, makinge melodie and singinge to the Lord in your hartes*, that surelie there is more cause to feare least the want thereof be a maime then the use a blemish to the service of god.[44]

In this heightened mood, Hooker simply rejoices in the glories of divine service itself and the interaction of minister with congregation, as they sing or recite the psalms and prayers together, answering one another "by course". And we see how it must have been for the ageing scholar in the pulpit of the little church of St Mary as he gazed upon his small peasant flock, or rather gazed shyly through them to the vacant spot above their heads. Here the writer is writing from life.

And if the Prophet David did thinke that the verie meetinge of men together, and theire accompanyinge one an other to the howse of God, should make the bonde of theire love insoluble, and tye them in a league of inviolable amitie, how much more may we judge it reasonable to hope, that the like effectes may growe in each of the people towardes other, in them all towardes theire pastor, and in theire pastor towardes everie of them, betwene whome there dailie and

248

interchangeablie passe, in the hearinge of God him selfe, and in the presence of his holie Angels so manie heavenlie acclamations, exultations, provocations, petitions, songes of comforte, psalmes of prayese and thankesgivinge, in all which particulars, as when the pastor maketh theire sutes, and they with one voice testifie a generall assent thereunto; or when he joyfullie beginneth and they with like alacritie followe, dividinge betwene them the sentences wherewith they strive which shall most showe his own and stirre up others zeale to the glorie of that God whose name they magnifie; or when he proposeth unto God theire necessities and they theire own requestes for reliefe in everie of them; or when he lifteth up his voice like a trumpet to proclaime unto them the lawes of God, they adjoyninge though not as Israel did by way of generalitie a cheerfull promise *All that the Lord hath commanded wee will doe*, yeat that which God doth no lesse approve, that which savoureth more of meekenes, that which testifieth rather a feelinge knowledge of our common imbecillitie, unto the severall branches thereof severall lowlie and humble requestes for grace at the mercifull handes of God to performe the thinge which is commanded; or when they wish reciprocallie ech others ghostlie happines; or when he by exhortation raiseth them up and they by protestation of theire readines declare he speaketh not in vaine unto them; these interlocutorie formes of speech what are they els but most effectuall partlie testifications and partlie inflammations of all pietie?[45]

We have seen how on a high holiday Hooker would lead his villagers joyfully round the parish boundaries, and how he would lock himself with sorrowful solemnity into the church for his ember day fasts. Both fast days and feast days (what he would call festival days) he embraced with equal fervour; both were opportunities to give service to God. A feast day was the day which the Lord had made, so let man rejoice and be glad in it. "So that generallie offices and duties of religious *joy* are that wherein the hallowing of festivall times consisteth. The most naturall testimonies of our rejoycinge in God are first his praises sett forth with cheerefull alacritie of minde, secondlie our comforte and delight expressed by a charitable largenes of somewhat more then common bountie, thirdlie sequestration from ordinarie labors, the toiles and cares whereof are not meete to be companions of such gladnes. Festivall solemnitie therefore is nothing but the due mixture as it were of these three elementes, praise, and bountie, and rest".[46]

In addressing the last of these in a serious tone, Hooker begins to expound his own personal philosophy of work. "Rest is the end of all motion and the last perfection of all thinges that labor. Labors in us are jorneyes, and even in them which feele no wearines by anie worke yeat they are but waies whereby to come unto that which bringeth not happines till it doe bring rest. For as long as anie thing which wee desire is unattained, wee rest not. Let us not here take rest for idlenes. They are idle whome the painefullnes of action causeth to avoide those labors, whereunto both God and nature bindeth them: they rest which either cease from theire worke when they have brought it unto perfection, or els give over a meaner labor because a worthier and better is to be undertaken. God hath created nothing to be idle or ill imployed. As therefore man doth consist of different and distinct partes, everie part indued with manifold habilities which all have theire severall endes and actions thereunto referred; so there is in this greate varietie of duties which belonge to men that dependencie and order, by meanes whereof the lower sustaining alwaies the more excellent, and the higher perfecting the more base, they are in theire times and seasons continued with most exquisite correspondence, labours of bodilie and dailie toile purchase freedom for actions of religious joy, which benefit these actions requit with the guift of desired rest: a thinge most naturall and fitt to accompanie the solemne festivall duties of honor which are done to God." [47]

Fast days, those days of "pensive humiliation and sorrowe" [48] linked by contrast to the festival days, they too have their own philosophy turning over in the mind of the old scholar as he locks himself inside his church for the duration. "The verie purpose of the Church of God both in the number and in the order of hir fastes hath bene not onlie to preserve thereby throughout all ages the remembrance of miseries heretofore susteined and of the causes in our selves out of which they have arisen, that men considering the one might feare the other the more, but farther also first to temper the minde least contrarie affections coming in place should make it too profuse and dissolute, in which respect it seemeth that fastes have bene sett as the ushers of festivall daies for prevention of those disorders as much as might be wherein notwithstanding the world alwaies will deserve, as it hath don, blame, because such evels being not possible to be rooted out the most wee can doe is in keeping them low; and (which is chieflie the fruite wee looke for) to create in the mindes of men a love towardes frugall and severe life, to undermine the palaces of wantonnes, to plant parcimonie as nature where riotousnes hath bene studie, to harden whome pleasure would melt and to help the tumors which alwaies fulnes breedeth, that children as it were in the wooll of theire infancie died with hardnes maie never afterwardes chaunge coulor; that the poore whose perpetuall fastes are necessitie maie with better contentment endure the hunger which vertue causeth others so often to choose and by advise of religion it selfe so farre to esteeme above the contrarie; that they which for the most part doe lead sensuall and easie lives, they which as the prophet David describeth them are not plagued like other men may by the publique spectacle of all be still put in minde what them selves are; finallie that everie man maie be everie mans dailie guide and example as well by fasting to declare humilitie as by praise to expresse joy in the sight of God...". [49]

Having dealt with churches, preaching and prayer, Hooker completes Book V and his review of public worship with a dissertation on the sacraments. He sets off on a long disquisition on the nature of sacraments: "it seemeth requisite that wee first consider how God is in Christ, then how Christ is in us, and how the sacramentes doe serve to make us pertakers of Christ. In other thinges wee may be more briefe, but the waight of these requireth largenes".[50] And largeness he takes – a further eight chapters – before coming down to the individual sacraments themselves. But when he reaches the sacrament in which we most partake in Christ, Holy Communion, he blenches to take further largeness on the thorny question of transubstantiation: "compared with that successe, which truthe hathe hitherto had, by so bitter conflictes with errours in this point, shall I wishe that men would more give them selves to meditate with silence what wee have by the sacrament, and lesse to dispute of the manner how?" [51]

When he comes to the sacrament of matrimony, leading on to sexual questions, Hooker shows himself, as we might expect from the tone of his theology, in all the conservatism of a true sixteenth century man. It is what we would see today as a nice balance of male chauvinism with patronising condescension, but for all that rather gently and beautifully put. Perhaps Mrs Hooker, after all, should have been endowed with those tougher attributes which Walton and history have (falsely) bestowed on her.

> In this world there can be no societie durable otherwise then onlie by propagation. Albeit therefore single life be a thing more angelicall and divine, yeat sith the replenishing first of earth with blessed inhabitantes and then of heaven with Sainctes everlastinglie praysing God did depend upon conjunction of man and woman, he which made all thinges complete and perfect saw it could not be good to leave man without an helper unto the forealleadged end: In thinges which some furder ende doth cause to be desired choice seemeth rather proportion then absolute perfection of goodnes. So that woman being created for mans sake to be his helper in regard of the end before

mentioned namlie the havinge and the bringing up of children, whereunto it was not possible they should concurre unlesse there were subalternation betweene them, which subalternation is naturallie grounded upon inequalitie, because thinges equall in everie respect are never willinglie directed one by another, woman therefore was even in hir first estat framed by nature not onlie after in time but inferior in excellencie also unto man, howbeit in so due and sweet proportion as being presented before our eyes might be sooner perceyvd then defind. And even herein doth lie the reason why that kind of love which is the perfectest ground of wedlock is seldome able to yeeld anie reason of it selfe.[52]

As we reach the marriage service itself, it can only get worse.

As for the delivering up of the woman either by hir father or some other, wee must note that in ancient times all wemen which had not husbandes nor fathers to governe them had theire tutors without whose authoritie there was no act which they did warrantable. And for this cause they were in mariage delivered unto theire husbandes by others. Which custom reteined hath still this use that it putteth wemen in minde of a dutie whereunto the verie imbecillitie of theire nature and sex doth bind them, namelie to be allwaies directed guided and ordered by others, although our positive lawes doe not tie them now as pupils.[53]

The sacrament of Holy Orders leads Hooker on into an interesting discussion of the motives of men in seeking the ministry, and in seeking preferment after their ordination. It has been a puzzle to historians why Hooker, given his crucial role in establishing the intellectual framework on which the Church of England was founded, was not given higher office in the Church during his lifetime. Even if he were only well known to the highest levels of the hierarchy, it was those men who handed out the ecclesiastical rewards. But it is not so puzzling when one recalls the eagerness with which he had sought to relinquish his duties at the Temple for the peace of a country parish. It can safely be said that, whatever ambition he might have nursed in his youth, once he had tasted church power and its responsibilities, he never sought high office again.

It was perhaps this natural detachment from the desire for preferment that enabled him to empathise with those who hungered after it. Ambition, he argued, was not of itself a retrograde aspiration, it was necessary for the exercise of power and often for the exercise of power competently and diligently. And here Hooker makes an acute observation – that those who claim not to seek preferment may be surreptitiously just as ambitious as those who do. This gives us the hint that the young Oxford tutor, though locked away in his college and keeping his head well down, may himself have secretly harboured thoughts of important offices in the wider world.

> ...wee ought not therefore with the odious name of ambition to traduce and draw into hatred everie poore request or sute wherein men maie seeme to affect honor; seinge that ambition and modestie doe not allwaies so much differ in the marke they shoote at as in the maner of theire prosecutions. Yea even in this maie be error also if wee still imagin them least ambitious which most forbeare to stirre either hand or foote towardes theire own prefermentes. For there are that make an idole of theire greate sufficiencie, and because they surmise the place should be happie that might injoy them, they walke everie where like grave Pageantes observing whether men doe not woonder why so smale accompt is made of so rare worthines, and in case anie other mans

advancement be mentioned they either smile or blush at the mervelous follie of the world which seeth not where dignities should offer them selves. Seinge therefore that sutes after spirituall functions maie be as ambitiouslie forborne as prosecuted, it remaineth that the evenest line of moderation betweene both is neither to follow them *without conscience*, nor *of pride* to withdraw our selves utterlie from them.[54]

Wise and balanced words from someone whose main ambition lay in putting words on a page rather than ordering the lives of others.

Suits for preferment leads Hooker naturally on to the results of such suits, that weak underbelly of Anglican practice which the Dissenters made so much of: the holding of benefices in plurality. This was sensitive territory to Hooker who had held plural absentee livings at Boscombe and Netheravon in the early 90s to allow him to continue with work on the *Polity*. Even more sensitive to his friend Saravia who, while fulfilling his duties as a canon of Canterbury cathedral, held four other livings to which he paid scant attention. As ever from Hooker, one gets a balanced view. He is not opposed to pluralism in principle; what counts is whether the dispensation is justified to meet a higher good, and the manner in which it is exercised. He vehemently objects in the clergy to "that three-fold blot or blemish of notable ignorance, unconscionable absence from the cures whereof men have taken charge, and unsatiable huntinge after spirituall prefermentes without either care or conscience of the publique good".[55]

This was a time when one of the reformed Church's priorities was to improve the quality of priestly instruction by increasing the number of educated clergy out in the parishes, and by the 1590s the policy was bearing demonstrable fruit. For Hooker, therefore, the intellectual quality of the clergy is important and to that end the universities play a vital role, even if those in holy orders there are not actually attached to a particular parish. This is very special Oxbridge pleading. "It hath bene thopinion of wise men and good men heretofore that nothing was ever devised more singularlie beneficiall unto Gods Church then this which our honorable predecessors have to theire endles praise found out by the erecting such houses of studie as those two most famous Universities doe conteine, and by providing that choice wites after reasonable time spent in contemplation maie at the length either enter into that holie vocation for which they had bene so longe nourished and brought up, or els give place and suffer others to succeed in theire roomes, that so the Church maie be allwaies furnished with a number of men whose habilitie being first known by publique triall in Church labors there where men can best judg of them, theire calling afterwardes unto particular charge abroad maie be according." [56]

Pluralism, justifiably in Hooker's view, helps to keep this particular intellectual ship afloat. The urgent problem of college costs and fees has a nicely twenty-first century ring about it. "A third thinge respected both in permittinge absence and also in graunting to some that libertie of addition or pluralitie which necessarilie inforceth theire absence is a meere both just and conscionable regard that as men are in qualitie and as theire services are in waight for the publique good [*who else, after all, could have written the* Polity?], so likewise theire rewardes and incouragmentes by speciall privilege of law might somewhat declare how the state it selfe doth accept theire paines, much abhorringe from theire beastiall and savage rudenes which thinke that oxen should onlie laboure and asses feed. Thus to Readers in universities whose verie paper and booke expenses theire ancient allowances or stipendes at this daie doe either not or hardlie susteine; to governors of colledges least the greate overplus of charges necessarilie inforced upon them by reason of theire place and verie sclenderlie supplied by meanes of that change in the present condition of thinges which theire founders could not foresee; to men cald awaie from theire cures and imploied in waightier businesses either of the Church or common-welth, because to impose upon them a burthen which requireth theire absence and not to release them from the dutie of residence were a kinde of cruell and barbarous injustice; to residentes in cathedrall Churches [*Saravia*] or upon dignities ecclesiasticall, for as much as these beinge roomes of greater hospitalitie places of more respect and consequence then the rest, they are the rather to be furnisht with men of best qualitie, and the men for theire qualities sake to be favoured above others, I say unto all these in regard of theire worth and merit the law hath therefore given leave while them selves beare waightier burthens to supplie inferior by deputation...". [57]

This is not to say that the author does not recognise the opportunities this opens up for abuse. "But, as it fareth in such cases, the gap which for just considerations wee open unto some letteth in others through corrupt practises to whome such favoures were neither meant nor should be communicated. The greatnes of the harvest and the scarcitie of able workmen hath made it necessarie that law should yeld to admitt numbers of men but sclenderlie and meanelie qualified." [58] Pluralism oils the wheels and therefore has its place. Without it the first four books of the *Polity* might not have been ready in 1593.

Before signing off, Hooker cannot resist a final sideswipe at the Puritans, forever finding fault in ecclesiastical matters, and sees them as one symptom of the defects of the modern world. He looks back once more to a golden age where "perfect" men roamed the planet and positive virtue ruled Christian society.

> There is crept into the mindes of men at this daie a
> secret pernicious and pestilent conceipt that the greatest
> perfection of a Christian man doth consist in discoverie
> of other mens faltes, and in witt to discorse of our
> own profession. When the world most abounded with
> just righteous and perfect men, theire chiefest studie
> was the exercise of pietie wherein for theire safest
> direction, they reverentlie harkned to the readinges
> of the law of God, they kept in minde the oracles and

aphorismes of wisdome which tended unto vertuous life, if anie scruple of conscience did trouble them for matter of actions which they tooke in hande nothinge was attempted before counsell and advise were had for feare least rashlie they might offende. Wee are now more confident, not that our knowledg and judgment is riper, but because our desires are an other waie. Theire scope was obedience, ours is skill; theire endevor was reformation of life, our vertue nothinge but to heare gladlie the reproofe of vice; they in the practise of theire religion wearied chieflie theire knees and handes, wee especiallie our eares and tungues. Wee are growne as in manie thinges els so in this to a kinde of intemperancie which (onlie sermons excepted) hath almost brought all other duties of religion out of tast. At the least they are not in that accompt and reputation which they should be.[59]

These are the words of a man in the last years of his life, who has seen action at the coalface of Elizabethan politics, but now looks out on the wider world from his sequestered village and does not relish what he sees and hears of it. Though this now completed book is ready for publication, his work is not yet over. Three more books wait in draft for his attention, and criticism is beginning to stir even of those he has already published four years before. He seems weary of religious controversy which has dogged the last years of his life, but knows he must continue with it until his work is finally complete. He would much prefer now to cast it all aside and walk the beautiful woods and fields caring for his flock, preaching to them in the village church, writing sermons of virtue rather than harsh polemic, as he looks out from his study window to embrace the real world – that of his tiny parish.

CHAPTER 10

Last Days

Do take care of yourself – or get someone to do it. People
keep on dying now and hideously.

Yvonne Kapp to Jocelyn Brooke 12 April 1965[1]

Almost four hundred years span the time the three writers lived in
the village, the latter two aware of its literary heritage but with no
particular interest in it. They had come there entirely by chance –
Hooker through his presentation to the living by the Queen, Conrad
on an afternoon house-hunting trip, and Brooke because his parents
happened to rent a holiday cottage. It became a part of all three lives
just because it was there. They had come as an escape from a life of
action: Hooker from the political turmoils of the Temple; Conrad,
though more distantly, from twenty years grappling with the dangers
of the sea; and Brooke from the hazards and futility of world war.
Each life of action had been the direct inspiration of their writing;
when they arrived in the village, it was principally to write.

But the place meant quite different things to each, and played a
different role in their writing lives. For Conrad, it was just another
village with a showy, but none too convenient, house; he could take
it or leave it, and indeed was just about to leave it when he died.
Its main attraction was its existence in the Kent countryside he so
loved, bringing back as he grew older nostalgic memories of The Pent
where his run of great novels was written, and Capel House where
his maturing family spent its happiest years. At the opposite end of

the spectrum stands Brooke. For him, the village was his childhood, and his childhood, which never left him, was the prime material of his books. To imagine Brooke without Bishopsbourne would be to imagine Proust without Illiers. The village sustained him directly as a writer, for in it he wrote all his major works: by writing in the birthplace of his nostalgia, though with the objectivity conferred by the present at forty years on, he had conquered the problem of time by removing the issue of space. He could write compellingly about the past with controlled emotion because he was, in a physical sense, still living in it. Hooker stands between these two extremes. What he desired in life was not a particular parish, or village, or rectory, but freedom from politico-theological wrangling which, from his minimal experience of parochial life, he knew could be found in a country living. His demands were generalised and simple: the countryside and peace. He found the perfect spot for both in the beauty of the Elham Valley and the stillness of the Barham Downs.

The impact of the place upon their actual writing there was a reflection of their feeling for it. Immersed in the religious and social duties of a parish priest, life in Borne was quite different for Hooker from his seven years in the tense and hectic atmosphere of the Temple. There he preached in abstraction about the finer theological points of the Christian worship; here he lived and directed that worship in its simple detail among the rustic peasantry who, rather than the middle-class lawyers of the Temple, formed the principal congregation of the English Church. Thus it was that he was able to take up the thin draft of Book V and, like Proust, swell it with new and riveting material created out of the lived experience. His loving descriptions in perfect English prose of church accoutrements and daily discipline, of the purpose of preaching, of prayer, of the holy sacraments, all sprang from the actual experience of what went on there within the walls of St Mary's church.

The place had little direct influence on Conrad's work, for his creative imagination was far away in time and place, taking its sustenance from the Mediterranean of the Napoleonic era as he

260

laboured painfully on with his two last books – *The Rover* and the unfinished *Suspense*. But these, as he knew, were not to be compared in the same breath with the great works of his literary youth; they were workmanlike and uninspiring, if not to say a little dull. His correspondence of this period, however, despite the usual theatrical moans, still retains all the vitality of expression and ironic wit of earlier days, and stand as the major literary output of these twilight years of his life – the genuine letters from Bishopsbourne.

For Brooke, there is nothing to add; the place and the writing were one, in the mind of the writer and the minds of his (relatively few) devoted readers. You did not need to visit the village or the woods and fields all around to experience the topographical power evinced by the author. This was his country and through his writing he made it his own.

Superficially, all three lived quiet and peaceful lives in the village where they drew their last breath. They had achieved a great deal in their lives, but what they had achieved was not enough. These last days were filled with a strong sense of literary frustration. For Hooker, it was the failure to put to bed the last three books of his great work, drafts still-born because of the sterile controversies that had dogged his footsteps at the Temple. For Conrad, it was the slow dying of his creative powers, a process he could not conceivably influence, and one which left him paralysed in his struggles to complete the great Mediterranean novel he had set his heart on many years before. For Brooke, perhaps a deeper sense of failure: in these last days, with rejection of his latest work by every publisher on his agent's list, and in the knowledge that his past work sold badly and was mostly out of print, he saw himself as now unpublishable, a forgotten author who had not made the grade. He had not the courage to write any more. Despite the palpable evidence to the contrary, it was a failed writing life.

The birds still sang from the tall beech trees, the Nailbourne trickled down the village street, the labourers returned from the fields at dusk, but imprisoned in their separate studies – in the old rectory, at Oswalds, in Ivy Cottage – three writing lives were slowly dying in despair.

In Lent of 1598, just after the publication of Book V of the *Polity*, the one book he completed in the village, Richard Hooker was summoned to court to preach before the Queen.[2] Whether it was the book that inspired this honour, whether he had been summoned before in like circumstances, we cannot know. It seems likely, however, to be the first and last time that the rector of Bishopsbourne has been, or will be, called upon to preach to the sovereign. He was well used to the journey to London, by road and sea, and to consorting with lords and archbishops there, but there must have been just a little flutter around the rectory dovecotes on the spring morning he set off. There is no record of what he preached to the Queen, one of his more intellectual sermons no doubt, but it was wholly fitting that the man who a century later came to represent the soul of the Elizabethan settlement should have stood before the woman for whom that settlement was the very pinnacle of her political achievement.

Meanwhile, the last three books of his great work sat for the remaining years of his life mouldering away in a forgotten corner of his study. It seems that all three were finished in his lifetime, but what has come down to us (Book VIII and the remnant of Book VI, published in 1648, and Book VII in 1662) was not in finished form and seems to have been tampered with along the way. From documentary evidence of the comments of Hooker's friends Cranmer and Sandys on the drafts, we can tell they were uneasy about certain controversial passages which they wanted expanding and elucidating.[3] They pressed for more detail to destroy the Puritan case while Hooker was happier with philosophic generalisation of the kind he had deployed so adeptly in the first four books. There may have been long discussions on those weekend visits to the rectory as to what to do with these three books, but Hooker does not seem to have succumbed to a major expansion of the texts as he had with Book V. Difficult to speculate for we do not know in what precise form the texts stood at the hour of their author's death.

It is possible to deduce the issues that divided the author and his friends in the last three books. The remnant of Book VI starts as a discussion of the role of lay elders in the Presbyterian polity but turns into a treatise on "the virtue and discipline of repentance". Sandys disagreed with Hooker's arguments for extending the jurisdiction of the church courts into the civil area (a contentious issue throughout the 16th century) and saw penitence as an especially Papist practice. Book VII is a stout defence of the episcopacy but goes far to imply that bishops were established by divine law, the strongly held conviction of Hooker's friend, Saravia. Its comments on the faults of contemporary bishops and claim that the episcopacy might, in very extreme circumstances, even be abolished would have given Sandys and Cranmer considerable pause before agreeing to immediate publication. Hooker's defence of the royal supremacy in Book VIII is likewise qualified by the admission of constitutional restraints on the royal power, for example, through the law-making powers of Parliament. This was tough meat to chew at the close of the Elizabethan age, let alone in the days of the Stuart dynasty that followed.

But whatever the detailed objections to publication, the division between Hooker and Sandys was essentially one of approach: Hooker wanted to make a personal appeal to the conscience of the Puritans (as he had done in the early chapters of the Preface) whereas Sandys wished to rub their noses in the stern arguments of a polemical debate. Though Hooker was never so meek and mild as Walton wished to depict him, he nevertheless believed firmly in tolerance and humility as prime virtues to be deployed from a position of strength – the strength conferred by faith and rationality. In the last three years of his life, his brain was still as alert as ever, as his writings of the time fully testify, but he became more disillusioned with the politics of religion, with the emphasis on criticism and scoring points rather than on understanding and quiet persuasion. So it was probably not the loss of any physical or mental power that resigned him, like Conrad, to the failure to complete his work, but rather a conscious recognition that battling on with contentious issues was not the best way to pass the last years of life in careful preparation for death.

For polemical attacks made on him at this period seemed to cause him more anxiety than they had in the past. Late in 1599 there appeared the anonymous *Christian Letter*, probably hatched in Cambridge, which attacked all five published books of the *Polity*, in general for its over-intellectualism and in detail on numerous points in its argument. It accused him of attempting to introduce Popery through the back door under pretence of attacking the Puritans.[4] He immediately set about penning a refutation of this new attack but was never vouchsafed the time to complete it. We can tell how much it upset him by the comments he wrote in the margins of the *Letter* itself: the author was attacking him "without eyes for he seems not to perceive the bare meaning of the Church's most basic teachings and doctrines. I think his godparents have much to answer to God for not seeing that he was better trained in his catechism class". Of his antagonist he also wrote "You rage yell and bellow as one that were carried beside him self". At a place where he was criticised for his ponderous style, Hooker wrote "How this asse runneth, kicking up his heeles as if a summerfly had stung him. Great corsing but to no end". In another place, he wrote angrily "Ignorant Asse" and in another "You ly, sir". His rational objections were acid in tone: "Sermons are framed by the witt of man: therfore all things framed by mans witt are sermons. If this be your skill in reasoning, let a whelebarrow be a sermon. For it is a thing made by mans witt".[5] So much for the archetype of meekness and mildness.

There were other occasions for disturbing his peace around this time. Walton talks of false accusations that were made of him but gives no details: "he lay under the great charge, and the anxiety of this accusation, and kept it secret to himself for many months".[6] The precise details are not known but it appears he was blackmailed by a prostitute and her accomplice, put up to it by a religious opponent,

264

and that Sandys in the end took charge of the affair and forced the accusers to confess. Walton implies that this happened in the Borne years, but it may well have been earlier.

Hooker by all accounts was never very strong and he had not lived a particularly healthy life in the disease-ridden cities of Oxford and London. As he reached his mid-forties, despite the healthier environment of a country village, the stress of his life, both writing and teaching, began to take its toll. Walton gives us the detailed circumstances of the illness that led to his death. "About the year 1600, and of his age forty-six, he fell into a long and sharp sickness, occasioned by a cold taken in his passage by water betwixt London and Gravesend; from the malignity of which he was never recovered." Walton places the completion of the *Polity* at the centre of his concerns: "he did not beg a long life of God for any other reason, but to live to finish his three remaining books of the Polity; and then, Lord, let thy servant depart in peace".[7] In fact, the books were by this time largely complete and he resigned to their posthumous publication; his greater anxiety was to complete his Answer to the malignities of the *Christian Letter*, and that he never did.[8]

As time went on, his condition worsened. "About a month before his death, this good man, that never knew, or at least never considered, the pleasures of the palate, became first to lose his appetite, and then to have an averseness to all food, insomuch that he seemed to live some intermitted weeks by the smell of meat only, and yet still studied and writ".[9] At this time he had the misfortune to suffer a burglary, but still the safety of the *Polity* was the first thing on his mind. "In this time of his sickness, and not many days before his death, his house was robbed; of which he having notice, his question was, 'Are my books and written papers safe?' And being answered that they were; his reply was, 'Then it matters not; for no other loss can trouble me'.[10]

His friend, Dr Saravia, attended at his bedside and administered to him absolution and Communion. Soon after which "the Doctor apprehended death ready to seize him; yet, after some amendment, left him at night, with a promise to return early the day following; which he did, and then found him better in appearance, deep in contemplation, and not inclinable to discourse; which gave the Doctor occasion to require his present thoughts. To which he replied, "That he was meditating the number and nature of angels, and their blessed obedience and order, without which, peace could not be in Heaven; and oh! that it might be so on earth!".[11] Hooker had always a gently philosophical approach to death: "As birth, so death is beneficial unto the state of the whole world. Birth doth stop death, and death doth ease birth. No reason therfore but that we should be contented to give place unto others by death, as by birth we have succeeded others dead".[12]

He died on 2 November 1600 in one of the great rooms of the rectory with its fine ceiling of moulded black oak beams. Walton gives him a few last words and a peaceful seventeenth century send-off: " 'I could wish to live to do the Church more service; but cannot hope it, for my days are past as a shadow that returns not'. More he would have spoken, but his spirits failed him: and, after a short conflict betwixt nature and death, a quiet sigh put a period to his last breath, and so he fell asleep".[13]

He was buried in the chancel of St Mary's church under a flat stone slab that was once the old altar. In his will he left three pounds for a new pulpit at Bishopsbourne and five guineas for the poor of the parish.[14] It was another sixty years before the last book of his great work was published, but by then he had become renowned, not just as one of the finest exponents of Elizabethan English prose, but as the image maker of the newly constructed Anglican Church, even though it was the image of a Church, with its established "middle way", that he would never have recognised in his lifetime.

In September 1922 Scott Moncrieff sent Conrad a copy of his newly published translation of the first volume of Proust which Conrad had, of course, already read in the original French.[15] By November he was deep in it ("I've lately read nothing but Marcel Proust")[16] inspired by news of Proust's death. Later that month John Squire asked him to contribute his signature to a collective tribute, and this got him thinking about the French writer in a critical way. In his years at Oswalds Conrad had himself begun to turn towards the past as an antidote to the barren feeling of the present and future, and the failure of his creative powers. But it was not so much the handling of the universal in the past that now attracted him to Proust: "I admire him immensely but not... because he has reproduced for us our own past, for our pasts have been very different and we have felt them differently. I should rather admire him for disclosing to us a past like nobody else's and thus adding something memorable to the general experience of mankind". It gave him pause for thought about the essence of Proust's creativity: "What compels my admiration for M. Proust's work is that it is great art based on analysis. All his greatness lies in that. Where he is unique and for ever memorable is in this: that he is a prose writer (to put it in French since we all have read him in French) 'qui a poussé la force de l'analyse jusqu'au point où elle devient créatrice'".[17] While Conrad immersed himself that winter in the work of the master of time and place, there would return the following spring to the little cottage just up the road another Proustian who would, in time, with a different kind of mastery, turn this village and its environs into a symbol of the power of the past.

Conrad had spare time enough now fully to immerse himself in the riches of Proust and thus forestall his continuing guilt for abandoning those riches of the Mediterranean he had left behind in the fragment of his latest great novel. 1923 had been a memorable year for the American tour but it marked too the effective end of his writing. In December, he took stock of his position in a frame of mind more resigned than disconsolate: "Neither do I expect to do any work this month, because it must take some time to recover the creative tone.... I have had a rather strenuous year".[18]

Just before Christmas he went down with the usual attack of gout and was confined to his room for a couple of weeks. He managed, however, to make the best of this (the last) Christmas at Oswalds by packing the house with family and guests: "Aubry arrived on the 22nd, to spend Christmas with us, and found me in bed; but on Xmas Day I came down to share in the Xmas middle-day dinner, the company being eight, including those two crocks the host and hostess, Aubry and our John, and the four Muirhead Bones, who came over from Canterbury, where they were staying in rooms over the Xmas week. It wasn't a rowdy revel, the major part of the company drinking water steadily, but there were mince pies and a certain affectation of cheerfulness".[19]

The writer Gertrude Bone, wife of the artist Muirhead Bone, has left us with a touching portrait of Conrad that Christmas afternoon sat beside the fire with his friends and reminiscing on his first literary champion, Edward Garnett.

> It was Christmas Day at Conrad's house and his last
> Christmas Day, it transpired, though the shadow was
> not then upon us. Muirhead, the boys, Jean Aubry and
> Jessie and I sat around the fire, a soft wet mist drawing
> the curtain from outside the windows of the salon.
> Conrad, less than anyone I have ever met, had the
> home-making faculty. He, the voyager, sought his home
> here and there in the mind of a friend. No furniture
> contained him for long. Seated on the other side of the
> fireplace from myself, he addressed me across it, his
> face winning and sweet.
> "*You* admire Edward do you not?"
> "Exceedingly," I replied.
> "But I am so frightened of him. Are not you too?" he
> asked.
> "I am always terrified," I replied.
> "Ah! So is everybody," he said triumphantly.[20]

With the depth of winter still to come, he wanted to escape to France but Jessie's pending operation made that an impossible dream.[21] On the first day of February, the start of a new month inspired him to a new push on his book, and returning to it filled him with new hope: "I have tackled the Novel to-day. What a lot of work there is to do yet! However I feel not so very much disgusted." [22] But the effort amounted to little more than further tinkering with the existing text, and soon petered out. He still seemed more interested in his past work, recollection of which demanded no effort. When the literary critic of the *Manchester Guardian*, in an article about something else, praised *en passant* the lasting quality of *Nostromo*, Conrad sent him a copy of the latest edition and its preface, together with a remembrance of things past: "My over-anxiety, passing often into a weary restlessness, while writing that book, is responsible for a frequent clumsiness of expression. I can look back at that time now with a smile. Not only the youngsters have their illusions about the importance of their work, which are ridiculous and also a little touching. I was 46 – but as an author still young – and I thought N. a big undertaking". [23]

He did a little more tinkering with the present novel that March but the failure to push on with new chapters left him again to all appearances more resigned than frustrated. And this resignation seemed also to extend to the continuance of life itself as references to death now began to enter unconsciously into his correspondence. When a fellow writer asked which was the favourite of his own books, he explained why he could not declare it in public, and ended "So I think that the secret of 'the book I like best' will have to go with me to my grave". [24] In thanking Frank Swinnerton for an article praising his work, he wrote "I prize most the thought that when the hour strikes I'll have it to leave behind me"; [25] and when he sat at Oswalds that spring for a bust by Epstein, his main reaction was "It is nice to be passed to posterity in this monumental and impressive rendering". [26] By the end of April, he had many unsettling worries, above all Jessie's new operation planned for a month's time, and the prospect of leaving Oswalds (now "this infernal house") [27] for a new home yet to be discovered. He wrote to a Polish relative: "You may take it for certain that we will be in this house up to September 1st unless something utterly unexpected happens to call us away".[28] Something did happen, but it was not all that unexpected.

Despite the scare about his heart the previous autumn, it seemed now to be working normally. His mind was still lively on all worldly matters, especially the literary, and he could still write affecting letters – like this, on the English climate in May and his pride in becoming a grandfather: "Here, at this moment, it is raining. I am sitting by the fire and looking at the young leaves shaking and shivering outside in the cold wind. Just now Jessie and I have nobody here but we expect the Borys' baby with all his attendants and escort down for the weekend. That won't break the peace. That baby is the quietest I have ever known. He seems to thrive exceedingly. I wonder how the world will look in twenty years' time when he will have to find his own little place in it".[29]

The long awaited operation on Jessie took place on 13 June in Canterbury and this time proved a lasting success. Conrad visited her for the first four days in the nursing home there, but then himself went down with a severe attack of bronchitis which kept him bed bound for the next two weeks. He had a miserable July, waiting at Oswalds, still not wholly well, for news of Jessie's return, which was delayed from week to week. He felt the loneliness of her absence – "It is dreadful to be laid up here away from the Missus".[30] He developed a new routine, that of a single man: "I go to see Jessie every afternoon and devote the morning to pen and ink either upstairs or down here, in the study, where I am writing this (1pm) just before sitting down to my solitary lunch".[31] He had lived close to Jessie for 28 years, and now for six of the last seven weeks of his life, she was absent. Loneliness developed into a wider depression: "I have been to see Jessie three times this week but when I get home I get to bed and give myself up to passive contemplation of no very cheerful kind. It is 18 months since I have done any work that counts".[32] Predictably, his anger turned on the house he had never loved. He told a French acquaintance: "Miss Hallowes being on holiday, I am languishing alone in this wretched hole [*horrible boîte*] which we hope to leave in September".[33] It was the urgent search for a new house that was now to lead to Conrad's death.

Jessie came home at last on 24 July but remained convalescing in the bedroom next to his. Immediately Conrad's spirits rose and, a week after her return, he invited Richard Curle down for the weekend. Curle arrived late, at 11 o'clock, on Friday 1 August, the eve of the opening of Canterbury Cricket Week which had been enlivened by Pinker's grand coach procession just three years before. After a solitary supper downstairs, he went up to Conrad's bedroom above the porch and sat and talked with him for an hour and a half, as had been their habit in the past. Conrad was in a cheery chaffing mood, buoyed up by Jessie's return. He had some other good news: his chauffeur, Vinten, had found a new house, just eight miles down the Dover Road from Oswalds. Conrad had inspected it, and spoke enthusiastically of its rooms, its gardens, its garage. He would take Curle there the following day.[34]

He was equally buoyant the next morning when, after breakfast, he talked in his study of the six different lines of treatment that might be followed with *Suspense*: "My mind seems clearer than it has been for months, and I shall soon get hold of my work again". They took the car at 11 o'clock and were four miles down the Dover Road when Conrad felt pains across his chest, similar to an attack he had had a few days before. It was another two miles before he could be persuaded to have the car turned round and head for home. There he went straight to bed and a doctor was called who diagnosed a severe bout of indigestion. The pains continued, in his chest and down his arms, and later in the day another doctor was called who ordered oxygen cylinders from Canterbury Hospital to assist his breathing. Difficult breathing had been his lot since the attack of bronchitis earlier that year, and nothing particularly untoward was diagnosed, certainly not the heart attack he had just suffered.[35]

He spent an uncomfortable night, mostly dozing on the chair in his bedroom, watched over by Foote, his manservant. At 8.30 next morning, when no-one else was in the room, Jessie next door heard a cry of "Here", perhaps "Here, you ...", and a fall. People rushed to the bedroom to find he had slipped from his chair and lay dead on the floor.[36] His health had been bad for most of his life, and in recent days his power and inclination to write had too slipped away. Just a few months earlier, on a pause in conversation, he had told Richard Curle: "I shouldn't be very sorry to be out of all this".[37]

To escape the death scene, Curle walked out into the garden to catch some morning air.

> I could not bear to look on him again in death... .
> I wandered out on to the drive. The soft morning,
> already warm in the full tide of summer, spoke only of
> teeming and joyous life. Everything was still and quiet,
> as it is on a Sunday in the country, and the thought of
> death seemed utterly incongruous. Dr. Fox, of Ashford,
> and Dr. Reid, of Canterbury, had been telephoned for,
> and their cars, standing empty before the door, gave a
> curiously festive effect to the solitude as though some
> social gathering were in progress within the house. As I
> stood there I saw several strangers enter the drive gates.
> They, too, suggested the arrival of guests for a party. I
> went forward to intercept them. They were Americans
> and they had come, they said, to look over the house
> with a view to renting it.[38]

The funeral took place four days later on a day of grey cloud following a night of heavy rain. As the little motorcade wound out of the Oswalds drive and up the beech-lined lane to the Dover Road, the bell in the tower of Hooker's old church tolled solemnly out in his honour. A similar courtesy was given to it as they passed through the village of Bridge, and then on to the simple funeral service for close friends and family held at St Thomas' Catholic church, nestling in the shadow of the great cathedral. The coffin was then driven through the bustling High Street, joyously beflagged for the cricket week crowds, up to the cemetery off the Whitstable Road where hundreds of distinguished guests, come down on the 12.30 train from London, awaited its arrival. With some prayers, a little singing, and a sprinkling of holy water, it was finally laid to rest.[39]

Conrad was an "English" writer, but never a topographical one. He knew little of the English countryside, but he knew Kent – it was the county that held his affections, and he would never have lived for long outside it.[40] In his last years he took great pleasure in being driven around the Kentish roads, as Curle remembered well. "I recall innumerable occasions on which he and I have motored about its lanes or through Romney Marsh, stopping here and there to admire some picturesque old church or beautiful vista. They gave him immense pleasure, these drives, and he even liked getting out of the car and having tea or a drink at some small wayside inn".[41]

It was fitting, therefore, whatever Jocelyn Brooke may later have thought, to raise a memorial to him in the main street of the village where he died. It was, as Curle said, "not a cold memorial, like a statue, but a memorial which enters, as Conrad would have wished, into the very life of the village... a porch added to the village hall, where people can sit and smoke in the evening and rest after the toil of the day ".[42] A village meeting was called to decide upon an appropriate inscription for the teak memorial panel and it was there that Frank Ashton-Gwatkin, the novelist son of the rector, proposed the quotation from *Suspense*, reciting it word for word.[43] At the opening ceremony three years after Conrad's death, Cunninghame Graham was accorded the honour of drawing down the Polish flag to unveil the memorial. Many came to see the unveiling and listen to the speeches, and Richard Curle, looking out to the edges of the crowd, saw, or almost saw, an apparition: "as I stood upon the steps of the memorial during the opening ceremony on that October afternoon of 1927 I had the strange sensation that, were I to turn my head, I should see Conrad coming towards us. He would be walking slowly, leaning on his stick, and his face would wear a slightly mystified expression. Why had we left him to himself, and what had brought us all there?" [44]

273

The sixties, that decade that (we now learn) opened doors for so many, marked the closing of most doors on Jocelyn Brooke. But even in the year of the *Dog* there came a warning of trials ahead. On a bright morning in September 1955 [45] he set off in a hired car plus driver, with Ninnie (now in her mid seventies) seated in the back, for a trip to the Isle of Thanet. They returned later that afternoon in a mist of sleety rain. On the Dover Road the driver stopped to turn right down the lane into the village, just as my father and I were to do on our bicycles at about the same time. A speeding Jaguar, unsighted by the dip in the road behind them, could not pull up in time.

> There was an appalling explosion, a series of explosions – then sudden darkness, and a crackling of red spiky flames like fireworks. "So this," I can remember saying to myself, in that instant of darkness and dissolution, "is *it*." It was my last conscious thought for several seconds. The world rocked, disintegrated into a roaring, splintering chaos, I was plunging downward through some abyss beyond the bounds of space or time... Then, as though a light had been switched on in a darkened room, I was suddenly conscious again: slewed sideways in my seat, staring out of the window at a field of kale, my head throbbing painfully. The driver, next to whom I was sitting, was sprawled forward over the driving-wheel; in the back seat my old nurse had fallen sideways and was moaning with pain and terror.

Here was an intimation of death, or to be precise, of the three deaths that were soon to strike in his life. But it was more than that, as he felt intuitively once the immediate crisis had passed.

> I sat up, feeling suddenly alert, almost euphoric, with a sense of vividly heightened consciousness; just so does one feel on coming to from a dose of nitrous oxide at

the dentist's: there was the same sense of returning from some region immeasurably remote, of having covered, in a matter of seconds, enormous distances. Analogous, too, was a curious sense of deprivation, a conviction that one had been on the point of grasping some cosmic secret which, at the last moment, had been tantalizingly withheld. It was just as well, perhaps, that the Riddle of the Universe remained unsolved, for if a solution had, after all, been vouchsafed to me, it is unlikely that I should still be here to record it.[46]

Brooke, being Brooke, began to write a new book, with the accident (from which all escaped without serious injury) forming the opening scene, the very last of the autobiographical "novels", well deserving of its place as fifth in the series that began with the trilogy and *The Dog at Clambercrown*. It starts, typically enough, with a simple yet atmospheric opening sentence, which plunges us back into the heart of the village, a worthy rival to that of *The Military Orchid* and Mr Bundock.

Driving up the lane from the village, I saw the stream licking its way through the dried-up, grassy river-bed towards the bridge; remembering that old Mr Iggulsden lay dying in his cottage among the hazel thickets.[47]

The stream, of course, is the Nailbourne, the woe-waters that in their irregular rising breed forebodings of a doom-laden future, the very same that flowed under Joseph Conrad's front door without his recognition. They are used in the book, together with the poisonous hellebore plant, as images of human apprehension of the sinister, in the author's pursuit of the meaning behind that feeling in the accident, of that "inimical power lying in wait to attack... this awareness of something existing beyond the limits of consciousness yet at the same time inexplicably familiar".[48]

Ninnie who, in the back seat, had taken the full force of the collision, was the only one who needed some hospital treatment – for a cut head and severe shock. Brooke went with her in the ambulance, now returning to her the attention she had given to him all his life.

> Returning home, we passed over the bridge, at the bottom of the lane, which spans the Nailbourne: that spring, which, flowing irregularly in winter and early spring through the Elham Valley, is known locally as the woe-water, and is said, when it rises, to presage disaster. This year the stream was in spate: a day or two ago, it had not yet reached our village; but I had noticed, only this morning, that it had already rounded the bend beyond the bridge; now it flowed turbulently along the river-bed, over the withered grasses and fallen tree-boughs, towards the lake and the park-lands of Bourne.[49]

It had not been seen for some time and was now flowing more fiercely than for many years past. The ill omen was to fall heaviest, as so often happens, upon the most vulnerable party to the expedition that day. But bad omens for Ninnie were bad omens for Jocelyn too.

The new book, following on from *Conventional Weapons* which in 1961 had been poorly received, was to be called "Furious and Deadly", from the designation of the deadly nightshade in Gerarde's *Herbal* "banish it from your gardens ... being a plant so furious and deadly: for it bringeth such as have eaten thereof into a dead sleepe wherein many have died".[50] Brooke was fond of this last book in proportion as publishers took against it; it was "a quasi-autobiographical book, rather like my earlier stuff, but it is also *meant* to be a study of the relation between sex and the supernatural (see Freud on "The Uncanny"). I can quite see why publishers would fight shy of this – too "bitty", and too like my other stuff. Of course *I* rather like it."[51]

276

Brooke had never sold well. Even in the early 1950s, as a new voice bursting on the scene to the critical acclaim for the trilogy, his popularity among discerning critics was not enough to shift the books. As whispers got round the publishing industry that even his celebrated works did not sell, a publisher now presented with a new Brooke work, particularly another quirky autobiography, would hear the warning bells. With the publication of *The Dog at Clambercrown* in 1955, his frenzied spate of ten years writing had produced enough books, one might have thought, to set most average authors up for life. But Brooke was not an average author. He now began to believe that his critical acclaim had perhaps been just a temporary phenomenon, partly dependent on the novelty of the voice, and that the world, now sated with his stuff, wanted to move on. Olivia Manning, ever the acerbic critic, thought he needed " a new subject";[52] but Anthony Powell was nearer the mark in recognising that Brooke's only subject was Brooke himself, a subject of endless resource, always of appeal to those fully tuned in: "I think it quite extraordinary... that you manage to tell what is virtually the same story over and over again, yet it is always fresh and always enthralling".[53]

"Furious and Deadly" now did the rounds of the publishing houses, but no-one with the discrimination of an Anthony Powell was to be found at home. The manuscript, together with a few others, took almost four years to come full circle back to Ivy Cottage "much battered after their ignoble Odyssey".[54] Such wholehearted rejection (his agents gave up when there was no-one left to send them to) fed that sense of inferiority that had dogged him since childhood and about which he had written so openly in his books, without egotism or self-pity. He told his fellow writer, Francis King, who in 1965 made one last effort to use his influence with a particular publisher, that he had become more or less resigned to his fate: "I had quite given up any hope of being published again – I'm just an old hack nowadays... But I suspect that in the past [I] wrote far too much: I should have stopped after the 4th or 5th, like Forster".[55] This last push for publication ended, swiftly and predictably, in failure. When

King brought the bad news, he met it with resignation tinged with justifiable bitterness: "I'm not a bit surprised that you were defeated by the editorial board: I honestly do think my name is mud in the publishing world nowadays – and obviously anyone from the Bodley Head [*his principal publisher whom he had left in high dudgeon*] would be able to fling an extra bit of mud in the grave".[56]

Perhaps most humiliating of all, the news of this final defeat soon got round his literary friends, many of whom (like Raymond Mortimer and Olivia Manning) had earlier agitated on his behalf. Olivia Manning had heard on the grapevine that this latest work was just "the mixture as before" [57] and shed some faint tears: "You know how much I enjoy your work and it saddens me that any of it should lie unread in MS form... I simply will not have them mouldering in darkness".[58] A more genuinely outraged message came from the writer and political activist, Yvonne Kapp, his lifeline in the last years: "I *am* sorry about that stupid editorial committee: what crass fools they must be... one only has to peep round the corner of one's little life and to see what happens to other people with not a *tenth* of your talent to feel very indignant. I know we've said all this before, but I *do* resent the fact that your writing should go unpublished at a time when literary excellence is at such low ebb. By what right are people deprived of reading you?" [59]

It was while these last manuscripts were doing the rounds, and before the final guillotine had come down on them, that the domestic disaster, perhaps predicted by the car accident and the rise of the woe-waters, struck its irreparable blow. On his return from the second stint in the army to write, the inhabitants of the cottage in Bishopsbourne had formed a, none too youthful, *ménage à trois* – with Ninnie in her sixties and The Owl then approaching eighty – and throughout the 1950s, while the books came churning out, Jocelyn was fully supported, as he always had been, by mother and nurse. But the latter were now ageing fast. In October 1957, two years after the ominous car crash, May Brooke could no longer be cared for adequately in the cottage and moved into a local nursing home. As a woman with a still active mind, the adjustment was difficult and the decision caused her son considerable pain and guilt. A friend tried to reassure him with his own experience of a similar trial: "There were awful moans and groans – and then she settled down contentedly".[60] But The Owl was not the person to accept second best, though she was to spend the next six years in this new and unwelcome environment.

Brooke and Ninnie lived on alone in the cottage together for another four years. Then in the early sixties, Ninnie developed cancer and in June 1961, after an operation, died at a nursing home by the sea at Westgate. She was eighty. This was the severing of his main umbilical cord: as a child, his dependency upon her had been total; as a writer, he had made her a central figure in his life story. It came at a particularly bad time when Brooke himself was ill and fretting over the lack of reviews for his latest (and last) published novel, *Conventional Weapons*.[61] He now had only his mother to visit at the nursing home just down the road at Barham, where the deadening regime was still a trial for a woman of such active intelligence. A sad little letter to her much loved son survives from her last days there.

> I can't remember whether it is Sat. or Sunday today! I get so dreadfully forgetful. The flowers you brought me are such a joy, they look lovely and of course are quite fresh still. There is really no news here, just as dull as ever. I keep myself alive with work and reading![62]

Five months later she died of a stroke, aged 96, on the last day of August 1963.

Brooke was alone in the cottage that had been his life, but now with little of the hope that writing had given him in the past. He still wrote quantities of material, but these were mostly reviews – for *The Scotsman*, *New Statesman*, *The Listener*, *Times Literary Supplement*. His literary criticism had always been admired, and gobbets of it had appeared quite naturally in his autobiographical works. But now, in these last days, he built up a special reputation as reviewer, and a Brooke review was prized by most of the major authors of the day, many of whom – Eric Linklater, Pamela Hansford Johnson, L.P.Hartley – sent him thank you letters, a little out of line with literary protocol.[63] The work kept him fed (he was always worried, unnecessarily, of running out of money) and a place in the literary world, but above all it kept his hand in. Whatever its quality, however, reviewing remained as distasteful as he had envisaged it would when he first contemplated the dire fate awaiting an "established" author. He would complain to Yvonne Kapp about the "bloody nature" [64] of work and the dread word "hack" appears frequently in his letters to his friends.

Confined in the cottage and growing older, his natural tendencies became more marked. He had enjoyed being sociable, but always on his own terms – "my temptation has always been to contract out of the rat-race". Although there were still friends in the village he could invite over for an evening of music and chat,[65] he was generally now more reclusive – less willing to go up to London or follow up new encounters; the spring holidays abroad, that had fed his creativity in the past, now became less frequent, for lack of money, he claimed, though his bank balance was perfectly healthy. He kept up his serious botany, however, and in the spring of 1964 spent a productive time, at the instance of Olivia Manning, among the marsh orchids of the west of Ireland.[66]

He had always enjoyed his drink – "Shall we be *beasts*, and now go to *my* club, and have another glass of port?" – but now with the loss of the lifelong emotional support at home, and the feeling that the world, particularly the publishing world, was against him, the drink grew out of control. Drink led to depression and depression called for more drink – the traditional cycle. He was still looked upon with great respect in the village, but most of the neighbours saw him in these last years as a sad and lonely man.[67] Friends tried to entice him up to parties in London with promise of copious booze, but even this did not work.[68]

Yvonne Kapp, that most active of letter-writers and (at this time) translators, did much to keep him alive in the final three years when he lived all alone in the cottage. She tried through her sharply amusing letters to dispel the aura of depression by pointing out the elements of pose involved – the modern world was not declining as never before, he enjoyed his reviewing work and had fun with his botany, he did still go on holiday.[69] She regaled him with lively news of her own work and holidays, reminding him of the key triggers of his existence, like Italy and his home village: "I also tried rereading Conrad (because of his associations with Bishopsbourne), but something about him quarrelled with the mood of a particularly indolent Italian summer and I abandoned him." [70]

She was right in many respects – he *did* still enjoy his reviewing and most of his complaints deliberately followed the model of crusty old bachelor. But at the same time he *did* feel the emptiness of the cottage now the other inhabitants had gone, and also (like Conrad) the loss of his real writing: in his last letter to Olivia Manning he confessed to be completely "written out".[71] His health was declining, not helped by the drink and his overall mental state. His friends rallied round with letters of concern, but it was Yvonne Kapp who gave the most moral support. In the spring of 1965 he was laid up with a high temperature and she was genuinely worried: "How dire to have fallen ill just when the sun was trying to come out. Are you feeling better now? Has the temperature come down?.. *Do* take care of yourself – or get someone to do it".[72]

A year later he had problems with his teeth and had to have them all out; she tried to encourage him out of his self-pity: "you shouldn't let this teeth business get the better of you. I share your horror".[73] At the same time the inexplicable temperature returned and she pressed him to see a consultant. She had an attractive remedy: "The garden looks adorable now. You must get well quickly and sit about in yours. Are you being carefully looked after? And given delicious food to tempt you? You ought to drink a pint of *champagne nature* every day. It sets one up better than anything else".[74]

These were the first of the alarums and excursions. Despite them, he worked hard through the summer and autumn of 1966, churning out the reviews week by week and keeping up a lively correspondence. Kapp ended her last letter to Bishopsbourne on a questioning note "How *are* you? You don't tell me. And are you doing any writing apart from the reviews? I want to know how you spend your time. If it's fit to tell".[75]

The end came swift and unexpected. A week later, on Friday 28 October, he went to bed in Ivy Cottage in the usual way and never woke up. He was found on the Saturday morning by his cleaning lady lying dead in his bed. The post mortem revealed he had died in his sleep from natural causes: he had suffered a heart attack.[76] A few days later, his remains were cremated and scattered in the cemetery at Barham at the centre of that country of the mind he gave to us as Brooke-land.

Perhaps Michael Powell was the winner in the end. Instant posterity has embraced him more kindly. Regular gatherings of *aficionados* pay homage at the farmhouse in Bekesbourne where he was born and visit the sites of his great Canterbury film to recite the screenplay and re-enact the feeling of it all. Which only serves to show the power the film has wrested from the book.

For our village is left in comparative peace today, perhaps a blessing after all. Not too many literary societies pound the quiet lanes in an effort to resurrect the bones of the dead. Ivy Cottage stands in the summer sun with a small unpretentious plaque, wholly fitting to the small unpretentious royalties that its one-time occupant continues to enjoy. Paperback reprints of his trilogy come and go, cause a minor stir but then fade away, never selling as they deserve. The Dog sits in Clambercrown awaiting a properly edited reprint of its own. There's an even longer wait for the biography, now on the stocks for almost thirty years, which may ensure that justice is done at last.[77]

The ghost of Conrad looks out of his study window, more susceptible to tourist curiosity than the others, with posterity well marshalled by millions of readers worldwide: and every aspect of his work and life tested to destruction in hundreds of books, the most definitive and readable the brilliant biography of a fellow Pole.[78] Oswalds stands guard still over the official entrance to the village across the Nailbourne bridge, and has shed none of its elegance in the past fifty years.

Hooker sleeps before the altar undisturbed by the thought that few clergymen in village rectories (now turned from great houses into modern bungalows) still read him today. Compensation has come in the form of the American (and some English) academics who over the past thirty years have disinterred the bones and given them one almighty intellectual shake. A man with an open mind, Hooker appears today, as to his contemporaries, all things to all men, and the disputes as to what he actually stood for remain as puzzling as in his own day, but not, hopefully, so full of vitriol.

The village remains deep down much as it has always done in the topography of woods and fields, right from the days when the king held court at Kingston and it formed a tiny Jutish kingdom all its own. The village awaits the future, but not with bated breath. It has had more than its share of famous writers; their books in different measure belong here, along with the memories that crowded their deathbeds: for Hooker, the vicious battles with Walter Travers and his followers at the Temple, the magic alchemy of priest and people joined together in solemn worship; for Conrad, the long years of combat with the sea and the ultimate horror of the Congo; for Brooke, the slumbering afternoons of village childhood, the joyous feasting with those civilised peasants of the Abruzzi. All these are memories that still float today on the village air for those who have hands to reach out and grasp them.

Other writers may come here to live, write and die; but whether remembered or forgotten, they will not change the surface of the land. For theirs is the country of the mind.

Notes and References

ABBREVIATIONS

CCL   Frederick R. Karl and Laurence Davies (edited) *The Collected Letters of Joseph Conrad, 9 vols.,* Cambridge University Press 1983-2007

Dog   Jocelyn Brooke, *The Dog at Clambercrown*, Bodley Head 1955

Folger   W. Speed Hill, general editor, *The Folger Library Edition of TheWorks of Richard Hooker, Vols. 1-5*, Belknap Press of Harvard University Press 1977–90; *Vol. 6*, Medieval & Renaissance Texts & Studies 1993

GC   Jocelyn Brooke, *The Goose Cathedral*, Bodley Head 1950

MO   Jocelyn Brooke, *The Military Orchid*, Bodley Head 1948

MS   Jocelyn Brooke, *A Mine of Serpents*, Bodley Head 1949

Texas   Harry Ransom Humanities Research Center, University of Texas at Austin

trilogy   Jocelyn Brooke, *The Military Orchid and Other Novels*, Penguin 2002

Walton   Izaak Walton, *The Lives*, Society for Promoting Christian Knowledge 1850

284

CHAPTER 1   The Village and the Historian

1   From a 1986 edition of ITV's *The South Bank Show*, quoted Paul Tritton, *A Canterbury Tale*, E.C.Parker & Co. 2006 146. Powell clearly based this on the extended version in his autobiography, *see* Michael Powell, *A Life in Movies*, Heinemann 1986 77–8. The power and beauty of the cathedral from wherever in the surrounding country you approached it had much the same effect on a film maker of the next generation, Michael Gill, *see* Michael Gill, *Growing into War*, Sutton Publishing 2005 37-8.

2   Writing in 1952, Jocelyn Brooke recorded the recent explosion of the plant on the scorched bombsites: "Rosebay Willowherb is, I suppose, known to everybody nowadays, since it is as much at home in Cheapside or the Tottenham Court Road as in the remotest corners of Dartmoor... it received a new lease of life during the blitz... but as lately as the [*eighteen*] sixties was, as Anne Pratt remarks, 'a rare plant in moist woods'" – Jocelyn Brooke, *The Flower in Season*, Bodley Head 1952 103 and also 121. Geoffrey Grigson confirmed the point three years later: "the Rosebay Willow-herb had to wait a long while before it could spread and become that familiar splash of colour in the landscape which we enjoy. Railways, industry, industrial waste land, and the felling of woodland – and then destruction by bombs – at last turned a local plant (and a plant of gardens) into a common one known to everybody" – Geoffrey Grigson, *The Englishman's Flora*, J.M.Dent 1955 (1987 edition) 196. Reviewing Grigson's work in the *New Statesman* (3 December 1955) Brooke, who could become highly pedantic on his pet subject of flowers, took exception to the author's phraseology: "Just occasionally he goes haywire, as when he describes Rosebay Willowherb, once a rare-ish plant, as becoming (after the blitz) 'brilliant and sharp throughout the country' – a phrase which leaves me baffled". This led to a nasty little spat

in the correspondence columns (*New Statesman* 10 and 17 December 1955) but the offending words were omitted from later editions.

3   Tritton *op.cit.* 62.

4   For a full account of the bicycle ride along the Pilgrim's Way *see* Powell *op.cit.* 72-77.

5   Powell *op.cit.*439-40.

6   Powell later assigned the decision to the fact that all stained glass had been removed from the cathedral and the windows boarded up, making lighting difficult – Powell *op.cit.* 448; but the decision letter from the Dean and Chapter in September tells a different story: "In arriving at this decision the Chapter are influenced by the fact that the film is being produced primarily as a commercial proposition and they do not feel able to allow the Cathedral and the Precincts to be made use of as a part of the background of a commercial film. As trustees of the building and its environs it is the duty of the Chapter to do all in their power to guard it from anything which might be deemed inappropriate. In fact the Chapter feel extremely doubtful if the Cathedral should ever be used as a scene of a film except perhaps one of a directly religious character" – quoted Tritton *op.cit.* 111.

7   This was a trial for his long-suffering director: "The only thing he was a bit loony about was clouds in the sky. He detested a clear sky, and it sometimes seemed to me that he forgot about the story and the actors in order to gratify this passion. 'Meekee, Meekee, please wait another few minutes,' he would plead. 'There is a little cloud over there and it is coming our way, I'm sure it is'" – Powell *op.cit.* 443.

8   Alternatively, he might have walked to the village, as did Michael Gill and his girlfriend Christine on the afternoon of the German raid which had destroyed so much of the city. Gill recorded in his diary: "I stayed with C. all morning as her people out. Glorious weather for first time this summer so

picked her up at 2.30 and went for long country walk round
Bishopsbourne and Bridge arriving back 5.30 pretty tired.
Strange such a beautiful afternoon should follow such a night
of grotesque horror" – Michael Gill *op.cit.* 132.

9   But being surrounded by stately homes was not a foolproof
protection. In 1960 the owner of Bourne House and Park, Sir
John Prestige, offered both to the County Council as a site
for the new University of Kent, an offer which was politely
declined – Ian Taylor (edited), *An Anthology of Kingston and
Bishopsbourne, Book 1*, Kingston Village Society 1982 41.

10   Edward Hasted, *The history and topographical survey of the
county of Kent*, 1778–99 – "Bishopsbourne". In his inventory
of the village, Hasted gives prominence to the houses of both
Hooker and Conrad: "In this beautiful valley, in which the
Lesser Stour rises, and through which the Nailbourne at times
runs, is the village of Bourne-street, consisting of about fifteen
houses, and near it the small seat of Oswalds, belonging to
Mr Beckingham, and now inhabited by his brother the Rev
Mr Beckingham, and near it the church and court-lodge.
On the rise of the hill is the parsonage, an antient building
modernised, and much improved by the present rector Dr
Fowell, and from its whiteness a conspicuous object to the
road and Barham downs". It was further "modernised" in
1846, *see* page 226.

11   Brian Hart and Eila Lawton, *Elham Valley Way*, Kent County
Council 1997 6.

12   *ibid.* 15. Ian Taylor (edited) *op.cit.* 9 and 24.

13   The pub was built in 1862 and named the Lion's Head, after
the assumed crest of Matthew Bell, the owner of Bourne
Park from 1844 until his death in 1903. It was changed to the
Mermaid in the mid-1930s since a mermaid was part of the
arms of Sir John Prestige (Prestwich) who owned the estate
until his death in 1962 – Ian Taylor (edited) *op.cit.* 22.

14   Anne Curry, *Agincourt, a new history*, Tempus 2006 284. Patrick

Morrah, *1660 The Year of Restoration*, Chatto & Windus 1960 147.

15   A special apartment of particular magnificence was built for George IV who regularly came down to review the troops on Barham Down – he "either took an exceptional interest in his army or Charlton possessed for him a special fascination". In the new-built apartment he put on theatricals co-produced by himself and Lady Conyngham – Charles Igglesden, *A Saunter through Kent with Pen and Pencil Vol. XXVI*, Kentish Express 1932 61–2.

16   F.T.Vine, *Caesar in Kent*, privately printed 1886 158–172. The Rev. Francis Vine was onetime vicar of Patrixbourne and Bridge, and also chaplain to the Marquess Conyngham at Bifrons; he had spent much time on the local archaeological sites. *See also* MS 199 (trilogy 261).

17   Most noteworthy of the local finds is the Bishopsbourne Vase, third century Roman of pale green glass, discovered in an excavation of the lake in Bourne Park in the early twentieth century – Ian Taylor and Peggy Hogben (edited), *An Anthology of Kingston and Bishopsbourne, Book 2*, Kingston Village Society 1987 40.

18   For a recent professional assessment of Witney's original work (from which he emerges well) *see* Ernest Pollard and Hazel Strouts, "The Dens of Benenden and a possible early lathe boundary", *Archaeologia Cantiana, Vol. CXXV*, 2005 43–65, and especially 56. For a recent popular assessment, *see* Adam Nicolson, *Sissinghurst, an Unfinished History*, HarperCollins 2008 329.

19   There is a biographical note by Joan Thirsk in the foreword to Kenneth Witney (edited), *The Survey of Archbishop Pecham's Kentish Manors 1283–85*, Kent Archaeological Society 2000 iii–vi: and a brief obituary in *Archaeologia Cantiana, Vol. CXIX*, 1999 434.

20   J.E.A. Jolliffe, *Pre-Feudal England – The Jutes*, Oxford University

Press 1933. *See also* J.E.A.Jolliffe, "The Origin of the Hundred in Kent" in J.G.Edwards, V.H.Galbraith and E.F.Jacob (edited), *Historical Essays in Honour of James Tait*, Manchester 1933 155.

21   K.P.Witney, *The Jutish Forest. A Study of the Weald of Kent from 450 to 1380A.D.*, University of London Athlone Press 1976.

22   The direct line of the Eskings died out in 762 but there followed a period of unstable government, in part under the rule of Offa of Mercia, until the merger with Wessex in 825. The traditional rites and customs of the Jutes, however, lived on in Kent beyond the Norman invasion; indeed, gavelkind survived well beyond the medieval period. Despite this, the unfortunate habit continues among some historians of lumping the Jutes in with the Anglo-Saxons from whom they are racially, socially and politically only too distinct. For a comprehensive account of the political history of the Jutish government of Kent *see* K.P.Witney, *The Kingdom of Kent*, Phillimore 1982.

23   Jolliffe, *Pre-Feudal England op.cit.* 57.

24   Witney, *The Jutish Forest op.cit.* vi. The jacket to Witney's *Kingdom of Kent op.cit.* refers to his "intimate knowledge of Kent, which to him is a haunted country". Jocelyn Brooke would have agreed.

25   *ibid.* 47. Witney, *The Kingdom of Kent op.cit.* 61–2 and 237–8.

26   The brooch was discovered on 5 August 1771 when the curate of Kingston, the Rev. Bryan Faussett, opened a tumulus on the downs near Ileden. It is now in the Liverpool City Museum with the rest of the Faussett Collection – Ian Taylor (edited) *op.cit.* 32. For an assessment of the significance of the brooch ("the masterpiece in this genre") *see* Witney, *The Kingdom of Kent op.cit.* 103; a coloured photograph is opposite 117.

27   Witney, *The Jutish Forest op.cit.* 43. Jolliffe, *Pre-Feudal England op.cit.* 50 and note 6.

28   The Domesday survey records "This manor Archbishop Stigand

held, but it was not part" (of the fief) "of the archbishopric but belonged to the demesne farm of King E" (Edward) – quoted Witney, *The Kingdom of Kent op.cit.* 237.

29   Philip Morgan (edited), *Domesday Book – Kent*, Phillimore 1983 2,17.

30   Kenneth Witney (edited), *The Survey of Archbishop Pecham's Kentish Manors op.cit.* ix–lxxxii.

31   *ibid.* 269–272.

32   *ibid.* 270.

CHAPTER 2   An Orchidaceous Pyrotechnician

1   Preface to *L'Envers et L'Endroit* (1958).

2   The picture is a little more complicated than this. The centre of the manor of Northwood could have been St Anne's Farm lying to the north of the present Church Street – in 1574 Queen Elizabeth referred to "our Manor of Whitstable of old called Norwood and now called St Annes and Courtleys". All Saints church may have been built just outside the boundary of Northwood manor. The settlement round the harbour, a thriving port in the Middle Ages and before, was called Harwich from which Whitstable-street extended south-eastwards. The Domesday entry for Harwich (or in modern terms Whitstable) comes under the name of Nortone (i.e. Northwood). *See* Flavia Taylor, *The North Wood*, Emprint Publications 1995 39–48 and 95; *also* I. W. Green, *The Story of All Saints, a history of the parish church of All Saints, Whitstable*, Elvy Bros. 1956 1–5.

3   Douglas West, *The Third Portrait of a Seaside Town*, Emprint Publications 1992 119.

4   Jocelyn Brooke, *The Wonderful Summer*, John Lehmann Ltd. 1949 14–15.

5   *ibid.* 13.

6   GC 69 (trilogy 354).

7   GC 35–6 (trilogy 330).

8 Dog 45.

9 *ibid.*

10 Dog 105–6 and 108–9.

11 *ibid.* 110–11.

12 Jocelyn Brooke, *December Spring – poems*, John Lane The Bodley Head 1946 21.

13 Dog 111–12.

14 MO 42 (trilogy 39).

15 MO 44 (trilogy 41). True to form, Vincent in *The Wonderful Summer* (page 133) also refuses to take part in kiss-in-the-ring.

16 Oliver Warner (British Council) to Jocelyn Brooke, 17 October 1951 and 4 August 1961, Texas.

17 Michael De-la-Noy, *Denton Welch, the making of a writer*, Viking 1984 31–2. James Methuen-Campbell, *Denton Welch, Writer and Artist*, Tartarus Press 2002 16–17. Brooke thought Welch did not write about his schooldays because he found the routine fundamentally boring. One aspect of St Michael's added to this: "St Michael's was also a very pure school: one heard little or none of the usual schoolboy smut, and when I left at the age of thirteen I was still firmly convinced that babies were excreted through the back passages of married ladies" – Jocelyn Brooke, *Introduction to Denton Welch, extracts from his published works*, Chapman & Hall 1963 ix–x.

18 MO 51–4 (trilogy 46–9).

19 MO 51 (trilogy 46).

20 The "Iggulsdens" here in "Furious and Deadly" had been the "Igglesdens" in the trilogy, which is the usual Kentish spelling.

21 Jocelyn Brooke, "Furious and Deadly", unpublished typescript, Washington University c.1961 215–20. MO 69 (trilogy 58–9).

22 Jocelyn Brooke, "Furious and Deadly" *op.cit.* 221–2.

23 *ibid.* 225–31.

24 Hugh Walpole, *The Crystal Box* (1924), quoted in Rupert Hart-Davis, *Hugh Walpole, A Biography*, Macmillan 1952 17–18.

25   MO 70 (trilogy 59).

26   Jocelyn Brooke, "Furious and Deadly" *op.cit.* 251–2.

27   *ibid.* 252–3.

28   MO 70 (trilogy 60).

29   MO 71–2 (trilogy 60).

30   MS 121–3 (trilogy 199–200).

31   MS 123 (trilogy 200).

32   MS 128 (trilogy 205).

33   Jocelyn Brooke, *Private View, Four Portraits*, James Barrie 1954 74.

34   MO 86 (trilogy 71).

35   MO 85–6 (trllogy 71).

36   Jocelyn Brooke, "The Wrong Side of the Blanket", *London Magazine*, July 1955, Vol.2 No.7.

37   Jocelyn Brooke. *Conventional Weapons*, Faber and Faber 1961 37. MS 151 (trilogy 221).

38   MS 152 (trilogy 221–2).

39   Jocelyn Brooke, *Conventional Weapons op.cit.* 69.

40   *ibid.* 86 and 95.

41   MS 153 (trilogy 223).

42   MS 177 (trilogy 243).

43   MS 178–9 (trilogy 244).

44   Jocelyn Brooke, *Conventional Weapons op.cit.* 122.

45   MS 179 (trilogy 245).

46   MS 154 (trilogy 223). The trilogy was, of course, to become the Proustian novel with most of the relevant ingredients: the childhood holiday home and its walks, the towers on the horizon (in Brooke's case water- not church-), delight in the detail of flowers, the seaside versus metropolitan life, the faithful male friend etc., and above all the relations of time and place.

47   Albert Heron to Jocelyn Brooke, six letters undated ending with a postcard postmarked 8 December 1933, Texas. Jonathan Hunt, preface to trilogy ix–x and xii.

48   MS 188 and 190 (trilogy 252 and 254). Jocelyn Brooke
      to Henry Brooke, three letters undated (1935) and two
      postcards, one postmarked 4 October 1935, Texas.

49   Jocelyn Brooke, *Conventional Weapons op.cit.* 145.

50   MS 191–2 (trilogy 255). Jocelyn Brooke, *Conventional
      Weapons op.cit.* 153. He was also then writing his full-length
      monograph on British orchids which "at that time (the Munich
      period) ... seemed almost an act of defiance" – MS 194
      (trilogy 257).

51   MS 189 (trilogy 253).

52   Jocelyn Brooke, *December Spring op.cit.* 28.

53   MS 189 (trilogy 253).

54   MS 95–6 and 99 (trilogy 178–9 and 181).

55   Jocelyn Brooke, *December Spring op.cit.* 49.

56   Jocelyn Brooke to Evelyn Urmston, postmarked
      28 October 1942, Texas.

57   Jocelyn Brooke, *December Spring op.cit.* 53.

58   *ibid.* 56.

59   Jocelyn Brooke to Evelyn Urmston, 18 February 1944, Texas.
      He had amused himself in recent correspondence by setting
      his sister quiz questions about the distant family past. Radnor
      Cliffe was the old family home at Sandgate.

60   Jocelyn Brooke, *December Spring op.cit.* 67.

61   MO 117 (trilogy 93). Jocelyn Brooke to Emily Ford
      (Benjamin Bouncer to Mrs. Nutt), 20 February 1944, Texas.

62   MO 125–31 (trilogy 99–104).

63   Jocelyn Brooke, *December Spring op.cit.* 68.

64   MO 123 (trilogy 97).

65   MO 131 (trilogy 103).

66   Jocelyn Brooke to Evelyn Urmston, 28 November 1944,
      Texas.

67   Jocelyn Brooke to Evelyn Urmston, 2 December 1944, Texas.
      Mr Barron was the chemist and photographer at Bridge – MS
      36–7 (trilogy 131–2).

CHAPTER 3   Jocelyn Brooke

1   Texas.

2   Texas.

3   GC 13–14 (trilogy 313). This specific journey is the one he took to Shorncliffe Barracks in October 1947 on re-enlisting in the army, but it typifies the feel of travelling down the Elham Valley at this period.

4   Jocelyn Brooke to Emily Ford, 10 December 1942, and 12 May and 5 August 1944, Texas.

5   Olivia Manning, "An Enemy in the Mind. Jocelyn Brooke: The Man and his Work", *Times Literary Supplement*, 8 May 1969.

6   Cyril Connolly to Jocelyn Brooke, undated but probably end 1942 – *see* Jocelyn Brooke to Jonathan Curling, 1 February 1943, Texas. Connolly had already accepted one poem, "Seaside 1942", for *Horizon* but then thought better of it and retracted. Brooke puzzled for some weeks whether to sue him for breach of contract. Six years later Desmond MacCarthy too had some astringent remarks on the Brookean verse: "many of them are too deeply rooted in private myths – it lessens their value for others...... You owe a lot to Eliot – I don't blame you for that; but don't persist too much in following little damp dark paths among the laurels, they too often only lead to the garden privy." – Desmond MacCarthy to Jocelyn Brooke, 10 April 1948, Texas.

7   Jocelyn Brooke to Jonathan Curling, 1 February 1943, Texas.

8   Jocelyn Brooke, *December Spring – poems*, John Lane The Bodley Head 1946 30.

9   His father, Henry Brooke, had died in 1936.

10   Although the imprint page of *The Scapegoat* gives 1948 as the date of publication, it was actually published in February 1949.

11   Jocelyn Brooke, *The Scapegoat*, The Bodley Head 1948 128.

12   On the first version of the book, John Lehmann wrote:

"there is something wrong with the conception of the book: the psychological and supernatural elements in it have not been successfully fused, – or as one of my readers said 'Freud and Druids will not mix'.... There is a deep psychological compulsion underlying the whole book which the author has tried to explain in terms of pre-Christian myth, – but I am left with the feeling that the compulsion remains obscure even to him himself – A.M.Heath & Company to Jocelyn Brooke, 1 August 1946, Texas. Brooke came up with a new ending where Duncan was burnt to death, but it received even less applause: "The death by heart failure in fire doesn't seem to me to come off. I thought Druidical sacrifices were blood and not fire sacrifices?" – A.M.Heath & Company to Jocelyn Brooke, 16 October 1946, Texas.

13 Jocelyn Brooke, *The Image of a Drawn Sword*, Secker & Warburg 1982 13.

14 *ibid.* 133.

15 *ibid.* 135–6.

16 *ibid.* 139–40.

17 Jonathan Hunt, preface to trilogy ix.

18 Jocelyn Brooke to Yvonne Kapp, 24 May 1962, London Metropolitan University, quoted Jonathan Hunt *op.cit.* ix. Unfortunately, the Kapp archive is uncatalogued and not as yet open to the public.

19 Nathalie Blondel, entry for Bernard Jocelyn Brooke in *Oxford Dictionary of National Biography*, 2004 7:906.

20 Christopher Scoble, *Fisherman's Friend, a life of Stephen Reynolds*, Halsgrove 2000 135–6. For an earlier academic discussion of this genre and Reynolds' contribution to its theory, *see* Peter Keating, *The Haunted Study: A Social History of the English Novel 1875–1914*, Secker & Warburg 1989 308–11. In recent days, the term autobiografiction has been elevated to a more formal position in the taxonomy of literature – *see* in particular Max Saunders, *Self Impression, Life-Writing, Autobiografiction, and*

the Forms of Modern Literature, Oxford University Press 2010.
Reynolds *would* have been pleased.

21 MO 15 (trilogy 19).

22 MO 23–4 (trilogy 25–6).

23 MS 20 (trilogy 118).

24 MO 50–1 (trilogy 46).

25 Jonathan Hunt op cit. x–xi.

26 MO 83 (trilogy 69).

27 Jocelyn Brooke to Jonathan Curling, 20 February 1943
(No 2), Texas.

28 MO 109–10 (trilogy 87–8).

29 MO 115 (trilogy 92). This vision of winter-spring, which
becomes the literary symbol of Brooke's passion for the place,
first occurs in his letter of 18 February 1944 to his sister and
then appears in more permanent form in the poem "Scerni"
in *December Spring* (see page 44 above). It carries with it, of
course, overtones of the first stanza of *Little Gidding*, published
in October 1942 when Brooke was embarking for the Middle
East.

30 MO 114 (trilogy 91).

31 Jocelyn Brooke to Emily Ford, 5 August 1944, Texas.

32 MS 135 (trilogy 210–11).

33 MS 136–7 (trilogy 212).

34 GC 164 (trilogy 422).

35 *ibid.*

36 MS 250 (trilogy 301).

37 GC 18 (trilogy 317).

38 Jocelyn Brooke to John Lehmann, 1 September 1948,
Texas.

39 "It has delighted me. Mr. Brooke has given me two treats
I love: the opportunity of reading good prose and the
privilege of borrowing sometimes poet's eyes, sometimes
of watching human nature through eyes certainly acute" –
Desmond MacCarthy, *Sunday Times*, 18 April 1948. This was

the beginning of a warm relationship with MacCarthy that continued through the latter's last illness and death in 1952, and with his widow, Molly, the following year.

40   Dust jacket of *A Mine of Serpents* (1949).

41   Desmond MacCarthy to Jocelyn Brooke, 13 March 1948, Texas.

42   Desmond MacCarthy to Jocelyn Brooke, 16 March 1949, Texas. MacCarthy had his own idiosyncratic answer to the problem of the ending with which Brooke had wrestled for the previous three years: "To my thinking, the end would have been better if the boy had hanged himself in the wood of ill-omens, after being whipped by his uncle for pilfering. That would have been quite bad enough. But to make his uncle flog him to death was not only unnecessarily hideous, but improbable. No: that was bad art."

43   Dog 232 and 234.

44   The main narrative of the early part of the book is less about the pursuit of the desired firework than the long wait for the First World War to end before a proper firework display could be held in Brooke's cottage garden – MS 50–3 (trilogy 143–6). But many of the later firework displays were held across the road at Nutgrove, the garden of the Huggett family (the fictional Igglesdens) on the corner opposite Oswalds, which was open and much larger than the Brookes'. The Huggett and other village children were delighted as Jocelyn set off his usual idiosyncratic display of crackers, rockets and assorted fireworks – Ian Taylor and Peggy Hogben (edited), *An Anthology of Kingston and Bishopsbourne, Book 2*, Kingston Village Society 1987 12. This explains an initiative of his mother's about which Brooke wrote to his sister Evelyn from Switzerland in 1935: "The latest joke is the owl's [*his mother, May Brooke*]. An article of mine (about fireworks) having appeared in the New Statesman [*"The British fire ritual", 14 September 1935*], she writes to say that she is sending a copy to Mrs. Huggett! It took

me several minutes to think why" – Jocelyn Brooke to Evelyn
Urmston, undated, Texas. The Huggetts' house was called
Nutgrove because it had "an immense orchard of nut-trees" –
MS 88 (trilogy 172).

45 Jonathan Hunt *op.cit*. xi.

46 MS 98 (trilogy 180–1).

47 MS 252 (trilogy 302–3).

48 Anthony Powell, *Jocelyn Brooke*, trilogy 1.

49 MS 12 (trilogy 112).

50 GC 13 (trilogy 309).

51 Stephen Reynolds, *A Poor Man's House*, Halsgrove 2001 1.

52 GC 13 (trilogy 309).

53 Desmond MacCarthy's wife, Molly, had her own curious
take on the title of the new book following a recent visit to
the bombsites of Canterbury: "The only place I went to this
summer was Canterbury! for the day – saw the Cathedral for
the first time in my life – came out of the gate ... turned to
the left – down a bomber waste on left of street, the bombing
having opened up a perfect vista of the Cathedral, but to
my horror disgusting cheap shops rising to completely shut
out this view, some already finished, with spurious 'Ye olde'
furniture in windows of the very worst and most vulgar kind
– then at the end of all the street, after some tea shops – a
life size portrait of Jocelyn in a photographer's window!! [*the
premises in Burgate of Fisk-Moore, Brooke's usual photographer*]...
'how very incongruous' I exclaimed to myself. It was early
closing so I couldn't go in to the photographer's. When I got
back to Hampton the first thing I saw on Desmond's table was
"The Goose Cathedral" by Jocelyn Brooke – as yet unknown
to me this book – and somehow I immediately connected it
with *Canterbury* and felt the Clergy must be *Ganders* anyhow
not to have perceived the disgusting commercial vandalism all
round the precincts. No one among them clever enough to
rouse up fuss enough, to cause National Trust to do something

about it. Really they have almost turned Canterbury Cathedral itself into a scone and tea shop, and I feel disgusted. The little square [the Buttermarket] is nice but everything west is as desolate and squalidly crowded with modern meanness as anything I have ever seen. I think your family's country cottage is near there and so you were photographed there in the nearest town? It was a very nice photograph – but the large size made it seem as if it said 'There you see! Stupidity, rife all along down here! I'm here in my photograph just to point this out!' Canterbury Cathedral – the *Gander* Cathedral! now to me when I think of the Clerics!" – Molly MacCarthy to Jocelyn Brooke, 2 January 1950, Texas.

54   GC 185–6 (trilogy 437).

55   Robert Kee, "Life Itself", *New Statesman*, 21 October 1950.

56   Brooke had a lot in common with Denton Welch: both were weakly youngest sons of Christian Scientist parents, went to the same prep school, homosexual, lacking in social confidence, and in their writings obsessed with the childhood past. In 1963 Brooke edited a selection of Welch's writings to which he wrote a revealing introduction emphasising these common identities. Brooke's description of Welch's writing life comes at times very close to home: "there might, if he had lived, have been other books – further fragments of autobiography, odd episodes and impressions which had not found a place in the previous works; yet there was always a danger of this particular vein becoming overworked..." – Jocelyn Brooke (edited), *Denton Welch, extracts from his published works*, Chapman & Hall, 1963 xxii–xxiii.

57   Selina Hastings, *The Secret Lives of Somerset Maugham*, John Murray 2009 491 and 510. The papers on the Maugham Festschrift are in the Jenman Collection in New South Wales.

58   Jocelyn Brooke, *December Spring op.cit.* 17.

59   Anthony Powell to Jocelyn Brooke, 23 January 1953, Texas.

60   Anthony Powell, *Jocelyn Brooke*, trilogy 11.

61   *ibid.*

62   Olivia Manning *op.cit*. Brooke clearly felt guilty about the
      incident of "Lesley's hair"; Manning wrote to him some time
      later: "I did not realise you felt I had anything to forgive. It
      was poor Lesley's hair and she speaks of you as tenderly as
      ever" – Olivia Manning to Jocelyn Brooke, 22 November
      1955, Texas. But for Manning the incident became a joking
      symbol of Brooke's social behaviour: "It is years since we sat
      on a banquette at the Salisbury, years since you dropped in
      respectably sober for a little light literary chat before going
      off to get drunk and beat up more long-standing friends, years
      since you pulled poor Leslie's [*sic*] hair at the Ordnance Arms.
      What has become of you? So much time has passed that poor
      old Leslie, whom you used to rape or so she said, is quite long
      dead and another black eyed charmer sleeps in her bed" –
      Olivia Manning to Jocelyn Brooke, 21 May 1963, Texas.

63   Anthony Powell, *Jocelyn Brooke*, trilogy 12.

64   Olivia Manning was firmly supportive: "Of course you will go
      on writing. You are just passing through one of those phases
      that we all know and that seem so permanent and hopeless but
      are just a necessary fallow time. You are so clearly a Writer,
      the real thing, that you could not come to an end like that.
      You have only to wait. The impetus will return. I know all
      about it" – Olivia Manning to Jocelyn Brooke, 8 January 1953,
      Texas. Ten years later she was still attempting to reassure
      him: "I do *not* think you are written out" – Olivia Manning to
      Jocelyn Brooke, 27 May 1963, Texas.

65   John Lehmann put his finger on one of the problems in
      commenting on *Private View:* "I have to admit, at the same
      time, that I find the tension in the writing has sagged a little
      since 'The Military Orchid'. I regret this especially, because I
      believe an intelligent 'editor' would have persuaded you to see
      and correct it before publication – so little really to be done
      to achieve again the beautiful balance of style of that first book

of yours" – John Lehmann to Jocelyn Brooke, 12 December 1954, Texas.

66   Olivia Manning *op.cit*.

67   Not as unprepossessing as all that – it was Brooke's great expectations in 1925 that produced the let-down. A neat little farmhouse peeping over a garden hedge, it stands alone at a crossroads of tiny lanes in the midst of woodland and open meadows – the nearest habitation at least a quarter of a mile away. Arriving on foot hot from a long walk, the visitor today senses much the same dream-like qualities about this isolated site. The house was built in 1603 and extended about 1700, the lower storey of red brick, and most of the upper, part timber, part rendering under Kent peg tiles. For a description of its interior in the 1980s, complete with oak panelling, beams and the statutory inglenook, but never a bar, see Ian Taylor (edited), *An Anthology of Kingston and Bishopsbourne Book 1*, Kingston Village Society 1982 27. Dog 193–5.

68   Dog 16–17. To be fair to Brooke here, he probably means "no fear of flying" once airborne and full of alcohol.

69   His friends, particularly his homosexual friends, were intrigued by the scene in the woods. John Lehmann was curious: "I particularly enjoyed the visit to the Bandit, the horrible experience in the wood (was this an actual *physical* result of it – surely extremely remarkable if so)..." – John Lehmann to Jocelyn Brooke, 1 November 1955, Texas. The writer and naturalist, Robert Gathorne-Hardy, was reminded of an evanescent passage in Proust: "Of your writing, my admiration was unsurprisedly enhanced by the book; the orgasm in the wood triumphantly realises Logan's [*a friend*] test of a fine style (had you got in mind Proust's immaculate paragraph about masturbating in front of the window? Logan showed it to me once, but I've never been able to find it again)" – Robert Gathorne-Hardy to Jocelyn Brooke, 18 April 1957, Texas. Even Raymond Mortimer had a good word for it: "I

enjoyed particularly also your Sicilian pages, and the account of the 'love-affair' with the Army, and the scene in the wood under the rain" – Raymond Mortimer to Jocelyn Brooke, 1 January 1956, Texas.

70   Interestingly, although Clambercrown is a mythical name not appearing on any map, the same area on the 1819 Ordnance Survey is entitled "The Dogs" – Timeline Historical Map No. 179 Canterbury and East Kent 2005.

71   Dog 173–4.

72   Dog 82 and 125.

73   Dog 25.

74   Dog 236.

75   Dog 234.

76   Jocelyn Brooke to John Lehmann, 30 October 1955, Texas. Lehmann would have preferred a separation into *two* books: "I still think there isn't quite enough connection between Sicily and childhood. I would, personally, have liked a book called, say, 'My Aunt Cock' entirely about the Forbidden Lands (there was surely enough material) and another about Sicily, more of a notebook in which you could have put all those observations about what you were reading, and so on. One fairly tight in structure, the other pretty loose" – John Lehmann to Jocelyn Brooke, 1 November 1955, Texas. In general, reviews of the Dog were mixed: one nasty one in the *Spectator* balanced by more flattering words in the *New Statesman* – "Mr. Brooke is a pleasure to read – a highly individual pleasure. Only he could have spun such a legend out of an unvisited and now defunct pub – for such is the "Dog" of the title; and only he, by some strange instinct for comedy, could so tenderly have linked himself with a VD unit of the RAMC in and out of war" – G.W. Stonier, "Rare Excursion", *New Statesman*, 24 December 1955.

77   Dog 132. While composing this paean to Bourne House, Brooke had been active in the campaign against Sir John

Prestige's proposal to demolish it (*see* Jocelyn Brooke to John Betjeman, 15 December 1955, Texas, reproduced here as illustration 13 – the television programme that night was the 10.15 broadcast of *Animal, Vegetable and Mineral* to which Brooke had no doubt been attracted by photographs of Betjeman, Ayrton and Bone in the *Radio Times*.). Though Sir John was supported once again by the county and district councils, this proved a more difficult object than the pushover demolition of the old rectory in 1954/5 (*see* note 4 to Chapter 9). The Ministry of Housing and Local Government decided to make a building preservation order on this important Queen Anne house and a copy of the decision letter of 14 August 1957 from Philip Allen (MHLG 1953/11/C2) was sent to Brooke, who had made representations to the public inquiry, and is preserved among the Brooke papers at Texas.

78 Dog 254–5.

CHAPTER 4 A Reluctant Occultist and a Looming Youth

1 Texas.

2 A.E. Waite, *Shadows of Life and Thought – A Retrospective Review in the Form of Memoirs*, Selwyn and Blount 1938 22.

3 *ibid*. 123.

4 *ibid*. 275–6. Sir Charles Igglesden also noticed Waite's distinctive house in the course of his perambulations in the early 1930s: "Nearing the end of the street we see a lane leading to a white cottage, half hidden by trees, and, opposite, the entrance gate to Charlton Park" – Charles Igglesden, *A Saunter through Kent with Pen and Pencil Vol. XXVI*, Kentish Express 1932 60.

5 Diary of A.E. Waite, May–August 1927, now in the possession of R.A. Gilbert.

6 *ibid*. 15 September 1928: "In the afternoon Sybil and I went to see part of a village cricket match in Charlton Park, having

received many requests all through the season, and this was the very last. It was Bishopsbourne v. Shepherdswell. The wind proved cold."

7   In a few diary entries for the summer of 1928 he refers to attending Evensong with Sybil and/or "Sung Eucharist".

8   Diary of A.E.Waite, 9 July 1932.

9   A.E.Waite, *The Secret Tradition in Alchemy*, Kegan Paul & Co. 1926 xxii.

10   Quoted R.A.Gilbert, *A.E.Waite, Magician of Many Parts*, Crucible 1987 159.

11   A.E.Waite, *Shadows of Life and Thought op.cit.* 6.

12   *ibid.* 248.

13   Diary of A.E.Waite, 30 August 1939.

14   Thomas Wild to Jocelyn Forestier-Walker, 8 June 1942, quoted R.A.Gilbert *op.cit.* 160.

15   R.A.Gilbert *op.cit.* 161.

16   Alec Waugh, *The Best Wine Last, An autobiography through the years 1932–1969*, W.H. Allen 1978 21.

17   Alec Waugh, *The Loom of Youth*, Richards Press 1955 244–5.

18   Alexander Waugh, *Fathers and Sons, The Autobiography of a Family*, Headline 2004 108–10.

19   Christopher Scoble, *Fisherman's Friend, a life of Stephen Reynolds*, Halsgrove 2000 46–9.

20   Alec Waugh, *The Early Years of Alec Waugh*, Cassell 1962 90.

21   *Nation*, 15 September 1917, quoted Grant Richards, *Author Hunting, memories of years spent mainly in publishing*, Unicorn Press 1960 196. This second edition of Richards' autobiography, first published 1934, has an introduction by Alec Waugh.

22   Alec Waugh, *Early Years op.cit.* 156.

23   Alec Waugh, *Best Wine op.cit.* 17.

24   *ibid.* 21.

25   *ibid.* 27. Alec turned out for the Charlton Park cricket club and on occasion brought down from London a team of

publishers and writers. The club was also supported by Lionel Troughton, the ex-captain of Kent, who arranged for the Kent groundsman at St. Lawrence to prepare the first rate wicket at Charlton Park. All this led to complaints from opponents that Charlton Park Cricket Club fielded MCC players (Alec was an MCC member) – Ian Taylor (edited), *An Anthology of Kingston and Bishopsbourne, Book 1*, Kingston Village Society 1982 7; Ian Taylor and Peggy Hogben (edited), *An Anthology of Kingston and Bishopsbourne, Book 2*, Kingston Village Society 1987 44. The Waughs had an earlier connection with Canterbury Cricket Week, Arthur's attempts at writing light operas turning up as prologues and epilogues for the Old Stagers' productions there – Evelyn Waugh, *A Little Learning*, Chapman & Hall 1964 69.

26 Alec Waugh, *Best Wine op.cit.* 22.

27 *ibid.* 21.

28 *ibid.* 27.

29 Alec Waugh, *The Balliols*, Tom Stacey Reprints 1972 publisher's blurb.

30 *ibid.* 1.

31 *ibid.* 259.

32 *ibid.* 488.

33 Alec Waugh, *Early Years op.cit.* 141.

34 Alec Waugh, *The Balliols op.cit.* 216.

35 *Kentish Gazette*, 9 September 1933.

36 Auberon Waugh, entry for Alexander Raban Waugh in *Oxford Dictionary of National Biography* 2004 57:749.

37 Alec Waugh, *Best Wine op.cit.* 21.

38 For much of the first half of 1934 Alec was in London and New York and Joan in Australia, though she remained at Oswalds for most of the following summer, giving birth to their second child there. Come the autumn, the village was sorry to see them go, but a little confused about the number of their progeny. The parish magazine recorded: "A large

number of friends attended at the christening of Mr. and Mrs. Waugh's infant daughter Veronica on Sunday September 23rd. We shall miss Mr. and Mrs. Waugh very much, but they will carry away with them happy memories of Bishopsbourne, which has been their first home and where their ten [*sic*] children have been born and christened."

CHAPTER 5   An Ancient Mariner

1   Gillian Tindall, *Countries of the Mind – the meaning of place to writers*, Hogarth Press, 1991 190.

2   This beautiful avenue, which features at large in the works of Jocelyn Brooke, rejoices in the name of Frog Lane.

3   Joseph Conrad, *Suspense*, J.M.Dent 1925 289. The sculptor, Dora Clarke, omitted "Though," before the first sentence and "don't you think, my friend, that" after "But" in the second.

4   MO 24 (trilogy 26). Brooke was worrying about this suburbanisation as early as 1944, before he had come home to witness the latest instalments – see page 46 above.

5   Joseph Conrad, "Poland Revisited" in *Notes on Life and Letters*, edited J.H. Stape, Cambridge University Press 2004 134.

6   *ibid.* 137.

7   Conrad to Spiridion Kliszczewski, 13 October 1885, CCL 1:12.

8   Conrad to Marguerite Poradowska, 29 March or 5 April 1894, CCL 1:151.

9   Conrad to Marguerite Poradowska, 29 October or 5 November 1894, CCL 1:185.

10   Conrad to Gerald Cumberland, 20 November 1919, CCL 6:530. The original version of this conversation was given in the author's note to *An Outcast of the Islands* (p.viii) which Conrad completed on 27 January 1919. The more widely quoted one comes from an account that Conrad gave Gertrude Bone four years later during his last Christmas at Oswalds – Edward Garnett (edited), *Letters from Conrad 1895–1924*,

Nonesuch Press 1928 vi–viii, and a fuller version in Carolyn G. Heilbrun, *The Garnett Family, The History of a Literary Family*, Allen and Unwin 1961 65 and note 1. As Najder has pointed out, the conversation with Garnett may not necessarily have been the decisive influence since at the time it took place Conrad had already been working on *An Outcast of the Islands* for two months. In later days, Conrad tried to play down his early self-motivation as a writer, pretending it all came to him by chance – Zdzislaw Najder, *Joseph Conrad, A Life*, Camden House 2007 196 and 199.

11 Edward Garnett (edited) *op.cit* ix.

12 Conrad to Stephen Crane, 16 January 1898, CCL 2:21.

13 Conrad to R.B. Cunninghame Graham, 27 August 1898, CCL 2:89.

14 Conrad to Edward Garnett, 13 August 1898, CCL 2:85.

15 Conrad to Aniela Zagórska, 18 December 1898, CCL 2:131–2.

16 GC 40 (trilogy 333).

17 Ernest Dawson, "Some Recollections of Joseph Conrad", *The Fortnightly Review*, August 1928, 205.

18 Conrad to Ford Hueffer, 12 November 1898, CCL 2:118.

19 Conrad to Edward Garnett, 7 November 1898, CCL 2:115–16.

20 Conrad to Ford Hueffer, 12 November 1898, CCL 2:119.

21 Conrad to John Galsworthy, 20 July 1900, CCL 2:284.

22 Conrad to Edward Garnett, 12 November 1900, CCL 2:302–3.

23 E.B. Eastwick, *Venezuela: or, Sketches of a Life in a South American Republic* (1868) and G.F. Masterman, *Seven Eventful Years in Paraguay* (1869).

24 Author's Note (1917) in Jacques Berthoud and Mara Kalnins (edited), *Nostromo*, Oxford University Press 2007 407.

25 Jacques Berthoud and Mara Kalnins (edited) *op.cit.* xiii.

26 *ibid.* 5.

27   Conrad to Aniela Zagórska, 18 December 1898, CCL
      2:131.

28   *ibid.* 132.

29   Borys Conrad, *My Father: Joseph Conrad*, Calder & Boyars
      1970 19.

30   *ibid.* 23 and 27.

31   Jacques Berthoud and Mara Kalnins (edited) *op.cit.* 407. The
      book in question was Frederick Benton Williams, *On Many
      Seas: the Life and Exploits of a Yankee Sailor,* 1897.

32   Conrad to John Galsworthy, 23 October 1902, CCL
      2:448.

33   Conrad to J.B.Pinker, 5 January 1903, CCL 3:6.

34   Conrad to J.B.Pinker, 4 and 6 February 1903, CCL 3:16.
      Conrad to John Galsworthy, 16 February 1903, CCL 3:17.

35   Conrad to John Galsworthy, 16 February 1903, CCL 3:18.

36   Conrad to J.B.Pinker, 17 March 1903, CCL 3:23.

37   Conrad to J.B.Pinker, 16 March 1903, CCL 3:23.

38   Conrad to Ford Hueffer, 23 March 1903, CCL 3:28.

39   Conrad to J.B.Pinker, 7 May 1903, CCL 3:33. Conrad to
      R.B.Cunninghame Graham, 9 May 1903, CCL 3:34.

40   Conrad to John Galsworthy, 4 June 1903, CCL 3:40.

41   Conrad to John Galsworthy, 7 July 1903, CCL 3:44.
      Conrad to H.G.Wells, 4 or 11 July 1903, CCL 3:43.

42   Conrad to R.B.Cunninghame Graham, 8 July 1903, CCL
      3:45.

43   Conrad to J.B.Pinker, 22 August 1903, CCL 3:55.

44   Conrad to J.B.Pinker, 7 or 14 October 1903, CCL 3:67.

45   Conrad to J.B.Pinker, 4 November 1903, CCL 3:72.

46   Conrad to H.G.Wells, November–December 1903, CCL
      3:80.

47   Conrad to J.M.Barrie, 23 November 1903, CCL 3:82.

48   Conrad to J.B.Pinker, 15 December 1903, CCL 3:92.

49   Conrad to David Meldrum, 26 December 1903, CCL
      3:100.

50   Conrad to H.G.Wells, 7 February 1904, CCL 3:112.

51   Conrad to David Meldrum, 5 April 1904, CCL 3:128.

52   Conrad to J.B.Pinker, 7 May 1904, CCL 3:137.

53   Conrad to William Rothenstein, 27 June 1904, CCL
      3:147.

54   Conrad to William Rothenstein, 3 September 1904, CCL
      3:163.

55   Conrad to John Galsworthy, 1 September 1904, CCL
      3:158.

56   Conrad to Ford Hueffer, 5 September 1904, CCL 3:165.

57   Conrad to John Galsworthy, 1 September 1904, CCL
      3:159.

58   Jacques Berthoud and Mara Kalnins (edited) *op.cit.* 408.

59   Conrad to William Rothenstein, 3 September 1904, CCL
      3:163.

60   Conrad to J.B.Pinker, 19 October 1904, CCL 3:171.

61   Conrad to J.B.Pinker, 31 October 1904, CCL 3:178.

62   Garnett observed that Conrad's subject was not the life of
      Nostromo nor the history of the San Tomé mine but " the
      great mirage he has conjured up of the life and nature of the
      Costaguanan territory lying under the shadow of the mighty
      Corderillas... .This great gift of Mr. Conrad's, his special sense
      of *the psychology of scene*, that he shares with certain of the great
      poets and the great artists who have developed it each on his
      own chosen lines, it is that marks him out for pre-eminence
      among the novelists. His method of poetic realism is, indeed,
      intimately akin to that of the great Russian novelists, but Mr.
      Conrad, often inferior in the psychology of character, has
      outstripped them in his magical power of creating the whole
      mirage of Nature." – Edward Garnett, *Friday Nights, Literary
      Criticisms and Appreciations*, Jonathan Cape 1929 78–84. This
      reproduces the original 1904 review article from the *Speaker*.

63   Conrad to John Galsworthy, 6 January 1908, CCL 4:9.

64   Gillian Tindall *op.cit.* 115.

65   Joseph Conrad, "Amy Foster" in *Typhoon, and Other Stories*, Heinemann 1903.

66   Conrad to J.B.Pinker, 3 August 1907, CCL 3:462.

67   Conrad to William Rothenstein, 21 August 1907, CCL 3:467.

68   Conrad to Harriet Mary Capes, 10 September 1907, CCL 3:473.

69   Conrad to Harriet Mary Capes, 20 August 1907, CCL 3:467.

70   Conrad to John Galsworthy, 23 August 1908, CCL 4:110.

71   Conrad to J.B.Pinker, 18 September 1908, CCL 4:124–5.

72   Conrad to R.D.Mackintosh, 26 March 1909, CCL 4:209.

73   Conrad to John Galsworthy, 7 September 1909, CCL 4:271.

74   Borys Conrad, *My Father op.cit.* 57.

75   Conrad to Stephen Reynolds, 26 June 1910, CCL 4:342.

76   Conrad to John Galsworthy, 17 May 1910, CCL 4:329.

77   Borys Conrad, *Coach Tour of Joseph Conrad's Homes in Kent*, Joseph Conrad Society pamphlet 1974.

78   Richard Curle, *The Last Twelve Years of Joseph Conrad*, Sampson Low, Marston 1928 4.

79   Joseph Conrad, "Poland Revisited" *op.cit.* 119.

80   Conrad to Edward Garnett, 7 July 1919, CCL 6:444.

81   Conrad to Captain Anthony Halsey, 5 May 1919, CCL 6:415.

82   Conrad to J.B.Pinker, 4 March 1919, CCL 6:379.

83   Conrad to J.B.Pinker, 29 March 1919, CCL 6:399.

84   Conrad to J.B.Pinker, 21 August 1919, CCL 6:472.

85   Conrad to J.B.Pinker, 7 October 1919, CCL 6:501.

CHAPTER 6   Joseph Conrad

1   Conrad to Stephen Reynolds, 14 February 1909, CCL 4:96, as corrected by CCL 9:287. Conrad to J.B.Pinker, 12 March 1920, CCL 7:50. Conrad had just asked Pinker for a

breakdown of all his past sales in the United States, book by book.

2   John Stape, *The Several Lives of Joseph Conrad*, Heinemann 2007 224.

3   Christopher Hussey, "Bourne Park, Kent – the home of Sir John Prestige", *Country Life*, 10 and 17 November 1944. Colonel Matthew Bell senior (1817–1903) was a regular soldier and later a director of Equitable Life. On purchasing the estate he engaged Andrew Nesfield to landscape the park with beeches and elms and create an ornamental lake by damming the Nailbourne – Ian Taylor (edited), *An Anthology of Kingston and Bishopsbourne Book 1*, Kingston Village Society 1982 4 and 33. He also changed the name from Bourne Place to Bourne Park – Charles Igglesden, *A Saunter through Kent with Pen and Pencil Vol. XXVI*, Kentish Express 1932 62.

4   Dog 113. Colonel Matthew Bell junior (1871–1926) served from 1898 to 1909 in the Rifle Brigade and the Somaliland Field Force. In 1905 he married Mary Dyke (born 1875), daughter of the Conservative minister, Sir William Hart Dyke and a maid of honour to Queen Alexandra – CCL 6:399 and 7:139; Ian Taylor (edited) *op.cit.* 4 and 9.

5   John Conrad, *Joseph Conrad: Times Remembered*, Cambridge University Press 1981 144–9. Borys Conrad, *My Father: Joseph Conrad*, Calder & Boyars 1970 147.

6   Richard Curle, *The Last Twelve Years of Joseph Conrad*, Sampson Low, Marston 1928 5.

7   Conrad to J.B.Pinker, 24 September 1921, CCL 7:342. Conrad to Eric Pinker, 10 August 1922, CCL 7:509.

8   Richard Curle *op.cit.* 175.

9   Borys Conrad, *Coach Tour of Joseph Conrad's Homes in Kent*, Joseph Conrad Society pamphlet 1974.

10 Conrad to Sir Sidney Colvin, 15 October 1919, CCL 6:504.

11 "We have now a team of servants – since Saturday – and you

would not be running an undue risk of perishing from hunger, cold and undue neglect if you managed to come here…" – Conrad to G. Jean-Aubry, 19 January 1920, CCL 7:10.

12 Conrad to Sir Sidney Colvin, 15 October 1919, CCL 6:504.

13 Conrad to William Rothenstein, 24 November 1919, CCL 6:537.

14 Conrad to Hugh Dent, 12 November 1920, CCL 7:202.

15 Conrad to J.B.Pinker, 17 November 1920, CCL 7:205.

16 Conrad to André Gide, 30 November 1920, CCL 7:212.

17 Major John Cecil de Veel Tattersall (1856–1930) was the eldest son of the Rev. W. Tattersall, Rector of Howe In Norfolk, and inherited Charlton Park on the death of his father. He was educated at Harrow and Oxford and took part in the 1882 campaign in Egypt where he was mentioned in despatches. He also served in India. In 1909 he married Nora Mary Dorothea Beatson (1867–1942), daughter of the Rev. L.B. Beatson of Pinchbeck Hall, Lincolnshire – Ian Taylor and Peggy Hogben (edited), *An Anthology of Kingston and Bishopsbourne, Book 2*, Kingston Village Society 1987 21 (there are two photographs of Major Tattersall opposite 18); CCL 7:88.

18 Conrad to J.B.Pinker, 15 July 1920, CCL 7:139–40.

19 *ibid.* 140.

20 The blacksmith, Luther Milward, told John: "Your Dad was a proper gentleman. He'd talk to you, not over your head or at you. He was always ready to learn and respect you and your opinions" – John Conrad *op.cit.* 185, also 153. Milward was a rather special blacksmith: his wrought ironwork can be seen in cathedrals around the world and he made the well-known Father Time weather vane at Lord's

21 John Conrad *op.cit.* 164.

22 Richard Curle *op.cit.* 140.

23 T.E.Lawrence to Bruce Rogers, 26 January 1935, in David

Garnett (edited), *The Letters of T.E.Lawrence*, Jonathan Cape 1938 843, quoted Ton Hoenselaars and Gene M. Moore, "Joseph Conrad and T.E.Lawrence", *Conradiana* 27(1995) 9.

24   Conrad to J.B.Pinker, 19 July 1920, CCL 7:143.

25   Conrad to Lord Northcliffe, 20 July 1920, CCL 7:144.

26   Conrad to J.B.Pinker, 20 July 1920, CCL 7:146.

27   Richard Curle *op.cit.* 13.

28   Richard Curle *op.cit.* 52–3 and 57.

29   Borys Conrad, *Coach Tour op.cit.* In the summer of 1922, he confessed to an American visitor, Hamlin Garland, that he took no joy in his home: "It has no outlook, no horizon. It is a hole – for me. My wife loves it and so – I stay" – Hamlin Garland, quoted Martin Ray (edited), *Joseph Conrad, Interviews and Recollections*, Macmillan 1990 42.

30   John Conrad *op.cit.* 159–60.

31   Richard Curle *op.cit.* 134–5 and 138–9.

32   *ibid.* 137. John Conrad *op.cit.* 144–6.

33   Richard Curle *op.cit.* 136. John Conrad *op.cit.* 144.

34   Richard Curle *op.cit* 68–70.

35   Rupert Hart-Davis, *Hugh Walpole, A Biography*, Macmillan 1952 195, quoted Hoenselaars and Moore *op.cit.* 3.

36   Conrad to J.M.Dent, 24 June 1920, CCL 7:116–17.

37   Conrad to J.B.Pinker, 2 May 1920, CCL 7:89.

38   Conrad to John Quinn, 17 July 1920, CCL 7:142.

39   Conrad to John Quinn, 25 September 1911, CCL 4:480.

40   Conrad to T.J.Wise, 2 October 1918, CCL 6:275 and 2 December 1918, CCL 6:316. To be fair to Conrad, he had offered *The Arrow of Gold* to Quinn before Wise snapped it up – Conrad to John Quinn, 6 October 1918, CCL 6:278.

41   Conrad to John Quinn, 29 September 1919, CCL 6:497.

42   Conrad to J.B.Pinker, 14 June 1921, CCL 7:301. Conrad to T.J.Wise, 21 June 1921, CCL 7:302.

43   Conrad to T.J.Wise, 20 May 1920, CCL 7:99.

44   Conrad to J.B.Pinker, 23 February 1905, CCL 3:219 and

24 January 1912, CCL 5:10. Conrad to Messrs Harper & Brothers, 27 October 1912, CCL 5:120.

45   Conrad to J.M.Dent, 29 October 1919, CCL 6:512.

46   Conrad to Stella V. Roderick, 27 March 1920, CCL 7:62.

47   Conrad to J.B.Pinker, 11 May 1920, CCL 7:94 and 15 May 1920, CCL 7:96.

48   Conrad to J.B.Pinker, 8 June 1920, CCL 7:107. Conrad to Richard Curle, 14 June 1920, CCL 7:108. Conrad to G.Jean-Aubry, 14 June 1920, CCL 7:109.

49   Conrad to J.B.Pinker, 14 June 1920, CCL 7:110.

50   Conrad to J.B.Pinker, 28 June 1920, CCL 7:121 and 30 July 1920, CCL 7:152. Conrad to John Quinn, 5 July 1920, CCL 7:129. Conrad to Richard Curle, 18 August 1920, CCL 7:161.

51   "My novel is hung up for the present. I am writing a cinema play based on Gaspar Ruiz" – Conrad to Richard Curle, 9 October 1920, CCL 7:188.

52   Conrad to Richard Curle, 22 November 1920, CCL 7:208.

53   Conrad to Edward Garnett, 16 December 1920, CCL 7:220.

54   Conrad to John Galsworthy, 17 January 1921, CCL 7:244.

55   Conrad to Eric Pinker, 5 February 1921, CCL 7:256.

56   Conrad to J.B.Pinker, 28 March 1921, CCL 7:268.

57   Conrad to J.B.Pinker, 10 May 1921, CCL 7:284 ("After you departed yesterday I made a good start with the novel") and 12 May 1921, CCL 7:285. Conrad to John and Ada Galsworthy, 10 May 1921, CCL 7:282. Conrad to J.B.Pinker, 24 May 1921, CCL 7:291.

58   Conrad to J.B.Pinker, 20 or 21 July 1921, CCL 7:318 and 23 August 1921, CCL 7:333.

59   Conrad to Bertrand Russell, 2 November 1921, CCL 7:365 and 18 November 1921, CCL 7:373–4.

60   John Conrad *op.cit.* 155–7. John Stape refers to Conrad as

a regular at the "Fleur de Lis Taproom of the White Horse Inn" at Bridge (John Stape *op.cit.* 161 and 321), but since his source, Fred Arnold (in Martin Ray (edited), *op.cit.* 220) refers specifically and with much internal detail to the "Fleur de Lys, Canterbury", a common misspelling used by both Conrad and his son, it seems clear that Arnold is referring to these lunch-time drinks and other late evening occasions at the hotel in Canterbury – Arnold is in fact writing to the *Daily Telegraph* to complain about the proposed demolition of the hotel, so the context is not in doubt. The idea that Conrad would walk up through Bourne Park of an evening to take a tot of gin goes flat against both his walking and drinking habits – whisky and soda was his usual tipple (see John Conrad *op.cit.* 157 and 159; Borys Conrad, *My Father op.cit.* 27).

61   John Conrad *op.cit.* 164. These were feelings wholeheartedly shared by his fellow villager, Jocelyn Brooke: "I loathed cricket with a pathological loathing, and I still do." – MO 53 (trilogy 48).

62   Conrad to J.B.Pinker, 18 July 1921, CCL 7:316.

63   *The Times*, August 1910, quoted Christopher Scoble, *Colin Blythe, lament for a legend*, SportsBooks 2005 29.

64   John Conrad *op.cit.* 178–83. Conrad was on best behaviour when the writer E. V. Lucas joined the party for an hour. Lucas was as surprised and delighted as all the other spectators by Pinker's grand entry: "I did not meet him again till two years ago, under very unexpected conditions, for it was in the St Lawrence ground during the Canterbury cricket week. For the most part this ground is a mass meeting of motor cars, but suddenly the modernity of the place was broken into by the notes of a guard's horn, and in rolled a coach-and-four driven by a benign gentleman in gold spectacles and a white hat, who might almost have come over from Dingley Dell. Behind him, on the next seat, was a distinguished bearded foreigner, tolerantly surveying the

scene through a single eyeglass. When I came to look again I saw that the driver was J.B. Pinker, the literary agent, since dead, and the distinguished bearded foreigner was Joseph Conrad. When the horses had been taken out and the vehicle was transformed into a private box, I joined the party, and for an hour or so sat with Conrad and did my best to qualify him to bat first for Poland. Cricket was strange to him, but he liked the crowd, and the excitement about such a trifle fed his sense of ironical humour. Again the thought struck me that there can be no defence like elaborate courtesy" – E.V.Lucas, quoted Martin Ray (edited) *op.cit.* 85–6.

65   Borys Conrad, *My Father op.cit.* 155.
66   Conrad to J.B.Pinker, 13 August 1921, CCL 7:327.
67   Conrad to Richard Curle, 31 August 1921, CCL 7:335.
68   Conrad to J.B.Pinker, 20 or 27 September 1921, CCL 7:341.
69   Conrad to J.B.Pinker, 4 October 1921, CCL 7:347.
70   Conrad to Karola Zagórska, 29 November 1921, CCL 7:387.
71   Conrad to J.B.Pinker, 19 December 1921, CCL 7:396–7. Conrad to Eric Pinker, 27 June 1922, CCL 7:482. Conrad to J.B.Pinker, 24 January 1922, CCL 7:409.
72   Conrad to Hugh Walpole, 10 February 1922, CCL 7:417.
73   Conrad to Richard Curle, 20 March 1922, CCL 7:434.
74   Conrad to Eric Pinker, 24 April 1922, CCL 7:455.
75   Conrad to Edward Garnett, 24 May 1922, CCL 7:472.
76   Conrad to Eric Pinker, 1 or 8 June 1922, CCL 7:475.
77   Conrad to Richard Curle, 29 June 1922, CCL 7:484.
78   Conrad to Eric Pinker, 13 July 1922, CCL 7:489.
79   Raymond Mortimer in the *New Statesman*, 15 December 1923.
80   Desmond MacCarthy, *Portraits*, 1931, quoted John Stape *op.cit.* 254.
81   Conrad to Edward Garnett, 24 May 1922, CCL 7:471.

Conrad to T.J.Wise, 20 July 1922, CCL 7:495. Conrad to Eric Pinker, 12 August 1922, CCL 7:510.

82 Conrad to Philippe Neel, 24 October 1922, CCL 7:552.

83 Conrad to Eric Pinker, 15 October 1922, CCL 7:534.

84 Conrad to John Galsworthy, 7 August 1922, CCL 7:505–6.

85 Conrad to G.Jean-Aubry, 9 August 1922, CCL 7:507.

86 Conrad to G.Jean-Aubry, 27 October 1922, CCL 7:557.

87 Conrad to Agnes Ridgeway, 7 November 1922, CCL 7:572.

88 Conrad to Eric Pinker, 8 November 1922, CCL 7:574 and 11 November 1922, CCL 7:579. Conrad to Arnold Bennett, 11 November 1922, CCL 7:581. Conrad to Major Gordon Gardiner, c.12 November 1922, CCL 7:582.

89 Conrad to Richard Curle, 14 November 1922, CCL 7:585.

90 John Conrad *op.cit.* 127. He uses the word "machin" which is presumably a slip of the pen.

91 *ibid.* 133. The electric plant was crucial to the running of the household; mains electricity did not arrive at Oswalds until April 1937 – Ian Taylor and Peggy Hogben (edited) *op.cit.* 26.

92 Conrad to Eric Pinker, 26 September 1922, CCL 7:527.

93 Conrad to Richard Curle, 1 October 1922, CCL 7:527.

94 Conrad to Elbridge L. Adams, 15 December 1922, CCL 7:619.

95 Conrad to F.N.Doubleday, 8 December 1922, CCL 7:610–11. Conrad to Eric Pinker, 21 February 1923, CCL 8:33.

96 Conrad to Kate Zuk-Skarszewska, 20 January 1923, CCL 8:12. Conrad to Eric Pinker, 3 January 1923, CCL 8:6. Conrad to Elbridge L. Adams, 22 January 1923, CCL 8:13. Conrad to T.J.Wise, 1 March 1923, CCL 8:36.

97 Conrad to Richard Curle, 2 February 1923, CCL 8:18. Conrad to Aniela Zagórska, 7 March 1923, CCL 8:42.

98 Conrad to F.N.Doubleday, 13 March 1923, CCL 8:49. Conrad to Eric Pinker, 14 March 1923, CCL 8:51.

99 Conrad to Eric Pinker, 23 March 1923, CCL 8:58.

100 Joseph Conrad, *Suspense*, J.M. Dent 1925 118.

101 *ibid.* 208.

102 Conrad to John Galsworthy, 22 February 1922, CCL 8:318.

103 Conrad to Karola Zagórska, 25 March 1923, CCL 8:61. On the voyage out, Conrad felt homesick particularly for Jessie, and the knowledge that Pinker had died in New York only a year before may have underpinned these anxieties: "I miss you more and more. As a matter of fact I am on the edge of worrying tho' I suppose there is no reason for it. It seems ages since I left you in that bedroom in the hotel. When I think of it I have a funny sensation under the breastbone" – Conrad to Jessie Conrad, 30 April 1923, CCL 8:86.

104 Conrad to Jessie Conrad, 4 May 1923, CCL 8:87.

105 Conrad to Richard Curle, 18 May 1923, CCL 8:100.

106 Conrad to G. Jean Aubry, 14 May 1923, CCL 8:98.

107 Conrad to Eric Pinker, 11 May 1923, CCL 8:95.

108 Conrad to Eric Pinker, 14 May 1923, CCL 8:99. Conrad to Jessie Conrad, 14 May 1923, CCL 8:96 and 18 May 1923, CCL 8:100.

109 Conrad to Eric Pinker, 2 July 1923, CCL 8:121. Conrad to G. Jean-Aubry, 7 July 1923, CCL 8:125.

110 Conrad to Eric Pinker, 9 July 1923, CCL 8:126. Conrad to G. Jean-Aubry, 5 August 1923, CCL 8:150.

111 Conrad to Lewis Rose Macleod, 21 July 1923, CCL 8:139.

112 Conrad to Lorna Watson, 15 July 1923, CCL 8:133–4.

113 Conrad to Florence Doubleday, 15 July 1923, CCL 8:132–3.

114 Conrad to Ford Madox Ford, 13 October 1923, CCL 8:195. Conrad to Lt-Colonel Matthew Bell, 22 October 1923, CCL 8:204. Conrad to Eric Pinker, 26 November 1923, CCL 8:230–1. Conrad to Richard Curle, 2 November 1923, CCL 8:210.

115 Conrad to Richard Curle, 12 November 1923, CCL 8:217.

116 Conrad to Eric Pinker, 26 November 1923, CCL 8:230.

117 Conrad to Richard Curle, 12 November 1923, CCL
8:217–18.

118 *ibid.* 217.

119 Conrad to Arnold Bennett, 5 December 1923, CCL 8:240.

CHAPTER 7 A Photographical Microscopist and a Political Cricketer

1 Poem by the Rev. John Duncombe in Frederick Lillywhite,
Cricket Scores and Biographies of Celebrated Cricketers, Lillywhite
1862 vol.1 1744–1826 9–11. *See also* Charles Igglesden,
A Saunter through Kent with Pen and Pencil Vol. XXVI, Kentish
Express 1932 65–7.

2 John Conrad, *Joseph Conrad: Times Remembered*, Cambridge
University Press 1981 152.

3 Conrad to Jessie Conrad, 29 June 1924, CCL 8:394. The
Ashton-Gwatkins had their own little literary circle. A
regular visitor to the old rectory was the romantic historical
novelist Stanley Weyman (pronounced Wyman) (1855–1928)
who held sway over the popular literary world in the 1890s.
Oscar Wilde recommended his novels as first-rate reading
for convicts – T.E. Welby (revised Clare L. Taylor), entry for
Stanley John Weyman in *Oxford Dictionary of National Biography*
2004 58:337.

4 Frank Trelawny Ashton-Gwatkin (1889–1976) wrote novels
about Japan (where he served as a consular official from 1913
to 1918) under the pseudonym John Paris. He transferred to
the Foreign Office in 1921 where, after an influential career,
he rose to become principal establishment officer during the
Second World War and presided over the Eden reforms – the
amalgamation of the Foreign Office, the diplomatic service,
the commercial diplomatic service and the consular service
into a single foreign service. Conrad did not get on with
intellectuals of this sort and their conversations together

were always very heavy going – John Conrad *op.cit*. 153. In fact, Gwatkin turned up on Conrad's doorstep one day in 1921 and proceeded to cross-examine the old novelist at length on the minutiae of his writing method, the kind of approach that Conrad abhorred. But he "answered his queries with painstaking patience, there being evident in his manner a feeling of the futility of giving this sort of information" – Walter Tittle, quoted Martin Ray (edited), *Joseph Conrad, Interviews and Recollections*, Macmillan 1990 160.

5   John Conrad *op.cit*. 152.

6   The quaint little statue of Richard Hooker, the work of an Italian sculptor copied from Exeter Cathedral, was installed by the Rev. Ashton-Gwatkin in a niche in the wall of the old rectory, and removed to the church after the rectory had been demolished – Charles Igglesden *op.cit*. 58.

7   For a fuller biography of Reade *see* Alan Major, "Bishopsbourne's Eminent (But Forgotten) Victorian, The Rev. Joseph Bancroft Reade", *Bygone Kent*, March 1989 171–7 and R.D. Wood, entry for Joseph Bancroft Reade in *Oxford Dictionary of National Biography*, 2004 46:230.

8   R.D. Wood, "J.B. Reade, F.R.S., and the Early History of Photography", *Annals of Science* 27 (1971) 13–83; "J.B. Reade's Early Photographic Experiments", *British Journal of Photography* 28 July 1972; "Straightening the Record on Reade", *British Journal of Photography* 3 July 1996.

9   Alan Major *op.cit*. 177.

10   C.H. Oakden, "Joseph Bancroft Reade: his contributions to microscopical science", *Journal of Royal Microscopical Society* (1926) 181–92.

11   J.B. Reade to J. Glaisher F.R.S., 20 October 1869, in "Account of Two Meteors seen at Bishopsbourne", *Proceedings of the Meteorological Society*, 5 (November 1869), quoted in Alan Major *op.cit*. 175. Jocelyn Brooke was fascinated by comets as much as fireworks – Dog 123–4.

12   J.B.Reade to Jabez Hogg, 21 and 27 September and 7 and 25 November 1870, Brotherton Collection, University of Leeds, MSS Misc. Letters 2 READE, 1868–70 ff 14.

13   Alan Major *op.cit*. 177.

14   Kentish Gazette, 20 December 1870, quoted Alan Major *op.cit*. 176. The obituary drew a direct comparison with Hooker: "Without being as deeply read a Theologian as his predecessor 'the judicious Hooker', he was no unworthy successor to that great man and by no means unlike him in his simple habits and retiring nature. The main difference between the two was, that Hooker was an earnest student of God's word, the last rector while holding firmly the same faith read as well another book, no less God's book, the book of nature."

15   Christopher Hussey, "Bourne Park, Kent – the home of Sir John Prestige", *Country Life*, 10 and 17 November 1944. The alienation of Dame Elizabeth Aucher was a sorry tale. Her foolish son, completely dominated by his evil legal adviser, John Corbett, reduced his mother to almost complete destitution and she ended up eating with the servants. After the court case restored her legacy, she still preferred to live in Canterbury rather than return to Bourne, the house she had built herself – *see* Bourne Park, John Corbett of Bourne, Kent, compiled by J.C.Noble, Elham Valley Website, www.elham. co.uk, as at 6 September 2009.

16   Robert W. Gutman, *Mozart – A Cultural Biography*, Secker & Warburg 2000 204. Stanley Sadie, *Mozart – The Early Years 1756–1781*, W.W.Norton and Company 2006 79.

17   David Underdown, *Start of Play – Cricket and Culture in Eighteenth-Century England*, Allen Lane The Penguin Press 2000 145.

18   J.Wilson (edited), *A biographical index to the present House of Commons* (1806) 363.

19   David Underdown *op.cit*. 11.

20   *ibid.* 127.

21   It was described by a contemporary as having "smooth grass… laid compleat… a sweet lawn, with shady trees encompass round" – John Burnby, *The Kentish Cricketers* (1773), quoted John Major, *More Than A Game, the story of cricket's early years*, Harper Perennial 2008 68–9.

22   David Underdown *op.cit.* 145.

23   *ibid.*

24   *ibid.* 146.

25   Ashley Mote (edited), *John Nyren's The Cricketers of My Time: The Original Version*, Robson Books 1998 79.

26   David Underdown *op.cit.* 146.

27   *ibid.* For a more detailed narrative of the actual cricket and a rather romanticised account of the death of Mann's wife – "fate cast a shadow over the idyllic life of the Manns" – *see* John Major *op.cit.* 69–76. For an account of the celebrated match of 1773 *see* Charles Igglesden *op.cit.* 65–7, although Igglesden mistakenly records Mann's second innings score as 1 instead of the 22 he actually made.

28   Christopher Hussey *op.cit.*

CHAPTER 8 A Learned and Judicious Divine

1   Pat Davis, *Kent Tellers of Tales*, Geerings of Ashford 1996 45.

2   James Boswell, *The Life of Samuel Johnson*, Everyman's Library 1973 557.

3   Walton 129–30.

4   Walton 136.

5   Walton 136–7.

6   Richard Symonds, *The Fox, the Bees and the Pelican – Some Worthies and Noteworthies of Corpus Christi College, Oxford*, Corpus Christi College 2002 9.

7   Walton 139–40.

8   Walton 145.

9   Millar Maclure, *The Paul's Cross Sermons 1534–1642*, University

of Toronto Press 1958 3–5.

10   Thomas Carlyle, *Oliver Cromwell's Letters and Speeches, with elucidations*, Chapman and Hall 1888 50.

11   Richard Newcourt, *Repertorium ecclesiasticum parochiale Londinense* (1708–10) I 4–5, quoted Millar Maclure *op.cit.* 11.

12   Walton 143.

13   Walton 147. Walton has Hooker uttering the same wish in much the same words when seeking to make his escape from the Temple six years later – Walton 175.

14   Christopher Haigh, *English Reformations. Religion, Politics, and Society under the Tudors*, Oxford 1993 241.

15   Philip B. Secor, *Richard Hooker, Prophet of Anglicanism*, Burns & Oates 1999 51.

16   Walton wrote : "I cannot learn the pretended cause; but that they were restored the same month is most certain" – Walton 141–2.

17   W. Speed Hill, "*The Evolution of Hooker's Laws of Ecclesiastical Polity*" in W. Speed Hill (edited), *Studies in Richard Hooker, essays preliminary to an edition of his works*, Press of Case Western Reserve University 1972 124.

18   *ibid.* 119–23.

19   Thomas Fuller, *The History of the Worthies of England*, J.G.W.L. 1662 I 264.

20   Walton 166.

21   Folger V 256.

22   *ibid.*

23   Folger V 253.

24   Walton 144–5.

25   Walton 173.

26   Thomas Fuller *op.cit.* I 264. Fuller took a rather harsher line in his *Church-History* three years later: "Mr Hooker his voice was low, stature little, gesture none at all, standing stone-still in the Pulpit, as if the posture of his body were the emblem of his minde, unmoveable in his opinions. Where his eye were

left fixed at the beginning, it was found fixed at the end of his Sermon: In a word, the doctrine he delivered had nothing but it self to garnish it. His stile was long and pithy, driving on a whole flock of several Clauses before he came to the close of a sentence. So that when the copiousness of his stile met not with proportionable capacity in his auditors, it was unjustly censured, for perplext, tedious, and obscure" – Thomas Fuller, *The Church-History of Britain from the Birth of Jesus Christ until the Year MDCXLVII*, John Williams 1665 III 127–8. Both passages are quoted Folger V 658.

27   Walton 174.
28   Walton 173.
29   Folger I 43.
30   Folger I 47.
31   Folger I 51.
32   Christopher Morris, Introduction to Richard Hooker, *The Laws of Ecclesiastical Polity*, Everyman edition 1965 v.
33   Folger I 61.
34   Folger I 99.
35   Folger I 171.
36   Folger I 56.
37   Folger I 82.
38   Folger I 132.
39   Folger I 183.
40   Folger I 191.
41   Folger I 302.
42   C. J. Sisson, *The Judicious Marriage of Mr. Hooker and the Birth of The Laws of Ecclesiastical Polity*, Cambridge University Press 1940 58–9 and 66–78.

CHAPTER 9   Richard Hooker

1   Walton 174–5. Another eminent cleric, Nicholas Ridley, the Protestant martyr, had sought the peace of Bishopsbourne during his later life. He had been curate there in the 1530s

before being appointed Vicar of nearby Herne – Charles Igglesden, *A Saunter through Kent with Pen and Pencil* Vol. *XXVI*, Kentish Express 1932 54.

2 Charles Igglesden *op.cit.* 58–9. In addition to the description of the old drawing of the original house which Igglesden had seen in the church, this provides a detailed portrait of how the house and garden looked in the early 1930s. There is a front elevation and first floor plan drawn up by a Canterbury architect in March 1813, as part of a petition by the then rector for repairs, which shows the length of the old house to good effect – Canterbury Cathedral Archives, CCA-Dcb-E/F/Bishopsbourne, St Mary/1.

3 Arthur Mee, *The King's England – Kent*, Hodder and Stoughton 1942 50.

4 In the early 1950s Sir John Prestige was looking out for an opportunity to pull down the Rectory and indeed Bourne House, neither of which was then occupied. It came in March 1954 when the tenant of Oswalds died and Prestige offered Conrad's old house to the Church for use as a rectory, on condition that he was permitted to demolish Hooker's house. He had little concern for the historical associations of the old rectory: "This building has a reputed interest as the residence of Doctor Richard Hooker, an Elizabethan Devine [*sic*] who wrote a book known as the 'Ecclesiastical Polity'. The house is about the worst possible example of how Rectors in years gone by, possessing wealth hacked about Rectories to give themselves larger accommodation regardless of their successors. This Rectory is enormous and extremely inconvenient and possesses no single architectural detail of any interest except an early Sixteenth Century moulded oak ceiling which is in a very large room facing North-East." (Sir John Prestige to J.W.R.Adams, County Planning Officer for Kent, 5 March 1954). The investigator sent down by the Ministry of Housing took a rather different view: "The main

features of interest lie in the small remains which still exist of the original Elizabethan house, the most important of which is the moulded oak-beamed Tudor ceiling in the dining room. Other features include the eighteenth century panelled doors set in deep recess openings in the dining room, the ceiling of the study, the stone mullioned and transomed window lighting the cloakroom, the plain Elizabethan panelling in the small bedroom over the front door, and the late eighteenth century marble mantelpieces in two other bedrooms The building also has historical associations with Richard Hooker who lived in the house when Rector of Bishopsbourne from 1595–1600. The house has considerable architectural importance, is regarded as worthy of preservation if this is practicable and we should like to see it preserved." But in the end the Ministry accepted the Prestige argument that the wholesale alterations since 1600 left preservation an open question: "It has however been so much altered since Richard Hooker's time, and bears very little resemblance to that in which he lived, that we feel this historical association is not sufficient to justify its preservation as a building of outstanding national importance. We consider therefore that its preservation is a matter which can be left to the local authorities to decide, as they are in a better position to assess its local importance and the wishes of the local people for its preservation." (Ministry of Housing to Kent County Planning Officer, 30 March 1954). The County Council and the Bridge-Blean Rural District Council swiftly rubber-stamped the Prestige proposal, and typically no local voices of dissent were raised until demolition actually began in March 1955 (C.S.Chettoe to County Planning Officer, 21 March 1955); it was completed in June. The County Planning Office file of 1954–5 (Centre for Kentish Studies, CKS-CC/C-PL/2/AH/-42/45) contains a photograph of the façade of the house and one of the Tudor ceiling at the time of demolition, the only compliance with the Ministry's injunction to obtain "full records by way of photographs and measured drawings of the principal features of interest". In addition to these minimal records of the old rectory, there is a watercolour painting of c.1935 executed by Margaret Mallorie, wife of the then Rector of Barham, which depicts the side of the house and the beauties of the garden on a full summer's day (Canterbury Cathedral Archives, CCA-DCc-PRINDRAW/4/B/4). Sir John's grandson built a mock Palladian house on the site, locally regarded as hideous, and sold it to live elsewhere in the village.

5   Rosemary Keen, "Inventory of Richard Hooker 1601", *Archaeologia Cantiana* LXX (1956) 231–6.

6   Peter Clark, *English Provincial Society from the Reformation to the Revolution: Religion, Politics and Society in Kent 1500–1640*, Harvester Press 1977 233. Local farmers were understandably reluctant to have their corn commandeered by the authorities and sold their stocks secretly for fear of public uproar. John Denn, a yeoman from the next village of Bridge, sold his in London (where demand was greatest) through a middleman because he was "loath himself to be seen to sell it" – *ibid.* 232.

7   *ibid.* 234. There were serious food riots in the neighbourhood (Canterbury, Hernhill and Wye) in the years 1595–6 – *ibid.* 250.

8   *ibid.* 243–4.

9   Walton 181.

10   Walton 184–5.

11   C.J.Sisson, *The Judicious Marriage of Mr. Hooker and the Birth of The Laws of Ecclesiastical Polity*, Cambridge University Press 1940 44.

12   The texts of Hooker's surviving sermons are in Folger V.

13   Walton 182. Fuller also notes this characteristic fixing of the eye (*see* note 26 to Chapter 8). Walton has the ingenuity to pray the myopia in aid to support his malicious view of Hooker's mother-in-law and wife: "and the reader has a

liberty to believe, that his modesty and dim sight were some of the reasons why he trusted Mrs. Churchman to choose his wife" – *ibid*.

14 Walton 183.

15 Walton 184.

16 *ibid*.

17 Walton 177.

18 Walton 181. The same was to happen to Conrad three hundred years later.

19 *ibid*.

20 Folger II 16.

21 Folger II 48.

22 Folger II 50 and 57.

23 Folger II 64.

24 Folger II 79.

25 Folger II 81.

26 Folger II 87.

27 Folger II 106.

28 Folger II 110.

29 Folger II 112–13.

30 Folger I 65.

31 For an extended academic account of his stylistic approach, *see* Georges Edelen, "Hooker's Style", in W. Speed Hill (edited), *Studies in Richard Hooker, essays preliminary to an edition of his works*, Press of Case Western Reserve University 1972 241–77.

32 Folger II 119.

33 Quoted Folger II 123.

34 Folger II 123.

35 Folger II 125.

36 Folger II 127.

37 Folger II 132.

38 Quoted Folger II 147.

39 Folger II 149.

40   Folger II 165.

41   He had been a chorister and knew music well, as Walton
     attests: "Nor was this excellent man a stranger to the more
     light and airy parts of learning, as music and poetry; all which
     he had digested and made useful" – Walton 141.

42   Folger II 150.

43   Folger II 151.

44   Folger II 158.

45   Folger II 154.

46   Folger II 363.

47   Folger II 364.

48   Folger II 383.

49   Folger II 400.

50   Folger II 208.

51   Folger II 332.

52   Folger II 401.

53   Folger II 403.

54   Folger II 435.

55   Folger II 472.

56   Folger II 465.

57   Folger II 483.

58   Folger II 484.

59   Folger II 487.

CHAPTER 10   Last Days

1   Texas.

2   A.S.McGrade, entry for Richard Hooker in *Oxford Dictionary
    of National Biography* 2004 27:973.

3   We have detailed notes (published in Folger III) by Cranmer
    and Sandys on a manuscript of Book VI which has not come
    down to us. For an illuminating analysis of these notes and
    the general concerns of Cranmer and Sandys that led to the
    breakdown of the project, *see* W. Speed Hill, "The Evolution of
    Hooker's *Laws of Ecclesiastical Polity*" in W. Speed Hill (edited),

Studies in Richard Hooker — essays preliminary to an edition of his works, Press of Case Western Reserve University 1972 135–53.

4   Anon., *A Christian Letter of certain English Protestants, unfained favourers of the present state of Religion, Authorised and profesed in England: unto that Reverend and learned man, Mr. R. Hoo. Requiring resolution in certain matters of doctrine (which seem to overthrow the foundation of Christian Religion and of the church among us) expresslie contained in his five books of Ecclesiastical Policie.* 1599 – Corpus Christi College, Oxford, Fulman MSS. 1682, 215b; reproduced Folger IV 6–79.

5   Folger IV 22–42. *See also* Philip B. Secor, *Richard Hooker, Prophet of Anglicanism*, Burns & Oates 1999 318–19.

6   Walton 186.

7   Walton 188.

8   Hooker's "Fragments of an Answer to the Letter of certain English Protestants" are cogently argued and display his mind at its best. They are comparable in length to any of Books 2 to 4 of the *Polity* – W. Speed Hill *op.cit.* 146.

9   Walton 188–9.

10   Walton 189.

11   Walton 189–90.

12   Richard Hooker, *A Sermon Fragment on Hebrews 2. 14–15*, Folger V 412.

13   Walton 190.

14   His will read: "I give and bequeath three pounds of lawful English money towards the building and making of a newer and sufficient pulpit and in the p'ish church of Bishopsbourne" – Charles Igglesden, *A Saunter through Kent with Pen and Pencil Vol. XXVI*, Kentish Express 1932 53–4.

15   Conrad to G.Saint-Aubry, 22 September 1922, CCL 7:523.

16   Conrad to Christopher Sandeman, 21 November 1922, CCL 7:599.

17   Conrad to J.C.Squire, 30 November 1922, CCL 7:605.

18   Conrad to F.N.Doubleday, 6 December 1923, CCL 8:242.

19   Conrad to Florence and F.N.Doubleday, 7 January 1924, CCL 8:260.

20   Gertrude Bone, enclosure to a letter to Edward Garnett, quoted in Carolyn G. Heilbrun, *The Garnett Family, The History of a Literary Family*, Allen & Unwin 1961 65 note 1.

21   Part of the desire for France was to reduce his income tax burden – Conrad to Richard Curle, 8 December 1922, CCL 7:609.

22   Conrad to Richard Curle, 1 February 1924, CCL 8:295.

23   Conrad to Allan Monkhouse, 8 February 1924, CCL 8:305.

24   Conrad to E.H.Visiak, 1 February 1924, CCL 8:295.

25   Conrad to Frank Swinnerton, 25 March 1924, CCL 8:332.

26   Conrad to Elbridge L. Adams, 26 March 1924, CCL 8:333.

27   Conrad to Eric Pinker, 21 January 1924, CCL 8:280. When Conrad sat for Jacob Epstein that spring, he told the sculptor it was "a prison set in a swamp" – Jacob Epstein, quoted Martin Ray (edited), *Joseph Conrad, Interviews and Recollections*, Macmillan 1990 170.

28   Conrad to Aniela Zagórska, 28 April 1924, CCL 8:347.

29   Conrad to F.N. Doubleday, 8 May 1924, CCL 8:354.

30   Conrad to Ernest Dawson, 3 July 1924, CCL 8:399.

31   Conrad to Eric Pinker, 8 July 1924, CCL 8:401.

32   Conrad to Sir Robert Jones, 10 July 1924, CCL 8:402.

33   Conrad to Auguste Gilbert de Voisins, 11 July 1924, CCL 8:403.

34   Richard Curle, *The Last Twelve Years of Joseph Conrad*, Sampson Low, Marston 1928 219–24.

35   *ibid.* 225–31.

36   *ibid.* 231–2.

37   *ibid.* 216.

38   *ibid.* 233–4.

39   Kentish Gazette, 9 August 1924. Richard Curle, *op.cit.* 182–3.
      Cunninghame Graham wrote a moving account for the
      Saturday Review of the atmosphere in Canterbury on the day
      of the funeral, and incidentally furnished a vivid picture of
      the environs of the cathedral twenty years before the German
      bombs: "Houses and yet more houses crowded in upon the
      cathedral, usurping what by rights should have been a grassy
      close, guarded by elm trees or by limes, with nests for rooks,
      who with their cawing supplemented the murmuring masses
      in the adjacent choir, for surely rooks in a cathedral close must
      ever praise the Lord for their quiet sheltered lives. Grouped
      round its dominating church the city huddled as if it sought
      protection against progress and modernity. Bell Harry in his
      beauty seemed a giant lighthouse pointing Heavenwards." –
      R.B. Cunninghame Graham, "Inveni Portum", *Saturday Review*,
      16 August 1924, quoted Martin Ray (edited) *op.cit.* 230–4.

40   When the American novelist, Hamlin Garland, visited
      Oswalds in August 1922 Conrad proudly boasted: "I have
      been here only three years, but I have lived in or near
      Bishopsbourne for thirty years. I am a Kentishman" – Hamlin
      Garland, quoted Martin Ray (edited) *op.cit.* 40.

41   Richard Curle *op.cit.* 194.

42   *ibid.*

43   John Conrad, *Joseph Conrad: Times Remembered*, Cambridge
      University Press 1981 153. Conrad had taken an interest in
      the building of the village hall and had contributed towards its
      construction – part of his local charitable giving. The scheme
      for the porch was masterminded by a small committee of the
      local notables – Canon Ashton-Gwatkin (chairman), Colonel
      Matthew Bell (Bourne Park), Major Tattersall (Charlton
      Park) and John Conrad himself. It also involved the laying
      out of a bowling green on the surrounding land. Much of the
      construction work was carried out by members of the Huggett

family – Jocelyn Brooke's "Igglesdens" – *Kentish Gazette*, 22 October 1927.

44   Richard Curle, *op.cit.* 194.

45   In "Furious and Deadly" Brooke places the accident in early January to fit in with the rising of the Nailbourne, but it in fact took place in September – a prime example of "autobiografiction". This involved a further tweak of time since the Nailbourne did not actually reach the village that year until the last week of January.

46   Jocelyn Brooke, "Furious and Deadly", unpublished typescript, Washington University c.1961, Part 1 An Accident 1–3.

47   *ibid.* 1.

48   *ibid.* 4–5.

49   *ibid.* 9–10. The Nailbourne was not to flow again until the opening of 1959, finally confirming the fate that was to overtake Brooke in the next few years. The local paper had a simple explanation for the question of ill omens: "For the first time since January 5, 1955, the Nailbourne is flowing again and has this week already passed through Barham. It is the strongest flow for many a long year, and at the present rate will soon reach the lake in Bourne Park and go on through Bridge to join the Lesser Stour. This intermittent stream is believed to have its origin in the overflowing of underground reservoirs – and after the weather of 1958 it is little wonder that they have overflowed. Its appearance, according to legend, presages a national or local disaster. While cases can be quoted as proof of the truth of this, the name of 'Woe Waters' is more likely due to the fact that in the past the flowing of the Nailbourne was a disaster for the occupiers of some cottages, long since demolished, that stood in its path and through which it inconsiderately swept" – *Kentish Gazette*, 2 January 1959. The next edition of the paper furnished a scientific explanation of the phenomenon: the Nailbourne could only flow when the water table in the chalk was higher

than the river bed – *Kentish Gazette*, 9 January 1959.

50   Marcus Woodward (edited), *Gerard's Herball*, Studio Editions 1990 74. Jocelyn Brooke, "Furious and Deadly" *op.cit*. 24.

51   Jocelyn Brooke to Francis King, 3 February 1965, Texas.

52   Olivia Manning, "An Enemy in the Mind. Jocelyn Brooke: The Man and his Work", *Times Literary Supplement*, 8 May 1969. "I do think … you should break out beyond the material you have used, and tend to use again" – Olivia Manning to Jocelyn Brooke, 27 May 1963, Texas.

53   Anthony Powell to Jocelyn Brooke, 11 June 1956, Texas.

54   Jocelyn Brooke to Francis King, 3 February 1965, Texas.

55   *ibid*. Even distant literary acquaintances, like Raymond Mortimer, had earlier been roped in to promote his work, following the dearth of reviews for *Conventional Weapons* – Raymond Mortimer to Jocelyn Brooke, 5 and 19 July 1961.

56   Jocelyn Brooke to Francis King, 19 February 1965, Texas.

57   Olivia Manning, "An Enemy in the Mind" *op.cit*.

58   Olivia Manning to Jocelyn Brooke, 6 May 1965 and undated [May 1965], Texas.

59   Yvonne Kapp to Jocelyn Brooke, 26 February 1965, Texas.

60   Robert Gathorne-Hardy to Jocelyn Brooke, 26 November 1957, Texas.

61   Olivia Manning was sympathetic: "I know exactly how you must feel about the reviews, and I feel for you. I can only say I am astonished by such neglect. I should have thought that apart from any question of whether the book is good or not, your reputation is such you would be reviewed automatically" – Olivia Manning to Jocelyn Brooke, 18 July 1961, Texas.

62   May Brooke to Jocelyn Brooke, postmarked 22 March 1963, Texas.

63   "It is supposed to be bad form, I know, to express appreciation to a reviewer of one's book, but in the circumstances, with paving-stones descending on my head and squeals of rage from all the people who have had it entirely their own way

for at least ten years, I think I might take the risk" – Pamela
Hansford Johnson to Jocelyn Brooke, 4 October 1965, Texas.

64   "Getting back to work – however much you sneer at its
bloody nature – has proved welcome and enjoyable" – Yvonne
Kapp to Jocelyn Brooke, 12 April 1965, Texas.

65   Peggy Hogben, the local amateur historian, recalls
entertaining evenings with Brooke in Ivy Cottage, listening
to his witticisms, his knowledgeable accounts of wild flowers
and his extensive collection of music, especially his favourites,
Poulenc and his contemporaries – Ian Taylor (edited), *An
Anthology of Kingston and Bishopsbourne Book 1*, Kingston Village
Society 1982 25. *See also* Peggy Hogben's article in *Book 2*
(1987) 3.

66   "I do not know whether you have ever been to the west of
Ireland, but I am sure, as a botanist, it would delight you. I
have never before seen so many rare-looking plants, most of
them quite unknown to me. I also saw orchids that looked
remarkably like your Military Orchid … " – Olivia Manning
to Jocelyn Brooke, 5 July 1961, Texas. He took up the
suggestion and brought back a number of specimens of the
Irish marsh orchid which he sent to Victor Summerhayes, one
of the Principal Scientific Officers at Kew, something he had
done regularly in the mid-Fifties but had not done for seven
years. He also wrote a scientific paper on the vexed question
of the taxonomy of these plants which was turned down for
publication by the botanical powers-that-be. It seemed as if
which ever way he turned rejection lay in his path – Victor
Summerhayes to Jocelyn Brooke, 23 June and 20 November
1964, Texas.

67   Pat Davis, *Kent Tellers of Tales*, Geerings of Ashford 1996 14.

68   Olivia Manning was one of the enticers: "I think Heinemanns
will give me a party on the 1st Nov – after all, it is the last
of the trilogy – and if there is any chance of your being in
London, I hope you will be able to come. Good drink and lots

of it" – Olivia Manning to Jocelyn Brooke, undated [June/July 1965], Texas. By contrast, Yvonne Kapp understood Brooke's aversion to literary parties which he had ridiculed so effectively in *A Mine of Serpents* – MS 250–1 (trilogy 301–2). She was not averse to a bit of ridicule herself: "They (Methuen's) gave a cocktail party to launch this series and, reluctantly as always, I went to it, on the 10th floor of a new skyscraper in a street which, as far as I can remember, never existed at all in the past but was the site of Thomas Wallis. From there the view of (clean) St Paul's is really *magnificent*, particularly when one is filled with drink at sunset. But the *people* you meet are so glossy and successful, so full of confidence and plans and in-the-know, so well-groomed, so wonderfully able to produce words of wisdom and erudition at the drop of a hat that I have to have a *great* deal to drink to be able to remain in their company at all. They bandy about talk of '4-figure advances' and being translated into 600 languages and performing rights (as though they were fleas) and what is and isn't 'worth while' (in the 4-figure sense) until if I weren't propped up by alcohol I, with my grubby struggles and dreary sense of failure, would sink slowly all ten floors and nestle in the woodwork (only it's probably plastic). Thanks to the alcohol, however, I remain standing, if not exactly in flaunting evidence, and quietly thank my stars that I've never had the chance to be as they are" – Yvonne Kapp to Jocelyn Brooke, 19 September 1966, Texas. A mirror image of Brooke's own feelings at this time, and he reacted accordingly: "I'm not surprised … that the Methuen party I told you about made you feel sick. It's not our world, old boy. Not at all" – Yvonne Kapp to Jocelyn Brooke, 7 October 1966, Texas.

69   Yvonne Kapp to Jocelyn Brooke, 26 February 1965, 29 May, 1 August and 19 September 1966, Texas.

70   Yvonne Kapp to Jocelyn Brooke, 13 July 1966, Texas.

71   Olivia Manning, "An Enemy in the Mind" *op.cit.* He had, of

course, been making the same claim for the previous thirteen
years – *see* page 80 above.

72   Yvonne Kapp to Jocelyn Brooke, 12 April 1965, Texas.

73   Yvonne Kapp to Jocelyn Brooke, 18 April 1966, Texas.

74   Yvonne Kapp to Jocelyn Brooke, 12 April 1965, Texas.

75   Yvonne Kapp to Jocelyn Brooke, 21 October 1966, Texas.

76   *Kentish Gazette*, 4 November 1966. The wheel had come full
circle: in *The Image of a Drawn Sword,* Reynard had found his
mother dead in her bed in the same cottage but, of course, in
far less peaceful circumstances.

77   The biography by Jonathan Hunt, the leading expert on
Brooke, is expected before long.

78   Zdzislaw Najder.

Bibliography

Brooke, Jocelyn, *December Spring – poems*, Bodley Head, 1946.
　　　The Military Orchid, Bodley Head, 1948.
　　　The Scapegoat, Bodley Head, 1948.
　　　The Wonderful Summer, John Lehmann, 1949.
　　　A Mine of Serpents, Bodley Head, 1949.
　　　The Image of a Drawn Sword, Bodley Head, 1950.
　　　The Goose Cathedral, Bodley Head, 1950.
　　　The Flower In Season. A Calendar of Wild Flowers, Bodley Head,
　　　1952.
　　　The Elements of Death and other poems, Hand and Flower
　　　Press, 1952.
　　　The Passing of a Hero, Bodley Head, 1953.
　　　Private View. Four Portraits, James Barrie, 1954.
　　　The Dog at Clambercrown, Bodley Head, 1955.
　　　Conventional Weapons, Faber & Faber, 1961.
　　　"Furious and Deadly", unpublished typescript, c. 1961.
　　　(edited) *Denton Welch, extracts from his published works,*
　　　Chapman & Hall, 1963.
Brydon, Michael, *The Evolving Reputation of Richard Hooker, An Examination
　　　of Responses, 1600–1714*, Oxford University Press, 2006.
Cecil, Hugh and Mirabel, *Clever Hearts, Desmond and Molly MacCarthy,
　　　a biography*, Gollancz, 1990.
Clark, Peter, *English Provincial Society from the Reformation to the
　　　Revolution: Religion, Politics and Society in Kent 1500–1640*,
　　　Harvester Press, 1977.
Conrad, Borys, *My Father: Joseph Conrad*, Calder & Boyars, 1970.
　　　Coach Tour of Joseph Conrad's Homes in Kent, Joseph Conrad
　　　Society pamphlet, 1974.
Conrad, John, *Joseph Conrad: Times Remembered*, Cambridge University
　　　Press, 1981.

Conrad, Joseph, *The Collected Letters of Joseph Conrad, 9 vols.* (edited Frederick R. Karl and Laurence Davies), Cambridge University Press, 1983–2007.

"Heart of Darkness" in *Youth, a Narrative, and Two Other Stories*, Blackwood,1902.

"Amy Foster" in *Typhoon, and Other Stories*, Heinemann, 1903.

Nostromo (edited Jacques Berthoud and Mara Kalnins), Oxford University Press, 2007.

Notes on Life and Letters, (edited J.H.Stape), Cambridge University Press, 2004.

Suspense, J.M.Dent, 1925.

Cooper, Robert M., *The Literary Guide & Companion to Southern England*, Ohio University Press, 1998.

Curle, Richard, *The Last Twelve Years of Joseph Conrad*, Sampson Low, Marston, 1928.

Davis, Pat, *Kent Tellers of Tales*, Geerings, 1996.

Drury, Nevill, *Magic and Witchcraft*, Thames & Hudson, 2003.

Edwards J.G. *et al* (edited), *Historical Essays in Honour of James Tait*, Manchester, 1933.

Fuller, Thomas, *The History of the Worthies of England, I*, London: J.G.W.L., 1662.

The Church-History of Britain from the Birth of Jesus Christ until the Year MDCXLVII, III, London: John Williams, 1665.

Garnett, David (edited), *The Letters of T.E.Lawrence*, Jonathan Cape, 1938.

Garnett, Edward (edited), *Letters from Conrad 1895–1924*, Nonesuch Press, 1928.

Friday Nights, Literary Criticisms and Appreciations, Jonathan Cape, 1929.

Gilbert, R.A., *A.E.Waite, Magician of Many Parts*, Crucible, 1987.

Gill, Michael, *Growing into War*, Sutton Publishing, 2005.

Green, I.W., *The Story of All Saints, a history of the parish church of All Saints,Whitstable*, Elvy Bros., 1956.

Grigson, Geoffrey, *The Englishman's Flora*, J.M.Dent, 1955.

Gutman, Robert W., *Mozart. A Critical Biography*, Secker & Warburg, 2000.

Haigh, Christopher (edited), *The Reign of Elizabeth I*, Macmillan, 1984.

Haigh, Christopher, *English Reformations. Religion, Politics and Society under the Tudors*, Oxford, 1993.

Hart, Brian and Eila Lawton, *Elham Valley Way*, Kent County Council, 1997.

Hart-Davis, Rupert, *Hugh Walpole, A Biography*, Macmillan, 1952.

Hasted, Edward, *The history and topographical survey of the county of Kent, second edition*, 1797–1801.

Heilbrun, Carolyn G., *The Garnett Family, The History of a Literary Family*, Allen and Unwin, 1961.

Hill, W. Speed, (edited), *Studies in Richard Hooker: Essays Preliminary to an Edition of His Works*, Press of Case Western Reserve University, 1972.

Hooker, Richard, (edited W. Speed Hill), *The Folger Library Edition of the Works of Richard Hooker* Vols. 1–5, Belknap Press of Harvard University Press, 1977–90; Vol. 6, Medieval and Renaissance Texts and Studies, 1993.

Igglesden, Charles, *A Saunter through Kent with Pen and Pencil Vol. XXVI*, Kentish Express, 1932.

Jolliffe, J.E.A., *Pre-Feudal England – The Jutes*, Oxford University Press, 1933.

Keating, Peter, *The Haunted Study: A Social History of the English Novel 1875–1914*, Secker & Warburg, 1989.

Lillywhite, Frederick, *Cricket Scores and Biographies of Celebrated Cricketers*, Lillywhite, 1862.

McGrade, A.S. (edited), *Richard Hooker and the Construction of Christian Community*, Medieval & Renaissance Texts & Studies, 1997.

Maclure, Millar, *The Paul's Cross Sermons 1534–1642*, University of Toronto Press, 1958.

Major, Alan, *Hidden Kent*, Countryside Books, 2003.

Major, John, *More Than A Game, the story of cricket's early years*, HarperCollins, 2007.

Martin, Jessica, *Walton's Lives. Conformist Commemorations and the Rise of Biography*, Oxford University Press, 2001.

Mee, Arthur, *The King's England, Kent*, Hodder and Stoughton, 1936.

Mote, Ashley (edited), *John Nyren's The Cricketers of my Time*, Robson Books, 1998.

Najder, Zdzislaw, *Joseph Conrad, A Life*, Camden House, 2007.

Novarr, David, *The Making of Walton's Lives*, Cornell University Press, 1958.

Powell, Michael, *A Life in Movies. An Autobiography*, Heinemann, 1986.

Ray, Martin (edited), *Joseph Conrad, Interviews and Recollections*, Macmillan, 1990.

Reynolds, Stephen, *A Poor Man's House*, Halsgrove, 2001.

Richards, Grant, *Author Hunting, memories of years spent mainly in publishing,* Unicorn Press, 1960.

Richards, Jeffrey and Anthony Aldgate, *Best of British. Cinema and Society 1930–1970*, Basil Blackwell, 1983.

Sadie, Stanley, *Mozart, The Early Years 1756–1781*, W. W. Norton & Co., 2006.

Saunders, Max, *Self Impression, Life-Writing, Autobiografiction, and the Forms of Modern Literature,* Oxford University Press, 2010.

Scoble, Christopher, *Fisherman's Friend, a life of Stephen Reynolds*, Halsgrove, 2000.
　　Colin Blythe, lament for a legend, SportsBooks, 2005.

Secor, Philip B., *Richard Hooker, Prophet of Anglicanism*, Burns & Oates, 1999.

Sisson, C. J., *The Judicious Marriage of Mr. Hooker and the Birth of The Laws of Ecclesiastical Polity*, Cambridge University Press, 1940.

Stape, John, *The Several Lives of Joseph Conrad*, Heinemann, 2007.

Symonds, Richard, *The Fox, the Bees and the Pelican, Some Worthies and Noteworthies of Corpus Christi College, Oxford*, Corpus Christi

College, Oxford, 2002.

Daring to be Wise, More Worthies and Noteworthies of Corpus Christi College, Oxford, Corpus Christi College, Oxford, 2004.

Taylor, Flavia, *The North Wood*, Emprint Publications, 1995.

Taylor, Ian (edited), *An Anthology of Kingston and Bishopsbourne, Book 1*, Kingston Village Society, 1982.

Taylor, Ian and Peggy Hogben (edited), *An Anthology of Kingston and Bishopsbourne, Book 2*, Kingston Village Society, 1987.

Tindall, Gillian, *Countries of the Mind – the meaning of place to writers*, Hogarth Press, 1991.

Tritton, Paul, *A Canterbury Tale. Memories of a Classic Wartime Movie*, E.C.Parker & Co., 2006.

Michael Powell's Canterbury Tales, Parkers, 2010.

Underdown, David, *Start of Play – Cricket and Culture in Eighteenth Century England*, Allen Lane. The Penguin Press, 2000.

Vine, F.T., *Caesar in Kent*, privately printed, 1886.

Waite, A.E., *Shadows of Life and Thought*, Selwyn and Blount, 1938.

Walton, Izaak, *The Lives*, Society for Promoting Christian Knowledge, 1850.

Waugh, Alec, *The Loom of Youth*, Grant Richards, 1917.

The Balliols (1934), Tom Stacey Reprints, 1972.

The Early Years of Alec Waugh, Cassell, 1962.

The Best Wine Last. An autobiography through the years 1932–1969, W.H.Allen, 1978.

Waugh, Alexander, *Fathers and Sons, The Autobiography of a Family*, Headline, 2004.

Waugh, Evelyn, *A Little Learning*, Chapman & Hall, 1964.

West, Douglas, *The Third Portrait of a Seaside Town*, Emprint Publications, 1988.

Witney, K.P., *The Jutish Forest. A Study of the Weald of Kent from 450 to 1380 AD*, University of London. The Athlone Press, 1976.

The Kingdom of Kent, Phillimore, 1982.

Witney, Kenneth (edited), *The Survey of Archbishop Pecham's Kentish Manors 1283–85*, Kent Archaeological Society, 2000.

342

Index

The index covers Chapters 1 to 10 and the notes and references. Main entries are highlighted in **bold**. Figures in square brackets denote illustrations depicting the subject of the index entry.